Hosea, Joel, and Amos

Westminster Bible Companion

Series Editors

Patrick D. Miller
David L. Bartlett

Hosea, Joel, and Amos

BRUCE C. BIRCH

Westminster John Knox Press
Louisville, Kentucky

Book design by Publishers' WorkGroup
Cover design by Drew Stevens

First edition

Published by Westminster John Knox Press
Louisville, Kentucky

This book is printed on acid-free paper that meets the American National Standards Institute Z39.48 standard. ♾

PRINTED IN THE UNITED STATES OF AMERICA

97 98 99 00 01 02 03 04 05 06 — 10 9 8 7 6 5 4 3 2 1

Library of Congress Cataloging-in-Publication Data

Birch, Bruce C.
 Hosea, Joel, and Amos / Bruce C. Birch. — 1st ed.
  p.   cm. — (Westminster Bible companion)
 ISBN 0–664–25271–0 (alk. paper)
 1. Bible. O.T. Hosea—Commentaries. 2. Bible. O.T. Joel—
Commentaries. 3. Bible. O.T. Amos—Commentaries. I. Bible.
O.T. Hosea. English. New Revised Standard. 1997. II. Bible.
O.T. Joel. English. New Revised Standard. 1997. III. Bible.
O.T. Amos. English. New Revised Standard. 1997. IV. Title.
V. Series.
 BS1565.3.B57   1997
 224′.607—dc21
                                             97–616

Contents

Series Foreword   vii

Introduction   1

HOSEA   5

Introduction   7
  Hosea Among the Prophets   7
  Hosea's Historical Context   8
  Hosea and His Family   10
  The Book of Hosea   11
  The Message of Hosea   12
  The Influence of Hosea   15
Commentary   16
  Go, Take for Yourself a Wife (Hosea 1:1–2:1)   17
  She Is Not My Wife (Hosea 2:2–23)   25
  Go, Love a Woman (Hosea 3:1–5)   39
  My People Are Destroyed for Lack
    of Knowledge (Hosea 4:1–11a)   45
  Though You Play the Whore, O Israel (Hosea 4:11b–19)   54
  Hear This, O Priests! (Hosea 5:1–7)   58
  I Desire Steadfast Love and Not Sacrifice (Hosea 5:8–6:6)   62
  They Call upon Egypt, They Go to Assyria (Hosea 6:7–7:16)   70
  They Have Broken My Covenant (Hosea 8:1–14)   77
  The Prophet Is a Sentinel (Hosea 9:1–17)   82
  Israel Is a Luxuriant Vine (Hosea 10:1–8)   89
  Since the Days of Gibeah You Have Sinned (Hosea 10:9–15)   93
  When Israel Was a Child, I Loved Him (Hosea 11:1–11)   96
  The Lord Will Punish Jacob (Hosea 11:12–12:14)   102
  I Will Destroy You, O Israel (Hosea 13:1–16)   109
  I Will Love Them Freely (Hosea 14:1–9)   116

JOEL   **123**

Introduction   **125**
  Joel's Historical Context   125
  The Book of Joel   126
  The Message of Joel   127
Commentary   **132**
  Tell Your Children of It (Joel 1:1–4)   133
  Cry Out to the Lord (Joel 1:5–14)   135
  The Day of the Lord Is Near (Joel 1:15–20)   138
  The Day of the Lord . . . Who Can Endure It? (Joel 2:1–11)   140
  Rend Your Hearts and Not Your Garments (Joel 2:12–17)   143
  The Lord . . . Had Pity on His People (Joel 2:18–27)   147
  Afterward I Will Pour Out My Spirit (Joel 2:28–32)   152
  I Will Restore the Fortunes
    of Judah and Jerusalem (Joel 3:1–21)   155

AMOS   **163**

Introduction   **165**
  Amos Among the Prophets   165
  Amos's Historical Context   166
  Amos, the Man   167
  The Book of Amos   168
  The Message of Amos   169
  The Influence of Amos   172
Commentary   **173**
  The Lord Roars from Zion (Amos 1:1–2)   173
  I Will Not Revoke the Punishment (Amos 1:3–2:16)   177
  Hear This Word (Amos 3:1–5:27)   188
  Alas, for Those at Ease in Zion (Amos 6:1–14)   224
  This Is What the Lord Showed Me (Amos 7:1–9; 8:1–3)   230
  I Am No Prophet (Amos 7:10–17)   237
  You That Trample on the Needy (Amos 8:4–14)   242
  Are You Not Like the Ethiopians? (Amos 9:1–10)   248
  I Will Restore the Fortunes
    of My People Israel (Amos 9:11–15)   255

For Further Reading   **261**

Series Foreword

This series of study guides to the Bible is offered to the church and more specifically to the laity. In daily devotions, in church school classes, and in listening to the preached word, individual Christians turn to the Bible for a sustaining word, a challenging word, and a sense of direction. The word that scripture brings may be highly personal as one deals with the demands and surprises, the joys and sorrows, of daily life. It also may have broader dimensions as people wrestle with moral and theological issues that involve us all. In every congregation and denomination, controversies arise that send ministry and laity alike back to the Word of God to find direction for dealing with difficult matters that confront us.

A significant number of lay women and men in the church also find themselves called to the service of teaching. Most of the time they will be teaching the Bible. In many churches, the primary sustained attention to the Bible and the discovery of its riches for our lives have come from the ongoing teaching of the Bible by persons who have not engaged in formal theological education. They have been willing, and often eager, to study the Bible in order to help others drink from its living water.

This volume is part of a series of books, the Westminster Bible Companion, intended to help the laity of the church read the Bible more clearly and intelligently. Whether such reading is for personal direction or for the teaching of others, the reader cannot avoid the difficulties of trying to understand these words from long ago. The scriptures are clear and clearly available to everyone as they call us to faith in the God who is revealed in Jesus Christ and as they offer to every human being the word of salvation. No companion volumes are necessary in order to hear such words truly. Yet every reader of scripture who pauses to ponder and think further about any text has questions that are not immediately answerable simply by reading the text of scripture. Such questions may be about historical and geographical details or about words that are obscure or so loaded with meaning that one cannot tell at a glance what is at stake. They may be about the fundamental meaning of a passage or about what connection a particular text might have to our contemporary world. Or a teacher preparing for a church school class may simply want to know: What should I say about this biblical passage when I have to teach it next Sunday? It is our hope that these volumes, written by teachers and pastors with long experience studying and teaching the Bible in the church, will help members of the church who want and need to study the Bible with their questions.

The New Revised Standard Version of the Bible is the basis for the interpretive comments that each author provides. The NRSV text is presented at the beginning of the discussion so that the reader may have at hand in a single volume both the scripture passage and the exposition of its meaning. In some instances, where inclusion of the entire passage is not necessary for understanding either the text or the interpreter's discussion, the presentation of the NRSV text may be abbreviated. Usually, the whole of the biblical text is given.

We hope this series will serve the community of faith, opening the Word of God to all the people, so that they may be sustained and guided by it.

Introduction

The books of Hosea, Joel, and Amos are the first three of twelve books that conclude the English Bible. Beginning with Hosea and ending with Malachi, these twelve books are often called the "minor prophets." This is an unfortunate designation, for many assume that "minor" is to be understood as "relatively unimportant" or "insignificant." Actually the designations "major" and "minor" for the prophetic books was intended to indicate only "long" and "short." All twelve of these prophetic books are rather brief as biblical books go. As it happens, two of the three books I discuss here are among the longer "minor" prophecies. Hosea has fourteen chapters, and Amos has nine. Joel has only three (unless you read it in Hebrew in which case the same material is divided into four chapters).

Unfortunately, the brevity of these books may have contributed to their obscurity. One hears few sermons on the minor prophets. For Hosea, Joel, and Amos combined there are only fourteen texts included in the Common Lectionary. Nevertheless, there are riches to be found in these books, and it is my hope that this book can help bring those riches to light. These are important voices from the biblical tradition of the prophets, and those voices address issues that still grip us in the church today.

Hosea and Amos have received a fair degree of attention among the minor prophets. Perhaps this is because they are considered to be the first of the great classical prophets. Preaching in the late eighth century B.C., Amos, followed a short time later by Hosea, was the first prophet to proclaim God's Word and have those words preserved in a book that bears his name. Thus, many of the features we have come to identify with the prophets are first defined by the preaching of Amos and Hosea. In this book, we will identify and discuss patterns of speech, concepts of God, and issues of judgment or hope in the life of the people that are first seen in these prophets but reappear in subsequent generations of the prophets as characteristic of Hebrew prophecy. To know something of the preaching of Amos and Hosea is to have a foundation for understanding all the prophets of Israel.

Amos is probably the most thoroughgoing prophet of judgment in the Old Testament. His role was to announce that Israel's sin had brought that nation to an end through God's judgment. It is a grim message, but one that makes clear the basis for such a judgment. It is the neglect of justice and righteousness that warrants the judgment of God. Amos's message is not easy to hear but we ignore it to our peril. In the struggles for justice that have marked our time, the prophet Amos has been a source of inspiration. Who can forget the rolling cadences of Martin Luther King, Jr. as he intoned the words of Amos in the hope of a new day of racial justice, "Let justice roll down like waters, and righteousness like an everflowing stream" (Amos 5:24).

Hosea is important for coupling the message of God's hope and redemption to the prophetic message of God's judgment. Many passages from Hosea are well known in the church without realization of their source in Hosea's preaching. In a recent adult Bible class, we were sharing favorite passages. A man spoke up to say that his grandmother had taught him a verse to emphasize that religious rituals were never more important than the living of a faithful life, but he had no idea where the verse was from. The verse was "For I desire steadfast love and not sacrifice, the knowledge of God rather than burnt offerings." It is from Hosea 6:6. Of course, the discovery of these prophets can also present us with new and difficult challenges. Most church members do not know the story of Hosea's marriage to Gomer and the important role it plays in his message. The discovery of the story of this marriage may be a bit of a shock and has, in fact, been problematic to the church over the centuries. Themes of prostitution, infidelity, authority, and abuse are part of this story. But so also are themes of love, redemption, fidelity, and renewal. Once again, these issues are difficult to face and understand, but they are at the heart of our daily struggle. There is much to learn from the prophet's words. To the concerns for justice and righteousness, Hosea adds the importance of love, both God's love and our own.

Joel is not as well known as Amos or Hosea. His date and setting are difficult to determine accurately, although most now agree on a date after the Babylonian exile in restored Jerusalem. The preaching of Joel is occasioned by the physical and spiritual crisis brought on by an invasion of locusts. Perhaps the neglect of Joel is from a sense that the issues arising out of such a crisis could not possibly be relevant to us. Yet, the book of Joel provided the text for what may be the single most important sermon in Christian history—the apostle Peter's Pentecost sermon (Joel 2:28–32;

Acts 2:17–21). Joel's vision of the egalitarian effects of the Spirit has new significance today in a climate of concern for greater inclusivity in the church and the society. We may not face plagues of locusts, but God's faithfulness and our trust in God's help are the perennial issues that arise out of any threat to the safety and well-being of the community. On these matters, Joel has a great deal to offer us.

These are three of the "minor" prophets, but they speak to us of "major" issues. As we read their words addressed to ancient Israel, what is surprising is how contemporary they sound. Their concerns are our own. Their God is our God. Thankfully, their proclamation of God's word addressed to those concerns is part of our scripture as the church, and we can be renewed by their preaching.

Hosea

Introduction

The book of Hosea is often seen as an embarrassment in the church. Recently a person who was taking a comprehensive Bible study program in the congregation I attend approached me to say, "Do you know that we actually studied a prophet who married a prostitute?" She was mildly shocked and more than a little surprised to find this in her Bible. She is not alone. Many in the history of the church have found understanding the book of Hosea difficult. Jerome, who translated the Bible into Latin in the fourth century, wrote, "If we have need of the Holy Spirit in understanding all of God's word, how much more when we come to Hosea must we pray 'O Lord, help us to understand these mysteries!'"

The central experience of Hosea's marriage to Gomer, and the way Hosea uses that experience in his preaching, is one of the most striking yet problematic images in all of prophetic literature. In some ways the reaction to this marriage imagery has obscured much of the rest of Hosea's message. It is Hosea who gives us some of the most compelling statements of God's judgment and the failure of God's covenant people. And it is Hosea who first among the prophets makes clear that judgment does not exhaust God's character. God's love speaks the final word. Hosea does all of this through use of some of the most imaginative imagery in all the prophets.

Hosea has much to offer, both for understanding the crisis in Israel in his own time and for seeing many of the same issues in the crises of our day. After a brief introduction to the book of Hosea we will turn to comment and reflection on the message of Hosea.

HOSEA AMONG THE PROPHETS

The book of Hosea is one of the earliest prophetic books. Hosea's preaching was preceded in time only by Amos among those prophets whose words were collected and preserved as prophetic books of the Old Testament. Like Amos, Hosea announced God's judgment against the Northern Kingdom Israel for failure to be faithful and obedient in relationship to God, in the covenant relationship that had helped establish them as a people. Although Hosea highlights different issues in this broken relationship, he like Amos sees the consequence of God's judgment as the death of the nation (see especially chapter 13). This was a new and shocking message in Israel (see the Introduction to the book of Amos). Hosea develops this theme of the end of the nation even further than Amos since his preaching extends on into the final, chaotic years of the Northern Kingdom, even to the brink of its final extinction. The actual conquest of Israel by Assyria in 722 B.C. served to vindicate the message of Hosea as well as his predecessor Amos. Other prophets carry on and develop this theme of God's judgment against the nation in ways appropriate to their settings (e.g., Isaiah, Jeremiah, Ezekiel, Micah, Zephaniah).

But Hosea, unlike Amos, coupled his message of judgment with a message of hope and renewal. He saw clearly that the character of God was not exhausted in divine anger and punishment. God's judgment was transcended by God's love, and although God would not turn back from the consequences warranted by the sin of Israel, the end of the nation would not be the end of relationship to God. Renewed life as God's people was possible beyond judgment. This coupling of God's judgment and love, wrath and redemption was clearly influential on later developments in the Old Testament tradition. Almost all the subsequent prophets develop themes of hope and redemption alongside their preaching of God's judgment. In particular, the books of Jeremiah and Deuteronomy use themes and emphases that seem drawn from Hosea, and in the midst of Babylonian exile the anonymous prophet we call Second Isaiah (Isaiah 40—55) uses Hosea-like language in developing a message to exiles entirely around themes of hope and renewal.

HOSEA'S HISTORICAL CONTEXT

Hosea began his preaching near the end of the relatively peaceful and prosperous years of the reign of Jeroboam II (786–746 B.C.) on the throne of the Northern Kingdom, Israel (1:1), probably around 750 B.C. Although there are occasional references to Judah, Hosea's preaching occurred entirely in the north and was almost entirely directed at the situation in Israel. Much of Hosea's early preaching (chaps. 1—4) reflects his conviction that in spite of outward appearances all was not well in the kingdom. The flourishing religious life was corrupted with idolatrous practices, and without its focus on relationship with the Lord the nation was without moral compass and headed in a disastrous direction.

Hosea's warning gave way to reality after the death of Jeroboam II. From 746 B.C. to the conquest of the kingdom by Assyria in 722 B.C. Israel's throne was occupied by six different kings (see 2 Kings 15—17). It was a period of bloody politics with the throne frequently changing hands by assassination. Few held the throne for more than a few years and some for only a few months. In this period Hosea's message frequently took note of the political intrigue that was creating national chaos and he blamed it on the kingship itself (7:7; 8:4).

Unfortunately for Israel, this period of chaotic rule coincided with a new period of Assyrian power. In 745 B.C., when Tiglath-pileser III came to the throne in Assyria, he opened a period of new ambition to empire. Israel's kings could not resist trying to play in the international political arena to their own advantage. Menahem (745–738 B.C.) paid a heavy tribute in submission to the Assyrian king, Tiglath-pileser, when the Assyrians were campaigning in the west in 743 B.C. This angered the heavily taxed landowners who supported Pekah in murdering Menahem's son and seizing the throne in 737 B.C. With the help of Egypt, Pekah formed an anti-Assyrian coalition with Syria and tried to force Judah to join them. Judah refused. So Syria and Israel joined forces against Judah and its king, Ahaz, in Jerusalem (this war plays an important role in the preaching of Isaiah). Ahaz appealed for help to Assyria, and Tiglath-pileser took this as an opportunity to invade the territory and subdue the rebels. In 733 B.C. Assyrian armies devastated Israelite territory, appropriating most of its land and deporting much of the population. The capital, Samaria, and the hill country of Ephraim were spared this fate when Pekah was murdered by Hoshea ben Elah who took the throne (732–724) and immediately paid tribute to appease Assyria. Much of Hosea's preaching in chapters 5—8 reflects this turbulent period and its politics of manipulation and murder.

For a time under King Hoshea things were relatively calm. Some of Hosea's oracles in chapters 9—11 may fit into this period. Perhaps Hosea hoped that final disaster could be averted. Some think the hope of chapter 11 comes from this time. But King Hoshea also eventually fell to the lure of international intrigue. He began to seek Egyptian support for revolt (11:5; 12:1). When the Assyrian throne changed hands in 727 B.C., King Hoshea withheld tribute. The preaching of Hosea in chapters 12—14 is to be seen against the background of this catastrophic decision. The end of the nation was near! The new Assyrian king, Shalmaneser V, soon invaded Israel (724 B.C.) and captured King Hoshea (13:10, see 2 Kings 17:3–4). He laid seige to Samaria, and although he died during the siege, his successor Sargon II completed the conquest of the capital and the final deportation of the Israelite populace in 722 B.C. The end of the nation was complete! Hosea's final chapters reflect these last days, but they do not seem to know of the final capture of Samaria. The prophet's last words must have come in the year or two prior to 722 B.C.

HOSEA AND HIS FAMILY

Little is known of Hosea as a person apart from the unique story of his marriage in chapters 1 and 3. He was the son of Beeri and lived in the Northern Kingdom of Israel where he also preached his message. No events are reported from his preaching career as a prophet. Hosea may be speaking autobiographically in chapter 9 in which his oracle (vv. 1–6) seems to be an interruption of an Israelite festival. Hosea 9:7–8 then seems to reflect the harsh criticism he received on this occasion and his own response to it.

The lack of other information on Hosea's life makes the intensely personal reporting of his marriage and the children of that marriage all the more unusual. The story of this marriage unfolds in two separate narrative episodes in chapters 1 and 3. Hosea reports that God commanded him to marry "a wife of whoredom and have children of whoredom" (1:2). From the beginning it is clear that Hosea understands this as a symbolic action related to a message about God's relationship to Israel, "for the land commits great whoredom by forsaking the LORD" (1:2). He marries Gomer, the daughter of Diblaim, and they have three children. All the children are given symbolic names that relate to God's judgment against Israel (1:3–9).

After an extended chapter of prophetic preaching in poetic form that develops the metaphor of God's relationship to unfaithful Israel (chap. 2), another narrative episode from Hosea's life appears in chapter 3. Hosea is commanded again by God to "Go, love a woman who has a lover and is an adultress." This is to be a sign that "the LORD loves the people of Israel, though they turn to other gods" (3:1). The prophet then "bought" an unnamed woman (as a slave or as a redemption from servitude) and shut her away from all men, including himself, as a symbolic representation of the period of broken relationship before Israel could return to the God who loves them (3:2–5).

The interpretive questions associated with these chapters are notoriously complex and have taxed the understanding of generations of interpreters in the church. What sort of promiscuity did Gomer engage in? Was she associated with the cult of Baal? Do the names of the children indicate matters of personal relationship between Hosea and Gomer? Is the unnamed woman of chapter 3 also Gomer? If so, what has brought her to this condition? What sort of transaction is this in chapter 3? Any answers to these questions are necessarily speculative because many details are not mentioned in the text. My discussion on chapters 1 and 3 will assess the possibilities in greater detail and draw some tentative conclusions.

In addition to the problems of interpreting these texts in their own terms, recent comment on Hosea has raised additional questions that cannot be ignored in the present context of the modern reader of these texts. The practices of arranged marriages, human servitude, and the purchase of women in conditions of servitude are all practices that are both alien and repugnant to those raised to think of ideal relationships as mutual and consensual. Further, the language used in Hosea 2 for God's judgment of unfaithful Israel, which uses the metaphor of the unfaithful wife and the aggrieved husband, is the language of abuse. It seems to reflect what would have been considered acceptable behavior by a husband toward an unfaithful wife in those times, but it is not acceptable at all in our own time. For modern readers, this language suggests Hosea may have acted in this way toward Gomer, although this is not explicitly said. It is certainly repugnant language to use for the activity of God. The effect is to leave the modern reader of Hosea 1—3 rather unsympathetic toward Hosea or toward God, whatever the particulars of unfaithfulness by Gomer or Israel. It also renders suspect the redemptive language of 2:14–23 and 3:1–5. My comments on chapters 2 and 3 will attempt to deal honestly with these issues as well.

THE BOOK OF HOSEA

The book of Hosea has been especially noted for its powerful images. These images appear in rich profusion as metaphors for Israel's sin, for the relationship between God and Israel, for God's judgment, for God's love or redemption, and for Israel's restored wholeness. Many of these images are drawn from nature or agricultural life, but others reflect common objects, military practices, or various human roles.

Unlike his predecessor, Amos, Hosea does not employ set forms or patterns of prophetic speech extensively. There are two chapters in narrative prose telling the story of Hosea's marriage (chapters 1 and 3). The rest of the chapters are collections of smaller poetic oracles, often grouped by theme within chapters or larger sections. There are two uses of a divine lawsuit pattern (4:1; 12:2). The oracle formula ("says the LORD") appears only in 2:13, 16, 21; 11:11, and the messenger formula so common in other prophetic books ("Thus says the LORD") is totally absent. An unusual number of Hosea's oracles are in the first person as if the Lord is speaking directly to Israel (for example, 4:1–14; 11:1–11). Some portions may reflect the influence of cultic liturgy (for example, the salvation response of the Lord to the people's prayer of repentance in 14:1–8).

Hosea is the only prophetic book written entirely in the language and idiom of the Northern Kingdom (Amos was a Judean who preached in the north). This may account for the different patterns of prophetic speech that are apparent when Hosea is compared to other prophetic books. It almost certainly is one of the reasons for the many problems of text and vocabulary encountered in translating Hosea.

The preaching of Hosea was collected and edited by others sometime after Hosea's time. This was undoubtedly done in Judah. The Northern Kingdom perished almost simultaneously with the end of Hosea's preaching. Several references to Judah seem added by later Judean editors, making Hosea's words applicable to their own time and place. We have already mentioned the tendency of the collectors and editors to group Hosea's oracles around common themes. A larger structure is also evident within the book. Three main sections are discernible: Chapters 1—3, which tell the story of Hosea's marriage and its meaning for his message; chapters 4—11, which are oracles from the time of Jeroboam's death until the final days of the kingdom (see the Introduction, "Hosea's Historical Context"); and chapters 12—14, which are from the very last days of Israel when it is evident that the nation's collapse cannot be averted. Each of these sections has been concluded with a chapter stressing hope and renewal of relationship between Israel and God (chaps. 3; 11; 14) so that God's love always has the final word beyond God's judgment.

THE MESSAGE OF HOSEA

Hosea's message will be discussed fully in my comment on the individual oracles in the book of Hosea, but it may be useful to identify some of the major themes we will find there.

1. *The Struggle with Idolatry.* Israel was God's covenant partner. Covenant

established a relationship between Israel and God with mutual obligations on both parties. The first and foremost obligation was loyalty to the Lord alone. Hosea's central indictment against Israel is that the covenant has been broken (8:1), and the most obvious of Israel's sins is that the people have engaged in idolatry, the worship of other gods who are not gods at all but human objects of wood or metal (4:12–13). Hosea describes this as harlotry (NRSV, "whoredom") and uses the metaphor of the unfaithful wife as a major image for Israel's dalliance with other gods (2:5; 4:13; 5:3; 9:1). In particular, Hosea saw the worship of Baal as apostasy against Israel's covenant God (11:2). Baal, the Canaanite god, was associated with rites intended to secure the fertility of the land. Sexual acts were probably involved in the cultic rites of Baal. In Hosea's message, this was both immoral and unnecessary. Israel's God provided the gifts of the land and idolatry was the path to death, not life (2:8–9; 13:1–2).

Israel's cultic sin of idolatry was compounded by priests who failed to teach the covenant law and ignored or participated in idolatrous practices (4:4–6; 5:1–2). Further, the attitude of the people seems to have been that sacrifices would cover their sins without the need to seriously alter their sinful behavior. Hosea makes clear that God desires not sacrifices but steadfast love and knowledge of God (6:6).

2. *The Corruption of Political Institutions.* Israel's cultic sin was coupled with the sins of its political life. Israel's disloyalty to the Lord was related to a failure to trust in God and a consequent breakdown in public life. Hosea charges Israel with general and widespread immoral behavior (4:1–2). He has an especially negative evaluation of Israel's kings and the self-centered, corrupt, and violent practices associated with the kings of the chaotic period following Jeroboam II (8:4; 9:11). Hosea believed that Israel's political maneuverings with Assyria and Egypt (7:11; 8:9; 12:1) and its reliance on its own military power (10:13–14) were failures of trust in the Lord. They were efforts at a false security that instead would destroy the nation.

3. *The Knowledge of God.* Israel's cultic and political guilt relate to a rupture in its relationship to God. The most central term for describing this relationship in Hosea's message is the "knowledge of God." The "people are destroyed for lack of knowledge" (4:6a). This is Hosea's term for normative covenant faith. It requires knowing and understanding the importance of Israel's historical traditions of relationship to God from Egypt through the wilderness and into the land (11:1–4; 13:4–5). Knowledge of God is the special responsibility of the priest (4:6) and is desired more than sacrifice (6:6). The term implies relationship and the experiencing of

relationship with God as a needed awareness in all of Israel's life. Knowledge of God is often associated by Hosea with steadfast love (sometimes translated as devotion or loyalty) and faithfulness (4:1; 6:6; 12:6). These two terms are also qualities of covenant relationship (see my comments on 4:1 for a fuller discussion of these terms). For Hosea, unlike his predecessor Amos, the terms *justice* and *righteousness* are not used or highlighted for covenant obligation.

4. *The Judgment of God.* Because of the guilt Israel had incurred for its idolatry, its political violence and corruption, and its lack of the knowledge of God, Hosea had no choice but to announce God's judgment. Often the images of judgment are appropriate to the sin itself. The people sought the gifts of the land from Baal, so the land would not yield its gifts (2:9; 4:3). The people sought security from treaties and military machinery, so they would fall victim to conquest (7:11–16). Often Hosea's announcement of judgment is by means of the metaphorical images for which he is well known, for example, Hosea 13:3, in which he states that the disappearance of Israel from among the nations will be as thorough as the dispersion of morning mist, early dew, swirling chaff, or smoke from a window.

Like Amos, Hosea saw God's judgment directed toward the entire nation and felt compelled to announce the end of the nation. Even God's people were not exempt from God's opposition to sin, and sin had become too constant and pervasive for the nation to be saved. Chapter 13 especially piles up one image after another of the end of Israel. "I will destroy you, O Israel, who can help you?" (13:9). Shortly after the preaching of this end to the nation, the Northern Kingdom of Israel was destroyed by Assyrian conquest. This fact no doubt contributed to the reputation of Hosea as one who truly spoke God's word and led to the preservation of his words for the edification of later generations (see 14:9).

5. *The Love and Salvation of God.* Unlike his predecessor, Amos, Hosea couples his message of God's judgment with an eloquent message of God's love and the renewal of relationship beyond judgment that is possible in God's love. Each major section of Hosea ends with a chapter devoted to hope based on God's saving and redeeming love (chaps. 3; 11; 14; see also 2:14–23). That these are placed as the final word of each section suggests that the love of God was considered to have the final word, transcending the wrath of God. Hosea is the first prophet to speak of God's love as a basis for relationship to God's people. In this respect he is especially influential on the later books of Deuteronomy and Jeremiah. Hosea's preaching of hope is also rich in images. Some of these depict God in mov-

ingly personal terms, for example, the images of God as the persistently loving parent of a rebellious son in chapter 11. In Hosea the word of death pronounced to Israel is fully balanced by a further word of life. For that reason, Christian preaching on Hosea has always found there a foreshadowing of the relationship between the seeming death of all hope on the cross of Calvary and the further word of life proclaimed from Christ's empty tomb.

THE INFLUENCE OF HOSEA

In the history of Christian biblical interpretation, Hosea has been used most often for the richness of his images of hope and God's love. Chapter 11 has been a favorite preaching text historically. The apostle Paul quotes Hosea 13:14 in 1 Corinthians 15:55 in support of his testimony to the meaning of Jesus' resurrection.

In general, however, the book of Hosea has suffered some neglect, probably because of difficulty and embarrassment associated with the themes of Hosea's marriage. Further, especially in modern times, there has been a tendency to treat the themes of idol worship in general and Baal worship in particular as archaic, and therefore of little relevance to the issues that face the modern church. Since these themes are central to Hosea, many dismiss his message as unimportant. In my judgment, this view represents a serious misunderstanding of the nature of idolatry, and we ignore the message of Hosea to our detriment. Idolatry is closely related to issues of cultural accommodation and materialistic religion, which are crucially important in the life of the modern church, especially in our North American setting. Further, for Hosea, idolatry is closely allied with self-serving political institutions and the growth of violence in the nation. The results of many current surveys indicate that U.S. citizens are becoming more concerned over increasing mistrust of political leaders and violence in our society. Could it be that Hosea's depiction of Israel's patterns of sin are more like patterns apparent in our own nation than we have heretofore recognized? My hope in the commentary on Hosea's preaching that follows is to suggest that his word, indeed, is still a word for us.

Commentary

We do not normally know much about the lives of prophets. Even when stories survive about them they are usually narratives drawn from their public ministries. We do not know a lot about the biography of Hosea either. But what we do know is drawn from the intimate personal experiences of his family life, and in its particulars it is likely to amaze if not shock us. The first three chapters of Hosea form a distinct section in which the marriage of Hosea to Gomer and the birth of their children are used as metaphor as for the relationship of the Lord to Israel. The nature of the marriage and the role of the children are not within the customary range of our own modern experience and were probably rather dramatic even in Hosea's time. Understanding the meaning of these texts and struggling with questions of meaning for the modern church are challenging tasks, and at the very least, it will require us to enter a world that is not our own and that in some particulars we certainly will not wish to make our own.

After a superscription in 1:1, the book of Hosea opens with one chapter of prose narrative recounted in the third person and tells of the marriage of Hosea to Gomer and the birth of their children (1:2–2:1), as well as suggests some meanings attached to these events for Hosea's prophecy. It is followed by a chapter of poetic material applying metaphors of marriage and unfaithfulness drawn from Hosea's marriage to Israel's relationship with the Lord (2:2–23). A brief third chapter (3:1–5) narrates in first-person prose another marriage of Hosea to an unnamed woman and the meaning attached to these events for his prophecy.

A feature of these chapters that seems significant for the book of Hosea as a whole is the way in which they alternate between material focused on God's judgment and material focused on God's redemption and renewal. Disaster as a consequence of Israel's sin is matched by renewal as a consequence of God's love. In chapter 1, verses 2–9 focus on judgment, but 1:10–2:1 have to do with promise and renewal. The harsh consequences of Israel's infidelity are the subject of 2:2–13, but 2:14–23 speak eloquently of the Lord's covenant-renewing love. The reflection of judgment in 3:3–4 is surrounded by the language of renewed relationship in 3:1–2, 5. The understanding reflected in these chapters that the Lord's love is not abrogated by divine judgment is a characteristic feature of the whole of Hosea. We will see at other points in the book that, for Hosea, the death that comes as the consequence of sin is never the last word, for God always has a further word of life-renewing love to speak beyond judgment.

GO, TAKE FOR YOURSELF A WIFE
Hosea 1:1–2:1

1:1 The word of the LORD that came to Hosea son of Beeri, in the days of Kings Uzziah, Jotham, Ahaz, and Hezekiah of Judah, and in the days of King Jeroboam son of Joash of Israel.

2 When the LORD first spoke through Hosea, the LORD said to Hosea, "Go, take for yourself a wife of whoredom and have children of whoredom, for the land commits great whoredom by forsaking the LORD." 3 So he went and took Gomer daughter of Diblaim, and she conceived and bore him a son.

4 And the LORD said to him, "Name him Jezreel; for in a little while I will punish the house of Jehu for the blood of Jezreel, and I will put an end to the kingdom of the house of Israel. 5 On that day I will break the bow of Israel in the valley of Jezreel."

6 She conceived again and bore a daughter. Then the LORD said to him, "Name her Lo-ruhamah, for I will no longer have pity on the house of Israel or forgive them. 7 But I will have pity on the house of Judah, and I will save them by the LORD their God; I will not save them by bow, or by sword, or by war, or by horses, or by horsemen."

8 When she had weaned Lo-ruhamah, she conceived and bore a son. 9 Then the LORD said, "Name him Lo-ammi, for you are not my people and I am not your God."

10 Yet the number of the people of Israel shall be like the sand of the sea, which can be neither measured nor numbered; and in the place where it was said to them, "You are not my people," it shall be said to them, "Children of the living God." 11 The people of Judah and the people of Israel shall be gathered together, and they shall appoint for themselves one head; and they shall take possession of the land, for great shall be the day of Jezreel.

2:1 Say to your brother, Ammi, and to your sister, Ruhamah.

Within this chapter are three distinct sections that deserve closer comment and reflection: the superscription in 1:1; the central section on

Hosea's marriage to Gomer and their children in 1:2–9; and the promise
of God's new future in 1:10–2:1.

Superscriptions (1:1)

The book of Hosea, like many other prophetic books (Jeremiah, Ezekiel,
Joel, Jonah, Zephaniah), opens with a superscription that names Hosea's
father and sets the time of his ministry in relation to the reign of Judean
and Israelite kings (1:1). These opening titles were the work of editors
who preserved and passed on the preaching of prophets like Hosea.

The perspective for our reading is made clear when the opening line
announces that the book in its entirety is to be understood as "the word
of the LORD that came to Hosea." It is typical of the prophetic books to
speak of God's word as something the prophets experienced (it "came" to
them) rather than heard. God's word is an event, not just a verbal communication. Thus, all we know of Hosea's life and his preaching in this
book is to be understood as the word of God to Hosea and through his
book to us.

We receive little personal information about Hosea, just the name of
his father, Beeri. We assume from references elsewhere in the book that
he was a citizen of the Northern Kingdom because he speaks primarily of
places in Israel, not Judah, and refers to Israel's king as "our king" (7:5).
This makes it somewhat odd that in identifying Hosea's time period the
kings of Judah are listed first. Furthermore, Hosea is said to have preached
during the time of four kings of Judah (Uzziah, 783–742 B.C.; Jotham,
742–735 B.C.; Ahaz, 735–715 B.C.; and Hezekiah, 715–687 B.C.), but he
lists only one king of Israel (Jeroboam II, 786–746 B.C.). Since all
prophetic books were edited and passed on in Judah, due to the destruction of the Northern Kingdom in 721 B.C., the superscription probably
reflects that Judean bias in listing Judah's kings first. But the listing of only
Jeroboam II may reflect the uncertainty over political events after his
reign. The years from 746 to 721 were marked by political chaos, with
kings being assassinated and overthrown at a dizzying pace. The compil-
ers of the book of Hosea may have been uncertain about the succession or
the legitimacy of the kings who followed Jeroboam II. We do know that
Hosea's ministry continued on into this chaotic period because many of
his oracles reflect the experience of that difficult time. Nothing in his
preaching, however, suggests the fall of Samaria, Israel's capital, in 721,
so Hosea's ministry is generally thought to have ended before that date.
Thus, Hosea's ministry began near the end of the reign of Jeroboam II,

but it quickly moved into a period of Israel's growing political crisis that was to culminate in the end of the Northern Kingdom.

Hosea's Marriage and Children
(1:2–9)

The book of Hosea opens with the report of four symbolic actions undertaken by the prophet at the command of the Lord. The first is a marriage (1:2–3), while the remaining three are the symbolic naming of three children born to this marriage (1:4–9). Symbolic actions are a common feature of prophetic activity. To reinforce and give dramatic impact to their messages many prophets undertook actions that they understood as commanded by God and that symbolically represented some element of the message they proclaimed in God's name (for example, Isa. 8:1–4; 20:1–6; Jer. 13:1–11; 27:1–15). Such actions might be thought of as enacted word, alongside the prophet's spoken word. The report of Hosea's symbolic actions is typical. It reports the giving of a command from God and an explanation of the symbolic meaning attached to the commanded action. Verse 3 reports Hosea's fulfillment of God's first command, but his carrying out of the command to name the three children is assumed.

Hosea is commanded by God, "Go, take for yourself a wife of whoredom and have children of whoredom" (1:2), and in response he married Gomer, the daughter of Diblaim (1:3). Immediately a host of questions are raised in our minds. Who was Gomer? What kind of a woman does this text suggest she was? What is the nature of such a marriage? What in the world must Hosea have thought of such a command? Why would God ask such a thing? Not all that we would like to know in answer to such questions can be known. The text is brief and undetailed. It is clear that the witness of this text is focused more narrowly than our natural curiosity about such a strange command.

The command to marry must mean that Hosea is relatively young, just at marriageable age, but what manner of woman is he being asked to seek? The early church fathers found this passage so awkward that they concluded the story must be allegorical and not in reality a description of the prophet's life. This is not supported by the straightforward reporting of the text. The story is narrated as events in Hosea's actual life. The phrase "wife of whoredom" has also been translated "wife of harlotry" or "promiscuous woman." From this single phrase an astonishing variety of suggestions have been made about the character of Gomer: She was a prostitute by profession; she was a cult prostitute involved in the fertility rituals associated with

Baal; she was a young woman who participated in a Canaanite ritual offering of her virginity to Baal; she is simply being described as a woman from
a harlotrous people (Israel); she is being described not in terms of what she
is but what she will become as an unfaithful wife. All these suggestions go
beyond what the spare terms of the text tell us.

The term translated in the NRSV as *whoredom* is a plural noun derived
from a Hebrew verb that means "to engage in sexual intercourse outside
of marriage." The verb can apply to adultery (married women), fornica-
tion (unmarried women), or prostitution (women who engage in sexual relations as a profession). There is a specific, related noun that designates a
prostitute, but this term is never used for Gomer in the book of Hosea.
To call Gomer a "woman/wife of whoredom" would seem to characterize
her as part of a group or class of women that does not include professional
prostitutes, either of the street or temple. Without further information we
can only conclude of Gomer that if she fulfilled the command given to
Hosea, she was a woman known by him to be promiscuous. She could perhaps be described as behaving like a harlot, but not as a prostitute by profession. As such a promiscuous woman, the children born to her were labeled "children of whoredom." The assumption of the text is that her
promiscuous behavior will not stop with her marriage to Hosea.

To read carefully only what the text tells us requires that we refrain
from fanciful scenarios about what led Gomer into promiscuity, what kind
of life she had led before this marriage, what her marriage to Hosea must
have been like, or how she felt to be married only because God commanded it. There is no information given to allow any of these issues to
be addressed. What is important to the witness of this text is that a marriage that should have been characterized by loyalty and commitment is
instead characterized by unfaithfulness.

This is the point at which Hosea's experience is intended from the beginning to symbolize God's relationship to Israel. God's command is
given with this intended meaning already attached, " . . . for the land commits great whoredom by forsaking the LORD (1:2b)." Hosea's experience
with Gomer is to become a metaphor for God's experience with Israel.
Gomer's unfaithfulness to Hosea dramatizes Israel's unfaithfulness to the
Lord. It is clear elsewhere in the book of Hosea that the unfaithfulness of
Israel is seen in its participation in Canaanite religion, particularly the
worship of the Baals. We will say more of Canaanite religion as Hosea describes it in discussions of chapters 2 and 4.

Three children are born to Hosea and Gomer in apparently quick succession. God commands that each child be given a symbolic name, a prac-

tice also known to us in the children of Isaiah (Isa. 7:3; 8:3–4). Whereas the marriage to Gomer was intended to symbolize Israel's sin, the names of the children are to symbolize the consequences of Israel's sin.

The first child is a son, and his name is to be Jezreel (v. 4a). Jezreel is the name for a beautiful and fertile valley situated between the hill country around Samaria and the hills of Galilee and the name of a city in that valley. The name itself means "God plants." As a name, this sounds pleasant enough, but Jezreel had become associated with violent events in Israel's story. At Jezreel, Jehu had culminated a bloody overthrow of the house of Omri and seized the throne of Israel for himself (2 Kings 9—10). He had killed both the king of Israel and the king of Judah there. It was at Jezreel that Jehu had Jezebel, the widow of Ahab, thrown down to the dogs, and displayed the heads of Ahab's seven sons. He also launched a mass extermination of Baal worshipers there. To name a child Jezreel in ancient Israel would be shocking and would certainly command attention. Imagine our own sentiments if we encountered children in our own time named after the places associated with violence and death in our history. What would we think of children named Wounded Knee, or Auschwitz, or Hiroshima, or My Lai?

God's command to name the child Jezreel is to symbolize God's coming punishment of the house of Jehu, the dynasty still on Israel's throne in the person of Jeroboam II. The bloody purge of Jehu had been undertaken in the name of a return to faithful covenant with the Lord and a turning away from idolatry. God's word to Hosea in the naming of the child Jezreel is that Jehu's dynasty now deserves to perish, and God "will put an end to the kingdom of the house of Israel" (v. 4b). The might of Israel (its bow) will be broken at Jezreel just as Jehu had done to the house of Omri (v. 5). The implication is that Israel is as deserving of judgment as those whom Jehu overthrew. As we shall see later in Hosea's preaching, God's judgment on the dynasty of Jehu is also largely for the sin of idolatry. The child Jezreel is to be a walking reminder of Hosea's word from God that Jezreel is the fate of idolatrous Israel in any generation.

The second child born to Hosea and Gomer is a daughter, and God commands her to be named "Lo-ruhamah," which translated from Hebrew means "Not pitied," or "No compassion" (1:6a). *Compassion* (a noun related to this verb) is an important term in the prophetic literature for God's care and regard for Israel. The noun is also related to the Hebrew word for "womb" and suggests that God's compassion is as encompassing and as nurturing as a mother carrying a child in her womb. Imagine the scandal of a child named "Not given compassion." God's word to Hosea is that the name of this daughter symbolizes the end of God's compassion on Israel. The time for forgiveness of Israel's sin has passed (1:6b). God's compassion and care for Israel has been exhausted, and the name of this daughter is a public reminder of this reversal of divine mercy.

Verse 7 promises the compassion (pity, mercy) denied to Israel will be given to Judah. This verse is almost certainly a later addition by the Judean editor who handed this book on to us. He seems to have a point he wishes to make to some later generation of Judah. God's mercy can be available to Judah but only by trusting in God and not the elements of their own military might (bow, sword, war, horses, horsemen, v. 7b).

A third child, a son, is born to Hosea and Gomer, and he is to be named "Lo-ammi," which translated from Hebrew means "Not my people" (1:1–9). In the covenant between God and Israel a common formula for expressing the closeness of covenant relationship was "I will be your God and you will be my people" (see variations on this formula in Deut. 26:17; Exod. 6:7; Lev. 26:12; 2 Sam. 7:24). Israel lived in the security of an identity that included the understanding that they were God's people. Now God announces that the name of this child symbolizes the undoing of that relationship, the reversal of the formula, "for you are not my people and I am not your God" (v. 9b). This child is to be a living reminder that the covenant is undone. God has declared it null and void because of Israel's sin.

The cumulative effect of the names of these three children is devastating. Through the prophet Hosea, these names symbolize God's word that Israel faces a future with no kingdom, no compassion, and no God. A bleak prospect, indeed! Like his slightly earlier contemporary, the prophet Amos, Hosea has become a messenger for God's word that Israel faces its own end as a consequence of its own sin. Unlike Amos, however, Hosea almost always has a word of hope beyond the prospect for judgment and we must go on to look at 1:10–2:1.

Before we move ahead in the text, however, it seems important to reflect on the use of Hosea's marriage and children as metaphors for the relationship between God and Israel. Can the strange circumstances of this family still speak to us? Does the intended metaphor still hold relevance for us today? Although there will be further development of these themes in chapters 2—3, we can make a preliminary assessment of the richness and the limitations of this metaphor.

The book of Hosea opens by offering us the portrait of a dysfunctional family as a way of understanding the dysfunctional covenant relationship between God and Israel. The images used have a power to shake us and confront us with depths of brokenness that other metaphors might not have.

We can identify with the pain and brokenness of a marriage commitment torn by infidelity. We can sympathize with children bearing names that symbolize broken relationship even as their own parents' relationship is being broken. No one in this story is without the experience of pain and rejection, neither Hosea, Gomer, nor the children. When this is the experience then used to understand the relationship between God and Israel, covenant and broken covenant become strikingly personal. We are forced to understand God as pained and vulnerable. Covenant cannot remain some abstract, judicial matter in the face of these images of unfaithfulness, rejection, and broken relationship. Marriage is a commitment that we still understand as requiring loyalty, fidelity, and trust, and we know as surely as did Hosea and Gomer that when these are absent the results are painful, futures once hopeful grow clouded, and relationships once meaningful are ended. When these images are used to understand the relationship between God and God's people, there is considerable power. Like Israel, we in the modern church are helped to understand that the commitment and loyalty asked by the first commandment ("You shall have no other gods before me") is not simply an abstract religious matter. It is a matter of commitment in relationship to God that requires faithfulness. In the book of Hosea, this imagery will allow us many opportunities to discuss the forms of idolatry that represent our unfaithfulness in relationship to God. The marriage and family metaphors force us to face the woundedness to God and ourselves that results from idolatrous unfaithfulness to our covenant commitment.

But the marriage and family metaphors of Hosea have limitations as well. We must acknowledge them from the beginning. Marriage in the eighth-century B.C. Israel was very different from our understandings of marriage in late twentieth-century North America. Marriages were arranged solely on the initiative of men. The freedom of women was under the control of fathers or husbands. Although a good marriage should be characterized by love, caring, respect, and commitment, women had no freedom of choice in relationships, and marriages were not thought of in terms of mutuality. Women certainly had no power to leave one relationship for another without the gravest of consequences. Thus, for Hosea's time, marriage suggested itself as an appropriate metaphor for the relationship between God and Israel. God is the superior partner and the initiator of relationship. Israel had no power to initiate that relationship itself. The limitation of this metaphor for us is that it necessarily casts husbands in the Godlike role in marital relationships. If God is like a husband, then husbands may be thought to be like God. Further, if God's people are unfaithful, as the human community in its sin always is, then the metaphor suggests that unfaithfulness and promiscuity are primarily identified with wives/women. Godlike authority for husbands who must control the promiscuous tendencies of their wives is in our time a formula for abuse, not a foundation for fulfilling marital relationships.

All this means that in reading and appropriating Hosea's message for the church in our time we must be aware of the need to translate the language of relationship into terms more appropriate to our twentieth-century understandings of marriage as a mutual partnership and not a patriarchal right. It is important not to abandon the language of commitment and love, unfaithfulness and brokenness that are introduced through the metaphor of marital relationship. This language of relationship applied to God and God's people is rich and promising, but it does not require us to accept the framework of a patriarchal society's practice of marriage as the necessary framework for our reflection on relationship to God. At many points in Hosea, we will have to ask what endures to speak God's word to us while transcending the limitations of ancient Israel's social practices— practices that cannot and need not be ours. We will return to some of these issues, particularly in relation to chapter 2.

The Promise of God's New Future (1:10–2:1)

All the preexilic prophets spoke of God's judgment, and we have particularly identified them with this message. But Hosea, as one of the earliest prophetic books, constantly reminds us that God's love has the last word. This pattern is set already in chapter 1 when the focus in 1:2–9 on Israel's sin and consequent judgment is followed immediately in 1:10–2:1 by a promise of restoration and renewal beyond judgment.

Israel, the nation, may come to an end, but for Hosea this does not mean God's love and grace are exhausted. He pictures a future time when the judgments symbolized by the children's names will be reversed. "Not my people" will become "My people" (2:1) and "Children of the living God" (v. 10b); "No compassion" ("Not pitied") will become "Compassion" ("Pitied," 2:1). The day of Jezreel will become great rather than disastrous (1:11b). None of this language suggests that God's judgment was softened or revoked. Hosea is deadly serious when he announces God's word that Israel's sin has brought them to the end of the kingdom itself. This is, in fact, the fate of Israel toward the end of Hosea's own lifetime. Samaria is destroyed and Israel perishes at the hands of the Assyrians in 721 B.C.

Hosea looks instead to a new future, beyond judgment. God is not finished with Israel, even though the nation itself perishes. The basis of that future is God's fidelity to the promise made first to Abraham. That promise is remembered in verse 10 by recalling the language of descendants too numerous to count (Gen. 13:16; 15:5; 26:24; 28:14). God has not forgotten the promise, but the future will be a new future. In verse 11, that new future will include the reunion of Israel and Judah into one people, and they will "appoint for themselves one head." By avoiding the word "king" and speaking only of a leader, "head," Hosea is foreshadowing a criticism, later in the book, of kings and kingdoms as part of Israel's sinful pattern. God's people need leadership, but perhaps not the imperial ways of kings and kingdoms.

It is well for us to observe from Hosea's opening chapter that judgment and hope are part of the workings of the same God. In the modern church we tend to treat judgment and hope as an either-or and to reduce these themes to mere pessimism versus optimism. Judgment is deeper and more crucial than griping and criticizing. It is a matter of accountability and responsibility and the real consequences when commitments are broken. Hope is more than a religion of positive thinking and happiness. It requires the ability to envision God's future in ways that take seriously the obstacles and struggles that impede and deny that future. Hosea saw clearly that the community of God's people needed to hear God's word both as judgment and as hope. We should take his witness seriously in our own efforts to speak God's word as the church to our time.

SHE IS NOT MY WIFE
Hosea 2:2–23

2:2 Plead with your mother, plead—
    for she is not my wife,
    and I am not her husband—
  that she put away her whoring from her face,
    and her adultery from between her breasts,
3 or I will strip her naked
    and expose her as in the day she was born,
  and make her like a wilderness,
    and turn her into a parched land,
    and kill her with thirst.
4 Upon her children also I will have no pity,
    because they are children of whoredom.

⁵For their mother has played the whore;
    she who conceived them has acted shamefully.
 For she said, "I will go after my lovers;
    they give me my bread and my water,
    my wool and my flax, my oil and my drink."
⁶Therefore I will hedge up her way with thorns;
    and I will build a wall against her,
    so that she cannot find her paths.
⁷She shall pursue her lovers,
    but not overtake them;
 and she shall seek them,
    but shall not find them.
 Then she shall say, "I will go
    and return to my first husband,
    for it was better with me then than now."
⁸She did not know
    that it was I who gave her
    the grain, the wine, and the oil,
 and who lavished upon her silver
    and gold that they used for Baal.
⁹Therefore I will take back
    my grain in its time,
    and my wine in its season;
 and I will take away my wool and my flax,
    which were to cover her nakedness.
¹⁰Now I will uncover her shame
    in the sight of her lovers,
    and no one shall rescue her out of my hand.
¹¹I will put an end to all her mirth,
    her festivals, her new moons, her sabbaths,
    and all her appointed festivals.
¹²I will lay waste her vines and her fig trees,
    of which she said,
 "These are my pay,
    which my lovers have given me."
 I will make them a forest,
    and the wild animals shall devour them.
¹³I will punish her for the festival days of the Baals,
    when she offered incense to them
 and decked herself with her ring and jewelry,
    and went after her lovers,
    and forgot me, says the LORD.

¹⁴ Therefore, I will now allure her,
        and bring her into the wilderness,
        and speak tenderly to her.
¹⁵ From there I will give her her vineyards,
        and make the Valley of Achor a door of hope.
    There she shall respond as in the days of her youth,
        as at the time when she came out of the land of Egypt.
¹⁶ On that day, says the LORD, you will call me, "My husband," and no longer will you call me, "My Baal." ¹⁷ For I will remove the names of the Baals from her mouth, and they shall be mentioned by name no more. ¹⁸ I will make for you a covenant on that day with the wild animals, the birds of the air, and the creeping things of the ground; and I will abolish the bow, the sword, and war from the land; and I will make you lie down in safety. ¹⁹ And I will take you for my wife forever; I will take you for my wife in righteousness and in justice, in steadfast love, and in mercy. ²⁰ I will take you for my wife in faithfulness; and you shall know the LORD.
    ²¹ On that day I will answer, says the LORD.
        I will answer the heavens
        and they shall answer the earth;
    ²² and the earth shall answer the grain, the wine, and the oil,
        and they shall answer Jezreel;
        and I will sow him for myself in the land.
    ²³ And I will have pity on Lo-ruhamah,
        and I will say to Lo-ammi, "You are my people";
        and he shall say, "You are my God."

Chapter 2 of the book of Hosea uses the metaphor of husband and unfaithful wife introduced through Hosea's marriage in 1:2–9 and develops it in detail as applied to God's relationship with Israel. The chapter is poetry (except for a portion in verses 16–20 that may be in prose) spoken in the first person as if the Lord is speaking directly. The entire chapter extends the metaphor of the marriage relationship with God speaking to or about Israel as the unfaithful wife. In this chapter, the husband represents God; the wife represents Israel (sometimes as people, sometimes as land); the children seem to be in the role of individual Israelites over against corporate Israel; the lovers of the wife are the Baals of Canaanite religion. The entire broken relationship between God and Israel is developed in this chapter through the metaphor of a husband and an unfaithful wife.

There are different ways of describing the structure of this long and sometimes complex chapter. It begins with an accusation reminiscent of legal language when formal charges are made. The word "plead" in verse 2 means "to argue a case." The first section (2:2–5) might almost be described as an indictment of an adulterous wife (Israel). Three subsequent sections of the chapter are introduced by the word "therefore" (vv. 6, 9, 14). They all deal with the husband's (God's) response and actions toward the adulterous wife. The first two of these sections (vv. 6–8, 9–13) are negative. They describe punishments and harsh consequences as response to the accusation of verses 2–5. But the third "therefore" section in verses 14–15 speaks of a response of love and renewed relationship. Two final sections begin with the phrase "on that day" (16–20; 21–23). They each elaborate a vision of a renewed future between husband and wife, God and Israel.

Overlaying this more complex structure of sections is a general mood to the chapter that divides it into two sections focused on judgment and hope, like the pattern observed in Hosea 1. In the first section (2:2–13), God speaks of the consequences to Israel of her unfaithfulness. In the second section (2:14–23), God speaks of restored and renewed relationship. We will use this two-part focus on judgment and hope as the simplest framework for continuing our discussion of the chapter.

The Consequences
of Unfaithfulness (2:2–13)

Verses 2–13 focus on the faithless behavior of Israel as an adulterous wife and the consequences of that behavior. The speaker and accuser is the Lord as the angry husband. The opening plea is to the children (presumably individual Israelites in this extended metaphor) that they might "plead with your mother" (v. 2a) to give up her promiscuous and adulterous practices (v. 2b). Injecting the children intentionally into the midst of a broken marital relationship would not, of course, be a procedure recommended by modern family counselors. Even in the text itself, this becomes ambiguous a few verses later when the very children appealed to are angrily labeled "children of whoredom" on whom God will have no pity (v. 4). This suggests the difficulty in the metaphor of condemning corporate Israel while appealing to individual Israelites. Further, we are alerted that the patterns of marriage and family relationships in ancient Israel, and behaviors that were approved in those relationships, will not conform to our own standards for marriages and families in many respects. Understanding and appropriating these texts for the modern church will require dealing often with the discontinuities between ancient and modern social practices.

One observation must be made from the beginning. The intent, even in the judgment section of the chapter (vv. 2–13), is not on the final severing of relationship. The goal is not divorce between God and Israel, but some kind of reconciliation and restoration of relationship. This might not be understood given the language of verse 2, "for she is not my wife, and I am not her husband." This is not a statement of what God desires, namely divorce, but a statement of the effect of infidelity on the marriage. The commitment of husband and wife is broken and is functionally inoperative. Israel is not fulfilling its responsibilities in relationship, so God cannot do so either. But everything about the chapter implies that the goal is to restore relationship, not to end it.

The problem as posed by this chapter is this: Israel has behaved like an adulterous wife. How does God, like an angry and wounded husband, respond to this broken commitment? We must seek to understand the testimony of this chapter in the images it draws out of its own ancient situation and then seek to determine the degree to which these images can still speak to our context as the modern church. To do this we must recognize that chapter 2 involves the intermix of two sets of images and language appropriate to those images. One of these languages is severely problematic to us, and the other is not well understood. We can identify these languages and their attendant issues as follows: (a) the language of marital discord in ancient Israel and the abuse of adulterous women and (b) the language of idolatry and interreligious conflict and the appeal of Canaanite religion. Almost the whole of chapter 2 must be understood through the intermix of these two languages and the interpretive issues they pose for us.

Adultery

The consequences for Israel of broken covenant with God are described in chapter 2 in terms of consequences for an adulterous wife in ancient Israel. Israel has gone after other gods as a promiscuous wife might have gone after other lovers. Once again we are operating out of ancient Israelite views of marriage and family that are rather different from our own.

Adultery in ancient Israel assumes that wives are dependent on husbands for material well-being and husbands are rightfully in control of wives' sexual behavior. For a woman to act promiscuously dishonors the husband and violates his rights. The penalties for such behavior are severe. Ancient Israelite law codes allow the giving of bills of divorce (Deut. 24:1ff), cutting women off from family connections and provisions, and even prescribe the death penalty for adultery in some cases (Deut. 22:13–29). Men can face severe penalties (even death) for adultery with another man's wife but are free to exercise sexual urges with unattached women (e.g., prostitutes) without penalty.

In the first section of this chapter (vv. 2–5), God speaks as an outraged husband accusing his wife, Israel, and imploring the children to intervene. The accusations include promiscuity (NRSV "whoring" [v. 2b] and "played the whore" [v. 5a]), adultery (v. 2b), acting shamefully (v. 5a), and taking lovers from whom she gains material benefit (v. 5b). In religious terms, the lovers are the Canaanite Baals whose worship promises fertility of the land (bread, wool, flax, oil, [v. 5b]). But the imagery is drawn from human experience with God as the outraged and dishonored husband. The accusations of adulterous behavior are accompanied by threats of physical abuse and humiliation: "I will strip her naked and expose her . . . and kill her with thirst" (v. 3). The threats extend to the children: "Upon her children also I will have no pity, because they are children of whoredom" (v. 4). God is pictured as the dishonored and humiliated husband who could not control his wife's behavior or satisfy her material and sexual needs.

The account moves from accusation to resolved actions in verses 6–13, a series of punishments (v. 13) for Israel's behavior as an adulterous wife. If we were to encounter these actions in our modern human experience, we would regard them as physically and emotionally abusive behavior. Unfortunately, such behavior was probably considered acceptable toward women in biblical times, especially if they were thought to have dishonored their husbands.

First, the husband isolates the woman by restricting her freedom and denying her access to her lovers (vv. 6–7a). The hope of this strategy is that she will recognize and acknowledge her proper dependence on her husband for her needs (v. 7b, "Then she will say, 'I will go and return to my first husband, for it was better with me then than now'"). The husband will withhold food and clothing (v. 9) and lay waste her vines and fig trees (v. 12). The husband carries out the earlier threat of public humiliation and nakedness: "I will uncover her shame in the sight of her lovers, and no one shall rescue her out of my hand" (v. 10). Her mirth and festivals are to be ended (v. 11), and she is to be punished because she "decked herself with her ring and jewelry and went after her lovers, and forgot me" (v. 13). Of course, in verse 13 with the naming of the Baals, it becomes clear that behind the human metaphors of broken marital relationship lies the Israelite pursuit of Canaanite deities. Some elements of the punishments have overtones of Israel as the land (vv. 8–9, 12). We will discuss this element of the chapter further below.

In verse 14, the tone shifts from punishment to reconciliation. The language is of a husband turning now to love and restored relationship. Traditionally, this redemptive turn is thought to make the harshness of the punishment irrelevant if not acceptable. But coming after such abusive behavior, such a pattern of affection and reconciliation is problematic for our reading in light of what we know now about patterns of marital abuse. It is typical of abuse, particularly in its early stages, to follow a threefold pattern of accusation, punishing/abusing behavior, and contrition/tenderness/reconciliation. It is the tenderness and loving expressions of this third stage that often lead to women remaining in abusive situations longer than advisable and sometimes with deadly or injurious results. It is true that Hosea 2 does not suggest an ongoing, repetitious cycle of these events but the juxtaposition of the three elements that make up such cycles is problematic for those in the modern church who are increasingly aware that marital abuse is far more widespread than any could have imagined. There are obvious limitations and problems associated with the language we encounter in Hosea 2. How can we deal with this problematic and yet ask if there is any word here that can legitimately or helpfully be appropriated for the modern church?

The first step in dealing with these texts is to recognize frankly the problems with the marriage metaphor when the assumption is the understanding of a patriarchal, Israelite society in which men were entitled legally to control the freedom and behavior of women, particularly their sexuality. We do not live in such a society.

A second step is to acknowledge as a truth we wish to preserve that relationships broken by unfaithfulness and promiscuity are painful to all involved—husband, wife, and children. Such behavior does have consequences. Anger and rejection as responses to such behavior are understandable. When metaphors of broken relationship are applied to our relationship with God, it allows us to understand God as wounded and vulnerable in ways other metaphors could not communicate. It is appropriate to save these understandings from our reading of these texts.

But in doing so, we must firmly and absolutely reject the appropriateness of abusive actions, physical or emotional, as responses to a broken relationship no matter what the circumstances. The language of a broken relationship as painful and wounding can be preserved. But we must say an absolute no to responses in broken relationships that justify abusive attempts to regain control no matter how painful the brokenness. Further, we must say no to the incorporation of these elements into metaphors for God's relationship to us (or to ancient Israel). To suggest that God, as husband, acts legitimately toward Israel, as wife, is to suggest that such behavior is appropriate in human marital relationships. This we cannot do. To reject the appropriateness of such language and behavior about God breaks the cycle in which love and tenderness are but intervals between episodes of abuse. It allows us to recover the redemptive language of Hosea 1:14–23 as rich and valuable in its own right and as appropriate in ruptured relationships when abuse is rejected and removed from the cycle. If with these texts we are to say "God is like a husband" then we must read them through the church's best *present* moral understanding of how husbands responsibly behave in crisis situations—not through the lens of ancient Israelite understandings of marriage.

Idolatry

The issue behind the marriage metaphor in Hosea 2 is the conflict between the worship of Israel's God, Yahweh, and the practices of Canaanite religion, particularly the appeal of the Canaanite god, Baal. To those defending the purity of Israel's religion, any of the practices or trappings associated with Baal or the Canaanite shrines constituted idolatry. The prophets were among the foremost of those defenders, and idolatry is a major concern in the preaching of Hosea.

Israel lived in the midst of Canaanite culture. In fact, Israel and its distinctive religion are considered by many historians to be a development out of Canaanite culture. They share similar languages and occupy territory that shares much in the way of common cultural patterns. Some would suggest that the conflict between Israelite and Canaanite religion is between two religions native to the area, and not between a native Israelite religion and an invasive, foreign, Canaanite religion. Much would suggest that it was natural for many Israelites to commingle elements of the two religions. It was against this that the prophets struggled and preached.

Canaanite religion possessed a pantheon of gods and goddesses, many of whom personified the forces of nature. Baal was the storm god and seemed to exercise chief influence both in the stories we know of the Canaanite pantheon and in the popularity of his worship among the populace. With his consort, the goddess Anat, the vitality of Baal played a chief role in the cycle of the seasons and the fertility of the land. Canaanite religion understood the rains as Baal's seed bringing life out of the earth. In winter, Baal was thought to die and go to the netherworld, from which he was rescued by Anat, and their sexual coupling restored life to the earth for the spring cycle of fertility. Canaanite ritual may have included ritual sexual intercourse to enact this fertility cycle of Baal. It is a matter of debate whether common worshipers participated in such rituals, but the prophets certainly regarded Canaanite ritual as immoral and obscene behavior (see Hosea 4:12–14). It was perhaps the sexual elements connected with the fertility religion of Baal that suggested the appropriateness of adultery with lovers as a metaphor for Israel's attraction to Baal worship. Canaanite deities, including Baal, were represented in carved and cast figures placed in shrines where rituals were carried out. These shrines were located on hilltops commonly with groves of trees to represent the fertility promoted by the worship of Baal and other Canaanite deities (hence the prophets preaching against high places and sacred groves). Although Baal was but one deity in the Canaanite pantheon, his local manifestations in these shrines were often called by the name of the place (for example, Baal-peor, Baal-zaphon). For this reason prophets like Hosea sometimes speak of Baal worship in the plural (for example, Hos. 2:13 "festival days of the Baals"). The word "baal" was also in use in Hebrew as an ordinary word for "master" sometimes used in the context of marriage to mean husband (in the sense of master of the household including the wife). We can already begin to imagine the plays on words that are possible where Hosea intermingles the language of the marriage metaphor with his concern for Canaanite idolatry. This sort of play on words is crucial for understanding 2:16–17.

The appeal of Baal worship is easy to understand in an agrarian society in which the fertility of the land is so centrally important. The Canaanite religion personifies the powers of nature and allows appeal to be made directly to those powers. Baal, the representative of the all-important rains and effective ruler of the gods, is the central figure in ensuring that those powers of nature will produce the crops necessary to life. If Baal is honored, celebrated, and perhaps even controlled by appropriate rituals, then the land will produce abundantly. If these rituals are sensual and sexual in nature to some degree, it simply ties the fertility of the land to the same sensual/sexual drives that produce life in human experience. To many Israelite peasants, it must have made sense to worship Baal even if one also worshiped Yahweh, Israel's God. The issue faced by the prophets was not so much the replacement of their God by Baal but the syncretistic combining of the two religions.

Hosea 2 certainly shows the conflict with Baalism clearly at many points. The central question is, "From whom do the gifts of the land come, the Lord or Baal?" Israel is charged with going after lovers (Baals) in the belief that bread, water, wool, flax, oil, and wine all come from the Baals (v. 5). But the Lord, speaking through the prophet Hosea, disputes this claim: "She did not know that it was I who gave her the grain, the wine, and the oil" (v. 8). To demonstrate that the land and its fertility are under the sovereignty of the Lord and not of Baal, God resolves to withhold the gifts of produce from the land (v. 9) or to give failed crops (v. 12). These verses perhaps suggest famines or droughts as chastisements from God. The harsh threat of verse 3 seems in part directed at Israel as land rather than as adulterous woman: "I will . . . make her like a wilderness, and turn her into a parched land, and kill her with thirst." The land will not be fertile because Israel has not recognized its true sovereign. Of course, the rituals giving honor to Baal are attacked and forbidden as well (vv. 11, 13). The religious conflict issue in this chapter is made clear in verse 13. Israel deserves judgment because in celebrating Baal (festivals, incense, jewelry) they "forgot me, says the LORD."

Does this conflict with Baalism still have meaning for us today? We are no longer primarily an agrarian society and not prone to deify the powers of nature. We do not make or worship physical objects of wood, stone, or metal (unless we count some persons' cars!). The tendency is to treat this enormous struggle in ancient Israel as an ancient curiosity, interesting but remote and unrelated to our own issues.

But the appeal of Baalism may not be as remote as it seems. Its basic appeal was the hope of controlling the forces that make for material well-being and allow for a life of sensual pleasure. We certainly live in a society that lures many with similar hopes. Perhaps the issues behind the struggle with Baalism are much like the church's struggle with the materialism and sensuality of our own culture. We are lured on every side by products, programs, settings, and schemes that promise us control in achieving the good life. They are idolatrous as surely as were the images of Baal. The church, like the ancient Israelite prophets, claims that the good life comes as the gift of God to be received and not to be manipulated by our own societal rituals for our own benefit. Many mistakenly believe that material well-being and pleasure are antagonistic to the God of the Judeo-Christian tradition. With Hosea, the church must say this is not so. We cannot come to church on Sunday to worship a "spiritual" God and then spend our remaining days pursuing wealth and pleasure as if these were separate gods deserving of our devotion. It is little more than attempting to worship the Lord and Baal. God desires that we live rich and full lives, where our needs are met. God gave us the gift of senses through which we experience pleasure, and God desires that we use them. But these are not ends in themselves. They are to be enjoyed together with other qualities that come from covenant relationship to God in the company of God's people. God gives us the possibilities of well-being and pleasure, but God does not intend that these possibilities be actualized in the individualistic, self-serving patterns so common in modern culture. For Hosea, the self-centeredness of Baal worship is to be replaced by a deeper relationship of God, community, and world marked by "righteousness, justice, steadfast love, mercy and faithfulness" (vv. 19–20). These qualities are no less needed in our time. The church offers them as a deeper vision of the good life than the idolatrous pursuit of materialism and sensuality for which so many are tempted to settle. To explore this vision further as it finds expression in Hosea, we must move from God's indictment of Israel to God's hope for restored and reconciled relationship.

Restored and
Renewed Relationship (2:14–23)

The final verses of chapter 2 (14–23) move us from harsh indictment to hopeful vision. They express a divine resolution for renewed and loving relationship ("therefore . . . " 14–15) and offer two developing word pictures of what the renewed future of that relationship might bring ("on that day . . . " 16–20 and 21–23). When these passionate speeches of renewal and love are taken out of the cycle of abuse toward an unfaithful wife, they are moving and eloquent. They are a vision of relationship that we want to claim and affirm. Left in that cycle of abuse, they are dangerous, for they suggest that hope for such a relationship is a false hope, held out only until the next crisis occasions new abuse. In keeping with our earlier argument in commenting on this chapter, we would argue that these verses must be claimed for the power of their vision, but only after saying no to the metaphors of abuse attributed to God earlier in Hosea 2. It is our interpretive responsibility to recast the context of this vision. It is an appropriate response to the pain and woundedness of broken relationship (for God, for marital partners, for ourselves), but not to abusive expressions of that pain and woundedness. That such language of abuse was used of God speaks a truth about ancient Israelite attitudes toward women but not a truth about God. The metaphor shows the limitations of the context in which it originated.

In this reframed context, verses 14–23 can be appreciated as one of the most moving portraits of divine love, reconciliation, and hope in the prophetic literature. The divine response shifts away from judgment. God resolves to woo Israel again. "I will now allure her, and bring her into the wilderness, and speak tenderly to her" (v. 14). One view of the wilderness time following deliverance from Egypt was that it was a time of harmony and rich relationship between God and Israel—a honeymoon. God proposes here a second honeymoon, a return to a time and setting where relationship was loving and whole. God's hope is that Israel will respond again in love as in those days when she came out of Egypt (v. 15b). God will "speak tenderly" to her (v. 14b, literally in Hebrew, God will "speak to her heart"). The richness of the land will return: "I will give her her vineyards" (v. 15a). The Valley of Achor lies southwest of Jericho, and its name means "valley of trouble." This place of "trouble" shall become a "door of hope."

Verses 16–20 offer a first portrait of God's hopes for that day of renewed relationship. The hope is for a different relationship of husband to wife. Israel will speak of God as "my husband" and not as "my Baal" (v. 16). The Hebrew word for "husband" is one of the common words for a man (*'ish*) and it is closely related to the word for a woman or a wife (*'ishshah*). These are the words used in Genesis 2:22–23 when God divides the first human creature into man and woman as partners to one another (Gen. 2:18). We have already mentioned that the word *baal* is not only the name of the Canaanite god but also a Hebrew word for husband that means "master." God's hope is not only the obvious hope that Israel will turn from the worship of Baal but that Israel's relationship to God will be that of marital partners and not that of master to subordinate.

In this new day, covenant will be renewed and the evidence of wholeness will be seen in harmony with all things in nature (v. 18a) and the end of war and conflict (v. 18b). Israel will "lie down in safety" (v. 18b). The harmony with nature reminds us of Eden when sin had not yet broken the harmony of creation. This vision of harmony and peace voiced in Hosea 2:18 is the first expression of a theme that reappears prominently in the prophets. Isaiah and Micah speak of a time when "they shall beat their swords into plowshares" (Isa. 2:4; Mic. 4:3). Isaiah hopes for the day of the "peaceable kingdom" when "the wolf shall live with the lamb" (11:6–9). Ezekiel envisions a "covenant of peace" marked by harmony with all of nature, and security and safety for Israel (34:25–31). The prophet of the exile talks of God's "covenant of peace" (Isa. 54:10) and envisions the mountains singing and the trees clapping their hands (Isa. 55:12). Hosea's imagery here is the beginning of a rich tradition of visionary hope in the prophets. It is an important early part of that biblical vision of God's future that has made the church a hopeful community when immediate circumstances are painful, difficult, and seemingly without hope. Hosea gives us the gift of vision as a response to brokenness and the church must reclaim it. Too often the church as institution wastes too much of its energy on diagnosing and griping about the ills of church or society and spends too little effort on reclaiming God's vision for a hopeful future.

Perhaps the most striking verses in this vision of God's future come in 2:19–20 when Hosea returns to the marriage metaphor again to speak of renewal between God and Israel. The marriage is to be renewed and it will be forever (v. 19a), but the terms of this renewed relationship will not be the traditional ones common in ancient societies. The phrase that appears three times as "take you for my wife" is a translation of the Hebrew word for "betroth." The concept of betrothal in ancient Israel includes the paying of a bridal price. This marriage relationship, this partnership of God and people, will be marked not by payment of material goods but by righteousness, justice, steadfast love, mercy, and faithfulness. These are God's gifts for the new marriage. These are all terms related to the covenant tradition and used to characterize the obligations in relationship to God and neighbor for covenant partners. They describe both what God chooses to give as the qualities of covenant relationship and what will be expected of Israel in renewed covenant relationship.

Relationship to God lived out of these qualities would look quite different from a life lived in pursuit of materialism and sensuality, whether sought in following the Baals or in modern desire for the good life. *Righteousness* is marked by actions taken to ensure the wholeness and well-being of the other in all our relationships. Here God offers relationship marked by divine righteousness that will act for Israel's wholeness (see also 10:12). *Justice* concerns the safeguard of rights and integrity in relationships, both personal and social. Here God guarantees those rights (see 10:4). *Steadfast love* is the covenant loyalty that marks committed relationship and the obligations that come with such relationships (see 4:1). This term is especially used to describe God's covenant commitment: "For [God's] steadfast love endures forever" (Psalm 136). *Compassion* (translated in the NRSV as "mercy") is a Hebrew noun related to the word for "womb," which is frequently used, as it is here, to describe God's encompassing care to those in need—a metaphor of care perhaps drawn from the image of a child in the womb encompassed by the mother's care. The compassion withdrawn from Israel in the symbolic naming of Hosea's daughter, Lo-ruhamah ("No compassion") is extended to Israel once again. *Faithfulness* is emphasized by appearing in its own separate sentence (see 4:1). It is the quality of fidelity and trustworthiness in relationship. The old covenant, the first marriage of God and Israel, may be broken, but God offers new covenant based on these five qualities and it is offered "forever" (v. 19a). This may suggest God is offering an unconditional covenant of love unlike the conditional covenant at Sinai, which has now been broken and nullified. This reminds us of Jeremiah's later hope for a new covenant written on the heart (Jer. 31:33).

The result of these qualities, offered as bride price in marriage to Israel again, is that "you shall *know* the LORD" (v. 20b). "Knowing" God will be a key concept in Hosea. The verb "to know" in Hebrew means more than the acquiring of cognitive knowledge. It implies an entering into and participation in that which is known. "Knowledge" of God is what Israel is expected to seek in relationship to God. They are to enter into and participate in the reality of relationship with God as it is now offered—in righteousness, justice, steadfast love, compassion, and faithfulness. These qualities are to characterize their learning and obeying of the will of God. Knowledge of God is Hosea's most inclusive term for what is expected of Israel in relationship to God (see 4:1, 6; 5:4; 6:3, 6; 8:2; 11:3; 13:4). Not incidentally, the verb "to know" is also used of the full participation of husband and wife in sexual relationship (for example, Gen. 4:1; 24:16). Hosea incorporates a term that reminds us of the marriage metaphor but has now been broadened to include the whole range of experience to be "known" in relation to God (see further discussion on 4:1).

This remarkable vision of full relationship (vv. 16–20) is an extraordinarily important text for the church and its ministry when our time and culture place so much value on individual self-fulfillment as the ultimate goal in relationships. The dual elements of husband-wife and God-Israel imagery suggests that the vision of these verses can apply to both personal and social relationships. These verses model what we can be in relation to spouses, families, friends, colleagues, and neighbors. They also model what we can be as communities, nations, congregations, and denominations. We live in a society with many evidences of broken relationships, at both personal and social levels. Much in our media and our popular cultural wisdom suggests that the appropriate response to such brokenness is self-protection and self-reliance. As children, we played neighborhood games with carefully drawn rules, but there often came a time in the game when the rules were suspended and someone would cry out, "It's everyone for himself." We live in a culture that often suggests that as the reality of our situation. We make best-sellers of books with titles like *Looking Out for Number One*.

What a different vision the church might offer through texts such as this one. The response to brokenness is not to be everyone for himself or herself. It is to be renewed relationships. And such renewal is not plucked out of the air. It is found by turning from mastery to partnership. It is found by acknowledging a need for relationships that extend to the whole of creation, the realm of nature along with the human. It is found by claiming the vision of peace and wholeness, the vision of shalom as the only true security. It is found by investing our relationships in the possibilities for righteousness, justice, steadfast love, mercy (compassion), and faithfulness. It is found in acknowledging that the only true way to know ourselves and our world is to know the Lord. Whether we speak of marriages (or other personal relationships to which we are committed) or of communities (political or religious), this is a vision rich in possibilities for new wholeness in a time when we experience many forms of brokenness. It is a distinct alternative to the individualism, the materialism, and the self-serving sensuality that characterize so much in our present culture. It is a vision the church can and must claim if it is to provide hope as God's covenant people.

The final verses of chapter 2 (vv. 21–23) are entirely devoted to the reversal of the brokenness of relationships between God and Israel symbolized by alienation from the earth and its productivity and by the names of the three children of Hosea and Gomer. When the marriage, that is, the covenant between God and Israel is renewed in the striking terms of verses 16–20, then the consequences of brokenness begin to be reversed. The chain of interrelationships in God's harmonious creation is reestablished. The chain of restored harmony is initiated from the heavens (the realm of God and the rain), then to the earth (the land, the soil), then to the produce of the land (grain, wine, oil), and finally to the people (Israel, humanity). When the restored chain of harmony reaches Israel, the names of Hosea's children (1:4–9) are reversed as the brokenness those names symbolized is reversed. Israel as Jezreel ("God sows") had become alienated from the land but now God says, "I will *sow* him for myself in the land" (v. 23a). God will have pity (compassion) on "Not-pitied" (No-compassion), verse 23a. God will say to "Not-my-people" that "You are my people" and he will answer, "You are my God" (v. 23b). It is a promise that reverberates far beyond the time of Hosea and has become part of the church's understanding of its life as God's covenant people. "Once you were not a people, but now you are God's people; once you had not received mercy, but now you have received mercy" (1 Pet. 2:10).

GO, LOVE A WOMAN
Hosea 3:1–5

3:1 The LORD said to me again, "Go, love a woman who has a lover and is an adultress, just as the LORD loves the people of Israel, though they turn to

**other gods and love raisin cakes." ² So I bought her for fifteen shekels of sil-
ver and a homer of barley and a measure of wine. ³ And I said to her, "You
must remain as mine for many days; you shall not play the whore, you shall
not have intercourse with a man, nor I with you." ⁴ For the Israelites shall
remain many days without king or prince, without sacrifice or pillar, without ephod or teraphim. ⁵ Afterward the Israelites shall return and seek the
LORD their God, and David their king; they shall come in awe to the LORD
and to his goodness in the latter days.**

Chapter 3 opens with another direct command from the Lord to
Hosea. He is told to "Go, love a woman who has a lover and is an adultress . . . (v. 1a)." We have moved back to Hosea's personal story, but
exactly where we are in his story is not at all clear. This is very reminiscent of God's command in chapter 1. It is clearly the account of a symbolic action the prophet is directed to undertake, but is it another one?
This brief chapter is, like chapter 1, in prose but this time in the first
person. It is Hosea speaking directly of his experience. Could this be
simply another version of the experience in chapter 1? Is this another
woman? Could God have asked Hosea to do this twice? Or is this woman
actually Gomer? If so, what has happened? What could have brought
Hosea and Gomer to these circumstances? These are natural and obvious questions, and we will raise some of them as we look more closely at
the witness of this brief and enigmatic chapter. But we can say from the
outset that the text does not seem concerned to answer all these questions for us. Apart from the central focus on the meaning of these events
for understanding the relationship between God and Israel little attention is paid to the circumstances that gave rise to this episode. Many of
our questions will go unanswered and all proposed explanations will be
conjectural.

The five verses of chapter 3 fall into three distinct sections. Verse
1 moves us back into the marriage story of Hosea and tells us that
God's story with Israel is similar. The marriage experience of the
prophet is being used again as a metaphor to help understand how
God relates to Israel. The next two verses (2–3) tell us of actions taken
by Hosea in the context of the circumstances described in verse 1. We
are in these verses wholly in the prophet's story. But in the last two
verses (4–5) the text speaks only of Israel and God. Presumably verses
4–5 are being suggested as analogous to the prophet's experience in
verses 2–3. We will discuss the message of each of these segments
more fully.

Hosea Loves a Woman Again (3:1–3)

It seems likely that the woman of 3:1 is Gomer. Although the word "again" is translated in the NRSV as referring to God's command, the Hebrew would allow it to apply to the following verb instead: "Go, again, love . . . !" God is commanding this of Hosea to symbolize God's own persistence in loving Israel, in spite of Israel's unfaithfulness. This would seem to require Hosea's persistence in loving Gomer rather than loving some different woman. In 1:2 God's command was to "take for yourself a wife," but here the command is to "love." The issue is not establishing a relationship but the quality of love that is necessary to maintain it even in the most difficult circumstances.

If this is Gomer, the practices that labeled her a "wife of whoredom" in 1:2 must have continued or resumed, since she is described in 3:1 as "a woman who has a lover and is an adulteress." The phrase "who has a lover" is in Hebrew more literally "loving a companion" (understood as a sexual companion; see Jer. 3:1, Song of Sol. 5:16), and this would make her guilty of adultery, the violation of the marriage covenant. As in chapter 1, we are given no particulars on behavior that would justify these characterizations.

The point of this symbolic action is made absolutely clear in God's command. Hosea is to love again "just as the LORD loves the people of Israel, though they turn to other gods and love raisin cakes" (3:1b). Hosea's action is to symbolize the persistence of God's love for Israel. Israel has turned to other gods, presumably the Baal worship alluded to in chapter 2. This behavior is to be understood through the marriage imagery as the taking of lovers by an unfaithful wife. The phrase "and love raisin cakes" refers to delicacies made of pressed and dried grapes that were perhaps used in cultic ceremonies to honor Canaanite deities (see Song of Sol. 2:5; 2 Sam. 6:19).

The central issue is once again the exclusive loyalty that God demands of those people who would be in relationship with God as covenant partners. There can be no other god, just as marriage requires a loyalty that allows for no other sexual partners. The loyalty God requires is related to an experience, marriage, that people knew and could understand. But an additional element has come into focus in chapter 3. When the covenant is broken what is to be the response? Already in the first verse of chapter 3, God suggests through the prophet that love is the ultimate response. Beyond the anger, pain, and judgment described in chapter 2 and symbolized by the naming of the children in chapter 1, it is love that must prevail. And the theme of God's love is a concern of Hosea's message to which we will return at later points as well. Here in 3:1, the verb "to love" is used four times. Hosea is sent to love, the woman (Gomer) loves, the Lord loves, and Israel loves. But the objects of love are different, and there lies all the difference. The focus of love for Gomer/Israel is on those objects and experiences that bring immediate pleasure and self-gratification. The focus is on the self. But God's love, and the love Hosea is asked to undertake (perhaps reluctantly), is one that is focused on the other, and the other's needs, in spite of pain and woundedness.

There is more to this story here, but already it should be clear that these are important matters not just for Hosea's time but our own. The cheapening of love to a mere synonym for self-indulgence and self-gratification is a readily observed phenomenon in our society. Is the object of love to be our own self-fulfillment, as much in our advertising and entertainment suggests? Or is the reality of love truly to be found in losing our focus on ourselves, even on our legitimate pain, to find focus in another? This is the self-giving love that God extends even to an unfaithful people. This is the love God asks of Hosea toward Gomer in spite of his own woundedness. This is the love God asks of us even in our most broken relationships. We must be clear, however, that this self-giving love does not require submission to wounding behavior. The call to love in spite of our woundedness is not a call to continuing victimization but a commitment to the possibility of whole relationship in spite of brokenness. Merely to accept brokenness and simply to endure wounding behavior is not genuine commitment to the other or to wholeness in relationship to the other. As we shall see in verse 3, Hosea's renewed commitment to love Gomer does not allow continuation of her hurtful behavior. In our relationships, this is also true whether the behavior is unfaithfulness, or abuse, or manipulation, or any other form of wounding that has broken the relationship in the first place. Commitment to love does not require submission to intentionally inflicted pain.

In verse 2, with no information at all on the circumstances, we are told: "So I bought her for fifteen shekels of silver and a homer of barley and a measure of wine." What has happened here? Who was selling her and for what reason? The woman that Hosea is to love again, presumably Gomer, must be purchased, but we are given no information to help us understand this state of affairs. There are possibilities. She could have resumed her unfaithfulness by practicing prostitution, and the price mentioned would have to be interpreted as purchasing her services indefinitely. Perhaps she had to be redeemed from a vow attaching her to a shrine. Or she may have fallen into slavery or become the legal property of another man through debt or criminal penalty. There are references (Exod. 21:32; Lev. 27:4) to values of thirty shekels set on women in similar circumstances.

The text is not interested in the circumstances that brought Gomer to this situation, but it is clear that the situation is a desperate one in which she has lost her freedom and is available for a price. It is the price that receives emphasis, its exact amounts in silver and barley and wine being reported. Her person and her circumstances have been displaced by her economic worth. The woman has become a commodity, and even Hosea cannot help her without paying the commodity price. It is a situation of considerable danger for Gomer, for presumably any man could have purchased her, and for any purpose.

Hosea does pay the price ("I bought her . . . , " v. 2a). If he was still legally her husband, and perhaps even if he were only her purchaser, he would have had the right by custom of the times to insist on conjugal relations with her, but he does not. Instead, he separates her from her life of adultery. She must live "many days" in his house, but will be denied the possibilities of sexual relationship with any man, and he also will not force such sexual contact on her (v. 3). As the interpretation of this act for the life of Israel seems to make clear (vv. 4–5), the purpose of this separation is to give Gomer the opportunity to turn back to Hosea in love.

Marriage in ancient Israel was not considered necessarily as a matter of love. Marriages were arranged and women were in many ways considered the property of their husbands. Again, the differences in understanding marriage give us some difficulty here. To be shut away, as Gomer is here by Hosea, seems to us like imprisonment. But we cannot assume for that ancient world the radical freedom of the individual that we assume as the right of all persons in choosing their associations with others (including husbands). What is unusual here is not that Hosea insists she stay at home "as mine" (v. 3a), but that, within the limitations of those ancient social patterns, he desires and provides opportunity for Gomer's love to matter to him. He does not wish a relationship with her as a husband's prerogative, but as an awakening of returned love from Gomer. His actions represent an opposition to continued sin (adultery) but also an unwillingness to coerce normal marital relationship as his due. He will wait while she remains with him, to see if the possibility of love can arise.

Israel Returns to God (3:4–5)

We do not know how this personal story turns out. Neither this chapter nor any other text in the book of Hosea suggests the outcome of this marriage story. But the text does make clear the meaning that Hosea and Gomer are symbolizing for God and Israel. In verses 4–5, the separation that Hosea imposes on Gomer is interpreted to symbolize a time when Israel must live apart from its normal interaction with the Lord. "The Israelites shall remain many days . . . " (v. 4a). In this time, Israel is to be "without king or prince, without sacrifice or pillar, without ephod or teraphim." King and prince represent the normal institutions of leadership, thought to have been ordained by God. Israel must live through a time deprived of leadership, perhaps deprived even of the possibility of governance. Sacrifice and pillar represent the normal institutions of worship connected with the shrines and holy places, thought to give access to God. The pillar, a standing stone, was more connected with Canaanite practice. The prophet may suggest Israel will live through a time when all cultic practices, legitimate or not, will not be possible. Ephod and teraphim are objects associated with inquiring after God's will. The ephod is a ceremonial garment the exact function of which is unclear. Teraphim are household images perhaps tolerated in Israel but tending toward idolatrous practice. It would seem here that Hosea is suggesting that Israel must also live a time without any customary means of divination, any of the common ways of seeking assurance of divine guidance. Israel must live without kings, holy places and rituals, divination—all the ways in which Israel felt connected to God—for a time, just as Gomer must live without men, even Hosea, for a time. How this time without is to come about we are not told in this passage, but elsewhere in the prophet's preaching are found images of judgment in the form of disruption of Israel's national and religious life by conquest and exile.

But the turning point comes in verse 5. "Afterward" (that is, beyond the time of judgment) God hopes for a day when the "Israelites shall return and seek the LORD." God will not coerce restored relationship, but beyond the brokenness and separation that result from sin and judgment, God holds out the hope of return. God hopes that Israel will love again in response to a divine love that has never been abandoned. (The phrase "and David their king" is surely a later addition by Judean editors who hoped for a return of Davidic kingship.)

The concept of return is a crucial element of Hosea's message. It is the turning away from Canaanite gods and their promises and the turning back to the Lord and the promises of covenant relationship. It is a return to the days of Exodus and Sinai as possibilities for restored community and not just original community. Hosea will use the verb "to return" many times as a central element of his preaching. Israel fails to return (7:10; 11:5). It is Israel's deeds that prevent their return (5:4). Hosea calls on them to return (12:6; 14:1–2). The Lord's judgment will enable Israel's return (2:7; 6:1;

14:7). The verb "to seek" used here with "return" is the common verb used throughout the Old Testament for approaching God in worship. Return is for the purpose of seeking God. The chapter ends with reference to God's goodness, almost in assurance that by returning and seeking, the gifts of God's blessing are still possible. The goodness of the land sought in worship of Baal was a false hope. True goodness lies with the Lord.

As a final reflection on this brief but compelling chapter, let us take note of the fact that love precedes return. Grace anticipates response. Hosea is asked to love Gomer again, as God loves Israel again. Love is not the reward for having returned to right relationship, but love makes return possible. In our society, love is often treated as the prize to be given if all our desired conditions are met. We are reminded by this story of Hosea and Gomer/God and Israel that relationships are made possible by love risked even in the face of brokenness. This is a story of the initiative of God's grace in spite of brokenness that cannot but remind Christians of a divine love that chose a path of grace that risked the cross for the sake of resurrection life.

MY PEOPLE ARE DESTROYED
FOR LACK OF KNOWLEDGE
Hosea 4:1–11a

4:1 Hear the word of the LORD, O people of Israel;
>   for the LORD has an indictment against the inhabitants of the land.
> There is no faithfulness or loyalty,
>   and no knowledge of God in the land.
> ² Swearing, lying, and murder,
>   and stealing and adultery break out:
>   bloodshed follows bloodshed.
> ³ Therefore the land mourns,
>   and all who live in it languish;
> together with the wild animals
>   and the birds of the air,
>   even the fish of the sea are perishing.

> ⁴ Yet let no one contend,
>   and let none accuse,
>   for with you is my contention, O priest.
> ⁵ You shall stumble by day;
>   the prophet also shall stumble with you by night,
>   and I will destroy your mother.

⁶My people are destroyed for lack of knowledge;
    because you have rejected knowledge,
    I reject you from being a priest to me.
And since you have forgotten the law of your God,
    I also will forget your children.

⁷The more they increased,
    the more they sinned against me;
    they changed their glory into shame.
⁸They feed on the sin of my people;
    they are greedy for their iniquity.
⁹And it shall be like people, like priest;
    I will punish them for their ways,
    and repay them for their deeds.
¹⁰They shall eat, but not be satisfied;
    they shall play the whore, but not multiply;
because they have forsaken the LORD
    to devote themselves to ¹¹whoredom.

Chapter 4 opens with two oracles that take the form of God's covenant lawsuit. The Hebrew word that means "lawsuit" appears in both verse 1 (NRSV "indictment") and in verse 4 (NRSV "contention"). This piece of vocabulary drawn from the law court is common in the prophets, who often used legal language to suggest that Israel (or its leaders) was under indictment by God for the breaking of covenant. The covenant itself was often pictured as a formally sealed agreement or contract between God and the people. When agreements are broken in Israelite life, the matter is taken to court. In similar fashion, the prophets many times appear as if they were covenant lawyers representing God as the aggrieved party in a lawsuit over a broken covenant agreement. In such cases, their oracles sometimes take the form of an indictment and a verdict rendered in a court of law (see also Hos. 12:2 and Mic. 6:1–8). Here Hosea announces first God's lawsuit against the people of the land (vv. 1–3) and then God's lawsuit against the priests of Israel (vv. 4–10).

The Lawsuit against the People
(4:1–3)

These three verses are a succinct but remarkably complete statement of the indictment against Israel that Hosea brings in God's behalf. Many have described these verses as a key summary of the portion of Hosea's message that deals with God's judgment against Israel.

The oracle begins with the command to hear (also in 5:1). This imperative in Hebrew (*shemaʿ*) carries overtones of the call to heed as well as to hear (note the famous *Shema* of Deut. 6:4–9). Hosea addresses this summons to the "people of Israel" and directs their hearing and heeding to his announcement of "the word of the LORD." "The LORD has a lawsuit," proclaims the prophet. And the people being sued are identified as "inhabitants of the land." In Hosea, land plays a crucial role. The land is where God bestows blessings to Israel and not the Baals (2:8–23). It belongs to God (9:3), but it has been given for Israel's use as God's covenant people. But this passage announces that Israel has broken covenant, and God now brings the case against her. The passage contains a series of negative charges (v. 1b), which are followed by a series of positive charges for violations of covenant (v. 2), and ends finally with a statement of consequences for this breaking of covenant (v. 3).

Israel's breaking of covenant first consists of its failure to observe the qualities of life consistent with covenant obedience. These are the sins of omission. "There is no *faithfulness*, or *loyalty*, and no *knowledge* of God in the land" (v. 1b).

The word "faithfulness" indicates trustworthiness, fidelity to one's commitments. The word used here for what Israel lacks is a synonym of the word discussed in 2:20 for the faithfulness to which God is committed in relation to Israel. Israel has not reciprocated the trust God has shown.

"Loyalty" here indicates the quality of life required of those who live in covenant partnership with God. The Hebrew word (*hesed*) is difficult to translate with any one English word. It is often translated as "kindness," "steadfast love," "mercy." It is also used frequently to describe God's covenant commitment as well (see the discussion on 2:19). "Loyalty" here indicates the quality that maintains wholeness in relationship. It consists of doing those things that are required to establish and maintain relationship. Hosea's charge seems to be that Israel has not exhibited loyalty in its relationship to God ("no knowledge of God," v. 1b) or in relationships to one another among the people (murder, lying, stealing, adultery, v. 2).

Finally, and most emphatically, Hosea charges that there is "no knowledge of God" in Israel. This is one of the most central themes in the book of Hosea. The terms *knowledge/know* appear throughout Hosea's ministry and the object of this knowing is God/the Lord (2:20; 4:6; 5:4; 6:3, 6; 8:2; 11:3; 13:4). To "know God" has both a content and a commitment. Knowledge of God is related to torah, or instruction, and is the special responsibility of the priest (4:6). It is in this respect related to Israel's memory of what God has done and the relationship that has been established between God and Israel. But the Hebrew words for knowing and knowledge imply more than a content. They imply an acknowledgment and participation in relationship.

The verb "to know" is, for instance, used to describe sexual union and the intimate relationship out of which such union should come. Perhaps the sexual imagery of the faithful or the adulterous spouse, which are such important metaphors in Hosea, suggested the centrality of this same term in covenant relationship to God. To know God is to acknowledge intimate relationship to God. Covenant is not for Hosea a matter of external obedience. It is a matter of intimate partnership. To keep covenant is to know God. Hosea uses the actual word *covenant* only twice, and each time it is to contrast the breaking of covenant with the knowledge of God (6:6–7; 8:1–2).

Verse 2 follows the sins of omission with charges of specific crimes that have been committed. If covenant relationship with God has been violated as described in verse 1b, then verse 2 suggests that relationships with the neighbor will become violent and dysfunctional as well. Hosea charges that life in Israel has now become marked by swearing, lying, murder, stealing, and adultery (see the similar series of charges in Jeremiah's temple sermon, Jeremiah 7:9). All five of these charges are violations of fundamental covenant responsibilities toward the neighbor laid down in the Ten Commandments and reinforced by Israel's covenant law codes.

"Swearing" does not refer to simple profanity. It might better be translated as "cursing," for it refers to the attempt to use God's name (or equally bad, the name of an idolatrous deity) to bring misfortune on another. As such, it is a violation of the commandment against taking God's name in vain (Exod. 20:7). "Lying" goes beyond the important matter of simply telling the truth. It was a special problem in maintaining the integrity of the legal system in which justice depends on the solemn commitment to truthful witness. One is reminded of the oath taken by witnesses in our legal system to "tell the truth, the whole truth, and nothing but the truth, so help me God." The commandment not to "bear false witness" refers to this need for judicial integrity (Exod. 20:16; see this concern also in the law codes, Exod. 23:1, 7). The prophets often voiced a special concern for the corruption of the law courts (e.g., Amos 5:12). "Murder," "stealing," and "adultery" are the same terms directly used in the Ten Commandments to prohibit such community-breaking actions (Exod. 20:13–15). Hosea ends his list of charges against Israel with the phrase "bloodshed follows bloodshed." He seems to suggest that in Israel of that time violence has become the norm.

The juxtaposition of these two sets of charges by Hosea against Israel is important. There is a necessary interrelationship between the rightness of our relationship to God and the rightness of our relationship to neighbor. Jesus' connection of these in summarizing the law was very much in keeping with Hosea's message here. Love of God and love of neighbor must go together (Matt. 22:34–40; Mark 12:28–34; Luke 10:25–28). Hosea charges that violence characterizes Israel's life because it is unchecked by a sense of right relationship to God, and the possibilities of right relationship to God are in turn undermined by the unchecked exploitation and violence in Israelite society. Israel is caught in a vicious cycle and the prophet speaks in the hope of breaking that cycle. For a covenant people, theology and sociology are interrelated.

In the lawsuit of God, the charges of verses 1b–2 are followed by the sentencing or the consequences in verse 3. Israel, characterized as the "inhabitants of the land" (v. 1), is to be denied the vitality of the land itself. The land as a source of God's blessing becomes a source of God's cursing as a consequence of broken covenant. Hosea understands the whole of God's creation as interrelated. It is not possible that relationship to God and relationship to neighbor can be broken without brokenness extending to the whole of creation. The land mourns; the wild animals, the birds, and the fish perish. Breaking of covenant is denial of the life that God gives, and, as a consequence, life flows out of creation itself. Sin has consequences for all our relationships, even to the earth itself. This understanding is close to that of the apostle Paul when he writes that the whole creation was "subjected to futility" and "groans in pain" while it awaits God's redemption (Rom. 8:19–22; see also Isa. 24:4–5).

This passage in which Hosea articulates God's lawsuit against Israel is an especially important text for reminding the modern church of the close and necessary interconnections among our relationships with God, with neighbor, and with creation itself. There are social and creational consequences that flow from the lack of the knowledge of God. And our inattention to matters of justice and right relationship in society and environment will create barriers that impede our full relationship with God.

It is not at all difficult to imagine that Hosea is addressing us as surely as he addressed ancient Israel. Many voices have called attention to our own crisis of the knowledge of God. *Secularization* has eroded our sense of divine presence in the midst of all life and substituted loyalties to nation, class, race, political persuasion, or interest group for what should have been our ultimate loyalty to God. *Compartmentalization* has removed our practice of covenant obedience to sanctuaries and church gatherings where we engage in explicit religious practices. We conduct our lives apart from such self-conscious gatherings as the church with little sense of being covenant people. We suffer as the church from *loss of biblical and historical memory*. Our knowledge of who God is and what God has done, as witnessed in scripture and tradition, is remarkably shallow. Almost all persons know more of their national, ethnic, or family history than their faith history. Even in a time when interest in our biblical roots is growing, we must speak of this as a recovery of that biblical witness to the knowledge of God.

One cannot but believe that this lack of the knowledge of God is connected to the alarming levels of violence and cynical manipulation of others that mark our present society. Children bring guns to school to settle arguments. Driveby shootings, carjackings, drug-related crimes, alcohol-related accidents, political- or issue-related violence, and violence-oriented entertainment are common elements of our communities. Character assassination is frequent in political campaigns. Our stock markets, savings and loans, corporations, and governments have experienced sensational exposures of fraud and corruption. Can any escape the effects of such realities on our sense of life, wholeness, and relationship to God?

It is also clear that the creation itself is affected by our lack of the knowledge of God and the social consequences that follow. Environmental sciences have given new scientific validation to the biblical notion that all creation is interrelated. Nature itself suffers the effects of human greed and self-indulgence. Acid rain, polluted waterways, depleted topsoil, toxic substance contamination, air pollution, disrupted ecological systems, species extinction, and the depletion of limited resources are realities in our time and are related to human exploitation of natural resources. The whole creation does indeed groan as a result of human sinfulness.

Hosea saw clearly that our relationships to God, to society, and to creation are part of one covenantal reality. We cannot seek to know God and remain unconcerned for the quality of our life together in human community or our life in harmony with nature and its resources. These are not simply interest groups optionally selected by the motivated few. Our concern for the welfare of all these relationships is part of what it means to be covenant community. To ignore this covenant commitment is to open ourselves to the lawsuit of God that Hosea announces.

The Lawsuit against the Priests
(4:4–10)

Again Hosea announces God's lawsuit (v. 4, "contention" NRSV), but this time it is directed to the priest. In verses 4–6, this indictment is directed personally to a singular subject identified only as "O priest" (v. 4). One can almost imagine that a religious official has stepped forward to take exception to Hosea's sweeping indictment of the people in verses 1–3, and the prophet turns the blaze of God's wrath on the priest and his neglected covenantal responsibilities (see also 5:1–2). We know of such a confrontation between the prophet Amos and Amaziah, the priest of Bethel (Amos 7:10–17). But if Hosea begins his indictment with reference to a single priest, he soon broadens it to include all those who had responsibility for leadership among God's covenant people. Verses 7–10 shift to plural address and demand covenant accountability of religious leaders in general.

Usually prophetic judgment speeches announce the charges or complaint against the people and then pronounce the sentence or judgment. In this oracle against the priests, complaint and sentence are alternated throughout. Hosea's principle seems to be stated in verse 9: "And it shall be like people, like priest." The sins of the priests against the people shall be revisited in similar fashion on the priests themselves. Thus, the verbs of sin and punishment appear in pairs: stumble (v. 5), destroy (vv. 5b, 6a), reject (v. 6), forget (v. 6), eat (vv. 8, 10), increase/multiply (vv. 7, 10).

The charges against the priests are harsh and the consequences equally so. The emphatic forms of address that open Hosea's speech in verse 4 suggest that he is responding to some sort of formal complaint against his preaching. Initially, he seems to be speaking to a single priest but broadens his indictment to include the whole of Israel's priesthood, which has failed in its role. Hosea says no priest should accuse him because God has a special case against the priest (v. 4). He who confronts Hosea so self-confidently will stumble, even in broad daylight, when God's judgment is leveled (v. 5). Mention is also made in verse 5 of "the prophet" who will stumble as well. This no doubt refers to cultic prophets associated with the sanctuaries and with priests, known to us best in the conflicts of Jeremiah with such prophets (Jer. 28:1–17). This is the only mention by Hosea of such prophets, and the focus of this oracle quickly returns to the priests.

Hosea goes straight to the central charge against the priests of Israel. They have "rejected knowledge" (v. 6a), and "forgotten the law of God" (v. 6b). We have discussed in connection with 4:1 the central importance of the knowledge of God for Hosea. It is at the heart of covenant commitment. Here Hosea places such knowledge as parallel to "the law [torah] of God." The Hebrew word *torah* means "instruction" both as process and as content. It is the way in which God's covenant will is made known and incorporated into Israel's life. The result would be a people filled with the "knowledge of God." And the priest had the leadership responsibility to see that this happened. The priest was to instruct the people. The priest was to know and teach the Torah. The priest was the custodian and steward of the "knowledge of God" in the midst of Israel. Hosea charges that the priests have failed in the central task given to them as priests. And because they have rejected knowledge, God will reject them from being a priest (v. 6). Further, because the result of this priestly failure is the destruction of God's people and the forgetting of the Torah, God will destroy and forget the family of the priest: "I will destroy your mother . . . and I will forget your children" (vv. 5b, 6b). The priest who has rejected knowledge will have no past or future in Israel.

Hosea charges that the priesthood, cut off from the knowledge of God, has become corrupt. Verses 7–8 seem to suggest priestly profiteering on the people's sin. People brought grain and wine and livestock to the sanctuaries for sin offerings. The priests kept a portion of these offerings and thus had a vested interest in the people's sin and their own priestly role in sacrificial release from sin. Ironically, the numbers of priests were increasing, the number of people coming to gain release from sin sacrificially was growing, and the profits of the priesthood were gaining accordingly. Religion was thriving while the knowledge of God languished. The priests were encouraging guilt and confession of sin to their own gain ("they are greedy for . . . iniquity," v. 8b) and then giving people an easy ritual release, with an accompanying profit ("they feed on the sin of my people," v. 8a), while neglecting to instruct them in the demanding knowledge of God's covenant way. Hosea frequently rejects sacrifice as a substitute for covenant obedience (see 5:6; 8:11, 13). Likewise, he announces God's rejection of priests with more interest in the people's sin than in their instruction in the faith.

Hosea's final decree of judgment on such priests (v. 10) is that their gain will not bring satisfaction. They have prostituted themselves. They do not serve the Lord; they have forsaken the Lord.

This text forces us to think about the accountability of leadership in the life of the church. The most direct parallel for this passage would relate to those who accept the responsibility to serve as ordained clergy in the church, but much of the message here applies to any who accept leadership office in the church, lay or clergy.

In 1972, James D. Smart wrote a book with the provocative title *The Strange Silence of the Bible in the Church*. It took note of the many signs that church members no longer knew their own biblical tradition, and many of those responsible for preserving and teaching that tradition showed little inclination to give that task a higher priority. Although there are some encouraging signs of renewed interest in biblical study in the church, there is still an embarrassing lack of biblical literacy in many segments of the church. For Christians, scripture is a primary source of our knowledge of God, and the biblical tradition shares much in common with Hosea's con-

cept of Torah. Without instruction in its stories, teachings, hymns, let-
ters, poetry, and visions, there can be no fully realized life of faith.

Yet, many clergy do not list teaching or instruction among their high-
est priority tasks. Historically, the ordained ministry has been mandated
to act as custodians and teachers of the tradition. There has been a decline
in the teaching role for those in pastoral ministry. Increasing emphasis on
professionalism in ministry has tended to make the pastor something like
the chief executive officer of a complex organization, and the time for this
has been purchased not from worship leadership and preaching, but from
the teaching ministries of pastors. Many clergy could hear themselves addressed in Hosea's indictment that the priest has "rejected knowledge."
Instead of knowledge, we often substitute management. As a result, "my
people are destroyed for lack of knowledge." The burgeoning adult education classes of the Sunday school movement earlier in this century are
now a thing of the past. Many congregations have little or no adult education. Some philosophies of church growth advise that new generations
of potential churchgoers are repelled by insistence on learning as a requirement for faith. They are consumers who want to be attracted not
challenged. There may be a place for new strategies to attract persons to
church, but if those attracted are to become people of faith, there is ultimately no substitute for the knowledge of God made available by those responsible for instruction in the faith.

Like the priests of Hosea's time, those clergy and lay leaders who are
deflected from their central task of promoting the knowledge of God are
prone to fall into other abuses. At the worst, there are those who profiteer
on sin. Multimillion-dollar ministries, often using the technology of the
mass media, have been exposed as guilty of outright criminal fraud and
moral hypocrisy, such as the celebrated cases of Jim Bakker and Jimmy
Swaggart. Others, not criminally liable, are morally bankrupt, maintaining elaborate and financially lucrative ministries from which only small
percentages of funds actually go to further God's mission in the world. But
we need not dwell on these more dramatic cases. Many clergy of ordinary
congregations find themselves lured by the rewards of a professionalism
purchased at the expense of people's genuine needs. They find themselves
locked into institutional systems that reward institutional needs over attention to instruction in the knowledge of God. Time spent in membership expansion brings salary and prestige, but hours of teaching and instruction rarely do so. Like the priests of Hosea's time, pastors often
create dependencies that suggest they are the sole possessors of knowledge
rather than those who are to impart knowledge to the people. Some clergy

"feed on the sin of my people" by fostering clergy-centered churches that do little to empower the people, personality cults that encourage reliance on the pastor and not on God.

It is well for us to heed again Hosea's warning. If the "people are destroyed for lack of knowledge," then the leadership of the church and its self-importance will perish as well. "It shall be like people, like priest."

THOUGH YOU
PLAY THE WHORE, O ISRAEL
Hosea 4:11b–19

4:11b **Wine and new wine**
> **take away the understanding.**
> [12] **My people consult a piece of wood,**
> > **and their divining rod gives them oracles.**
> **For a spirit of whoredom has led them astray,**
> > **and they have played the whore, forsaking their God.**
> [13] **They sacrifice on the tops of the mountains,**
> > **and make offerings upon the hills,**
> **under oak, poplar, and terebinth,**
> > **because their shade is good.**
>
> **Therefore your daughters play the whore,**
> > **and your daughters-in-law commit adultery.**
> [14] **I will not punish your daughters when they play the whore,**
> > **nor your daughters-in-law when they commit adultery;**
> **for the men themselves go aside with whores,**
> > **and sacrifice with temple prostitutes;**
> **thus a people without understanding comes to ruin.**
>
> [15] **Though you play the whore, O Israel,**
> > **do not let Judah become guilty.**
> **Do not enter into Gilgal,**
> > **or go up to Beth-aven,**
> > **and do not swear, "As the LORD lives."**
> [16] **Like a stubborn heifer,**
> > **Israel is stubborn;**
> **can the LORD now feed them**
> > **like a lamb in a broad pasture?**
>
> [17] **Ephraim is joined to idols—**
> > **let him alone.**

¹⁸ When their drinking is ended, they indulge in sexual orgies;
   they love lewdness more than their glory.
¹⁹ A wind has wrapped them in its wings,
   and they shall be ashamed because of their altars.

Hosea returns here to the imagery of adultery as a metaphor for Israel's idolatry and unfaithfulness to the Lord. There are two sections here: The first is in the form of a speech of the Lord (vv. 11–14), and the second seems to be a speech of the prophet (vv. 15–19).

The Speech of the Lord (4:11–14)

The speech of the Lord in verses 11–14 deals with the damaging effects of fascination with Canaanite religion. The speech begins and ends with proverbial sayings. Verse 11 suggests that indulgence of the senses in harlotry and wine drinking can only lead to impaired judgment. (Notice that the word "whoredom," which belongs to v. 11, is used in the NRSV to complete verse 10. Probably this word appeared twice and it should also be used to start verse 11. The whole speech is about Israel's "whoredom" with Canaanite religion. It is not just wine that "takes away the understanding.") The speech ends with another proverb, "a people without understanding comes to ruin" (v. 14b). Earlier in this chapter, Hosea has decried the lack of the knowledge of God in Israel and the priests' failure to teach that knowledge. This is related to the loss of understanding in these two proverbs and may be the reason for arranging these oracles next to each other. Here we are meant by Hosea to see the connection between this lack of knowledge or understanding and the indulgent practices of Canaanite religion. Prostitution and intoxication rob Israel of the knowledge and discernment required for covenant relationship to the Lord.

Between these two proverbs lies a description of the fascination and appeal of Canaanite practices among the Israelites of Hosea's time. Hosea attributes the loss of understanding to a "spirit of whoredom" that has led Israel astray (v. 12b). It is as if Israel has become collectively possessed by this spirit alien to the worship of their covenant God. The result is a fascinated participation in things Canaanite.

Israel engages in practices of *divination*. Seeking guidance, the people turn to wooden objects that have no divine power of their own (v. 12a). "A piece of wood" may refer to a wooden idol, but "divining rod" suggests the wooden pole, called an Asherah, which often stood by Canaanite altars and commemorated one of the Canaanite goddesses associated with

Baal (see Judg. 6:25). There may have been some technique for seeking divine guidance from such objects. The exact process is not known to us, but the fascination of such a process should be familiar. Every generation is lured by the appeal of a "quick-answer religion." Canaanite religion promised a system for understanding the world that was appealing in its simplicity and its immediacy. What could be more appealing to agriculturists than worship focused on nature itself as inhabited by divine powers. Further, Canaanite divination practices promised access to these powers. Who has not wanted all the answers at some time in life, and we often want those answers immediately. Even today, many are taken in by religious programs and leaders who promise simple and immediate solutions to all our problems in return for allegiance (money, participation) to their program or ministry. Such promises cannot ultimately be fulfilled, and the effect is often to insert loyalty to some human structure in place of the loyalty owed only to God. This is little more than a modern guise for the idolatry Hosea condemned in his time.

Hosea goes on to single out the practice of sacrifice and rituals conducted in the *sacred groves and high places* (v. 13a). The shrines of Canaanite religion were located on hilltops covered with groves of trees and often possessing an altar and possibly other sacred objects, such as the Asherah mentioned above and standing stones or pillars (see Deut. 12:2; 1 Kings 14:23; Jer. 2:20). No doubt these were pleasant and appealing places in the often hot climate of the area. Why not gather with friends and neighbors for appealing outdoor rituals in such pleasant surroundings? No doubt sociability was part of the appeal of Canaanite practices. This too must sound familiar. In a time when many denominations and congregations worry over the need to grow, there has been a distressing tendency to substitute sociability for the challenge of living as God's faithful community. A pastor recently mentioned the experience of a family who approached her, asking for their baby to be baptized but who hoped the ceremony would not have to mention the word *God*. When we gather in church buildings for sociability around interesting rituals in appealing surroundings and fail to hear any call to faithful covenant life, then this too is little more than a guise for the idolatry Hosea condemned in his time.

Finally, Hosea points to the *sexual practices* that seem to have been part of Canaanite ritual. In Canaanite mythology, the storm god, Baal, is rescued from the underworld by his consort, the goddess Anath. They engage in sexual intercourse and the result is the renewed springtime fertility of the land that had languished in winter while Baal was in the underworld. The cycle of the seasons and the fertility of the land are seen as sexual in character, and ritual sexual intercourse was apparently part of Canaanite ritual. Verse 14b suggests that "temple prostitutes" were available and used by Israelite men at Canaanite cultic places. But Hosea is also observing that sexual disorder has come to mark the general life of Israel. In verse 13b, he says that Israel's daughters and daughters-in-law "play the whore" and "commit adultery." This may be just a rise of general immorality or perhaps some ritual sexual practices to which women are submitted, such as dedication of virgins at shrines. In any case, it is startling that Hosea observes this behavior but refuses to condemn the women (v. 14a) because the men's sexual practices in the fertility religion of Canaan have promoted such a licentiousness. "The men themselves" are the guilty parties according to Hosea. The sexual focus of idolatrous religion has created the climate for a sexually disordered society. Again we should not be surprised at the appeal of such a sexually oriented religion, since we live in a society that sells an astonishing array of products by use of sexually oriented images. Hosea refuses to judge the symptoms when the guilt lies with a disorientation of values on the part of those who held power and control in his society, the male leadership. Unlike Hosea, we often hear religious leaders condemning sexually explicit books, music, and entertainment as if eliminating these symptoms alone would be enough. Hosea suggests that the practices of whoredom (society's sexual dysfunctions) have something to do with the spirit ("a spirit of whoredom has led them astray"). For example, we want to restrict adolescent sexual behavior without addressing the pressures—loss of self-esteem, exploitation of youth imagery, poor job prospects, and excessively materialistic culture—that are part of adolescent reality today. As another example, we decry sexually explicit expression in our culture but want to give up little of the material and individual freedom to "do our own thing" in other ways. Hosea's message is that sexual disorder is a crisis of religious values not just of bodily behavior. We cannot idolize sexuality and then decry the results.

The Speech of the Prophet
(4:15–19)

The final section of this chapter (vv. 15–19) seems to be Hosea's own speech of reproach to the people. It continues the themes of the Lord's speech in verses 11–14: "whoredom" (v. 15), sexual license and drunkenness in cultic rituals (v. 17b), and idolatry (v. 17a). There is a reference to Judah in verse 15 that has led some to see here a later Judean editor, but Hosea mentions Judah several times in his preaching (5:5, 10, 13; 6:4), and the suggestion here is that Israel is already judged for its sin so Judah should beware! In fact, the warning in verse 15b for Judah not to visit the well-known Israelite shrines is a potent indictment meant for the ears of Israelites who did worship there. Gilgal receives Hosea's scorn in later passages as well (9:15; 12:11) not only for its current sinful practices but perhaps also for its connection with the start of kingship in Israel (1 Sam. 11:14–15). Hosea had a low view of the kingship. Bethel was one of the royal sanctuaries in Israel, and its name means "house (*beth*) of God (*'el*)." Hosea now scornfully names this shrine "Beth-aven," which means "house (*beth*) of evil (*'aven*)." Amos makes the same play on words in Amos 5:5, and it is in Bethel that Amos was confronted by the priest Amaziah (Amos 7:10–17). Perhaps Hosea suggests knowledge of Amos's ministry here. Not only should these sanctuaries be avoided, according to Hosea, but one should also avoid swearing on the life of the Lord (v. 15b). This seems odd, but perhaps God's name is being put to idolatrous use. When the Canaanite god Baal returns from the dead, the cry goes up that "Baal lives!" Perhaps the oath "As the LORD lives" is being used to identify Israel's God with Baal.

Verses 16–18 are difficult to translate, but it seems clear that Hosea sees the people as becoming stubborn in their ways. Thus, it is impossible for the Lord to lead them as a shepherd would lead to pasture (v. 16). The kingdom of Israel (Ephraim here) is joined to idols (v. 17), and their worship practices have become orgies of drunken licentiousness (v. 18). They are caught up in a wind that has entangled them in its wings (currents?) and will carry them only to their shame (v. 19). That these things are associated in this passage with official sanctuaries such as Gilgal and Bethel suggests that official religion in Israel has become no different from the popular religion of the high places described in the previous passage (vv. 11–14). This only bears out what seems to be the theme of the whole of chapter 4, namely, that when the knowledge of God is neglected, it is only a matter of time before religious institution and cultural practices alike are eroded by idolatry and sin. The desire for simplistic answers, the substitution of sociability for faithfulness, the indulging of the senses without regard to covenantal values—these are all signs of idolatry and the rejection of the knowledge of God, not only in Hosea's time but also in our own.

HEAR THIS, O PRIESTS!
Hosea 5:1–7

5:1 **Hear this, O priests!**
　　　Give heed, O house of Israel!

Listen, O house of the king!
　　For the judgment pertains to you;
　for you have been a snare at Mizpah,
　　and a net spread upon Tabor,
2　and a pit dug deep in Shittim;
　　but I will punish all of them.

3　I know Ephraim,
　　and Israel is not hidden from me;
　for now, O Ephraim, you have played the whore;
　　Israel is defiled.
4　Their deeds do not permit them
　　to return to their God.
　For the spirit of whoredom is within them,
　　and they do not know the LORD.

5　Israel's pride testifies against him;
　　Ephraim stumbles in his guilt;
　Judah also stumbles with them.
6　With their flocks and herds they shall go
　　to seek the LORD,
　but they will not find him;
　　he has withdrawn from them.
7　They have dealt faithlessly with the LORD;
　　for they have borne illegitimate children.
　Now the new moon shall devour them along with their fields.

This section falls into two distinct parts. The first (vv. 1–2) is a direct speech of judgment by the Lord to the leaders of Israel. The second (vv. 3–7) is a speech of Hosea himself testifying to his own witness of Israel's sin and elaborating on the experience of God's judgment.

The Speech of the Lord (5:1–2)

The speech of the Lord in verses 1–2 is in the form of a verdict rendered in a lawsuit (see the comments on 4:1–3). God is both the injured party and the judge announcing that "the judgment pertains to you" (v. 1a) and "I will punish all of them" (v. 2b). The "you" whom God addresses in this case are the leaders of Israel. They are commanded to give attention in a threefold summons (v. 1a). Two of the three groups are clear. Hosea's divine oracle names the priests and the royal household. The second group is less clear. "House of Israel" normally refers to the whole nation, yet the intent of this speech to single out those in leadership seems clear. Perhaps, as some suggest, the phrase implies representatives of the people or, as others argue, the phrase should read "elders of the house of Israel." In any case, the commanding language demands that those responsible for leadership must attend to the announcement of their guilt and punishment.

The threefold demand for attention is matched by three charges leveled against the leaders (vv. 1b–2a), and concluded by a blunt statement of punishment (v. 2b). The charges are metaphorical rather than literal. God uses images from hunting to suggest that instead of protecting the people, Israel's leadership has turned them into prey. The leaders of Israel have been a snare, a net, and a pit, each being deadly for the animal caught in its clutches. Further, the ensnaring behavior of Israel's leaders is in each instance connected with the name of a place where a shrine is located. All these places (Mizpah, Tabor, Shittim) were shrines at one time or another connected with Baal worship. The snares into which Israel's leaders have caused them to fall are the snares of idolatry. It may even be that, in Israel's time, these places called to mind specific instances where leaders had corrupted their offices and engaged in idolatrous practices.

This is not the only time Hosea's oracles single out those in leadership (see 4:4–6 on priests and 8:4 on kings). His words remind us that seldom is the crisis of a nation not also a crisis of leadership. And frequently the crisis of leadership and nation involves the co-opting of the religious centers to purposes that are not in keeping with loyalty to a covenant Lord. Our nation, as all nations, has a long history of those who would enlist religious language about God in the service of narrow, partisan purposes. Hosea's word reminds us that such practices are idolatrous and lead to God's judgment. This is not to say that God has no place in the public arena. Quite the contrary. Leaders are called to faithful loyalty to covenant values. For Hosea, those include justice, knowledge of God, righteousness, compassion, and love. True leadership refuses to sacrifice these qualities to expediency or popular demand. These qualities are not the property of political parties or ideological groups. These qualities are not at home with policy and rhetoric that promote suspicion, intolerance, and hate. Hosea lived in a period of the history of Israel that saw the Northern Kingdom degenerate into a politics of suspicion, mistrust, violence, and assassination that eventually led to the permanent destruction of the nation. We would do well to heed Hosea's warning about the consequences of leadership that becomes a snare to the people.

A Speech of Hosea (5:3–7)

In verses 3–7, Hosea speaks as prophet, claiming energetically to know the reality of Israel's sin. "I know Ephraim, and Israel is not hidden from me" (v. 3a). The specifics of Hosea's charges against Israel and in behalf of God's judgment are the central themes already seen in chapters 1—4. Israel has "played the whore" (v. 3b), and the "spirit of whoredom is within them" (v. 4b). The central imagery of Israel as the harlot going after her lovers, the Baals, is used again by Hosea. In its idolatrous behavior, Israel cannot "know the LORD" (v. 4b) or "return to their God" (v. 4a). To know God is, for Hosea, the basic quality of orientation to God's covenant and its demands for loyalty to the Lord and following of God's revealed will (see the discussion on 4:1–3). Idolatry (here in the image of harlotry) is evidence of the lack of the knowledge of God and will prevent any return to God. (This short speech of Hosea may be placed in this location by the editors of the book because the inadequate speech of repentance by the people [see 6:1–3] makes use of the themes of return to the Lord and knowing the Lord.)

Verse 5 uses some of the courtroom language we saw at the beginning of this chapter. It is as if Hosea sees Israel in a lawsuit, but the case is not going well. Israel's pride *testifies* against them; Israel's *guilt* trips them up. Further, Judah, the Southern Kingdom, is no better off and stumbles in the case along with Israel.

Verse 6 is probably the major reason this speech is placed here. It prepares for the section to follow. Hosea describes Israel and Judah as going to "seek the LORD." But how do they go about this? They go with flocks and herds. Their idea of seeking the Lord is through ritual sacrifice, presumably at the shrines where much of their idolatrous behavior has been located. They seek the Lord by redoubling their religious behavior. As we will see in our discussion of the famous text in 6:6, this is not what God truly desires. We will discuss this further in the next section. But here Hosea indicates that such a seeking will not find the Lord. Indeed, God has *withdrawn* from them. (This theme is also taken up in the next section, 5:15.) In their sin, they must now face the absence of God. God's presence and the presence of sin are not compatible no matter how faithfully religious practices (sacrifices) are carried out. Verse 7 simply indicates that judgment is the lot of those who deal "faithlessly with the LORD."

It is sobering to realize how often we think that our religious practices of church attendance and support ensure the presence of God. Perhaps we are even tempted to think that pious practices obligate God. Hosea reminds us that God will not remain where we have turned away from faithfulness to

God and toward idolatrous loyalties in our lives. It will not matter how outwardly religious we appear.

I DESIRE STEADFAST LOVE
AND NOT SACRIFICE
Hosea 5:8–6:6

5:8 Blow the horn in Gibeah,
            the trumpet in Ramah.
        Sound the alarm at Beth-aven;
            look behind you, Benjamin!
    ⁹Ephraim shall become a desolation
            in the day of punishment;
        among the tribes of Israel
            I declare what is sure.
¹⁰ The princes of Judah have become
            like those who remove the landmark;
        on them I will pour out
            my wrath like water.
¹¹ Ephraim is oppressed, crushed in judgment,
            because he was determined to go after vanity.
¹² Therefore I am like maggots to Ephraim,
            and like rottenness to the house of Judah.
¹³ When Ephraim saw his sickness,
            and Judah his wound,
        then Ephraim went to Assyria,
            and sent to the great king.
        But he is not able to cure you
            or heal your wound.
¹⁴ For I will be like a lion to Ephraim,
            and like a young lion to the house of Judah.
        I myself will tear and go away;
            I will carry off, and no one shall rescue.
¹⁵ I will return again to my place
            until they acknowledge their guilt and seek my face.
        In their distress they will beg my favor:
6:1 "Come, let us return to the LORD;
            for it is he who has torn, and he will heal us;
        he has struck down, and he will bind us up.
    ²After two days he will revive us;
            on the third day he will raise us up,

that we may live before him.
³ Let us know, let us press on to know the LORD;
      his appearing is as sure as the dawn;
he will come to us like the showers,
      like the spring rains that water the earth."
⁴ What shall I do with you, O Ephraim?
      What shall I do with you, O Judah?
Your love is like a morning cloud,
      like the dew that goes away early.
⁵ Therefore I have hewn them by the prophets,
      I have killed them by the words of my mouth,
      and my judgment goes forth as the light.
⁶ For I desire steadfast love and not sacrifice,
      the knowledge of God rather than burnt offerings.

With verse 8, the subject abruptly changes. The focus is no longer on idolatry and its attendant follies in Israel. The subject now is war! Both Israel (often referred to by Hosea as Ephraim) and Judah are involved and subject to the prophet's indictment and God's judgment. It is the follies of misguided political opportunism and miscalculation that lead Hosea to speak. Many believe the concern with cultic sin (idolatry, apostasy, hypocrisy) to this point in the book of Hosea comes from the politically calm period of the last years of the reign of Jeroboam II (786–746 B.C.) in the Northern Kingdom, Israel. After the death of Jeroboam II, political events became turbulent and chaotic, with disastrous and tragic consequences for both Israel and Judah. This section and many subsequent passages in Hosea seem to reflect this more tempestuous time.

It is generally agreed that this section of Hosea's preaching reflects events at the time of the Syro-Ephraimite War. Following the death of Jeroboam II (746 B.C.) the Northern Kingdom of Israel (Ephraim) fell into a period of politics by murder. Three different kings were deposed by assassination after only brief periods on the throne. During this same time Assyria, under its king Tiglath-pileser III, began to extend its empire westward. One of the kings of Israel, Menahem (745–738 B.C.), sought to buy peace by paying a great sum in tribute to Assyria, a move that placed a heavy economic burden on landholders. King Pekah of Israel (737–732 B.C.) seized the throne by assassinating the young son of Menahem, and he began to form a coalition in opposition to Assyria. He formed an alliance with Rezin, the Aramaean king of Syria. They probably had Egyptian encouragement (see, for example, 7:11). Together, Israel (Ephraim) and Syria sought to enlist the kingdom of Judah into their plot. King Ahaz of Judah refused to join them, and in anger Israel and Syria laid siege to Jerusalem. Ahaz appealed for help to Assyria. Tiglath-pileser was happy for an excuse to enter the area. The Assyrian army conquered Damascus and in 733 captured a large portion of Israel's territory, deporting much of the population. To save what was left of the country (largely the territories of Ephraim and Benjamin), Hoshea (king of Israel, 732–724, not to be confused with our prophet) assassinated Pekah and then threw himself on Assyria's mercy, paid tribute, and became a vassal of Tiglath-pileser. It is against the backdrop of these complex and tragic events that we should understand the oracles of 5:8–15, and much of the later material in the book, to have been preached. (For a fuller treatment of this historical background see the Introduction.)

There are several separate units of material in 5:8–6:6, but they form a clearly related sequence. In 5:8–15, we find Hosea's warnings and announcements of judgment on the folly of Israel and Judah in the practice of their violent politics. In 6:1–3 we find a song of penitence by the people. Finally, in 6:4–6 Hosea voices God's impatience with the people's response and reveals God's true desire (6:6).

War Comes to Israel
and Judah (5:8–15)

The section in 5:8–15 is composed of several shorter pieces that, taken together, show Hosea's growing alarm over the violent politics of Israel and Judah and the consequences of such policies. In verses 8–9, Hosea seems to take the role of watchman, shouting the alarm for an invasion into Israelite territory from the south. Gibeah, Ramah, and Bethel (Beth-aven is a derisive name for Bethel; see 4:15) are strategic locations on a direct route from Jerusalem into Israelite territory. Hosea seems to be warning of a possible counterattack from Judah, which had been attacked by the Israel-Syria coalition trying to force them into an alliance against Assyria. Hosea warns that Israel's violent policy could boomerang against them. Ephraim, the heart of Israel, can be desolated (v. 9a), and, as a prophet, Hosea boldly declares this as a certainty (v. 9b).

There follow two brief judgment speeches (vv. 10–12 and vv. 13–14) each with an accusation followed by an announcement of penalty or punishment. In the first of these (vv. 10–12) there is a separate indictment for each of the two kingdoms, Judah and then Ephraim (Israel). Judah is condemned for violating boundaries (v. 10). To "remove the landmark" is to change the fixed boundaries of another's land for one's personal gain.

Such a practice is strictly forbidden in the law codes (for example, Deut. 19:14; 27:17). This is especially serious when it takes place between covenant brothers. It appears that this is a condemnation of Judah at the time Ahaz is counterattacking and seizing Israelite territory in reprisal for the attack of the Ephraim-Syria coalition against Jerusalem.

But Ephraim (Israel) is not to be held the innocent party in this matter. Hosea seems fully aware of the entire sequence of events and condemns both kingdoms for a politics of self-serving violence. Ephraim is already experiencing judgment (v. 11a). If Judah is counterattacking from the south, this means that the Assyrian king, Tiglath-pileser, is invading from the north. Ahaz of Jerusalem had appealed to Assyria for help when confronted with the threat of the Israel-Syria coalition. In Hosea's view, this misbegotten alliance with Israel's ancient Aramaean enemy, Syria, is indeed to "go after vanity" (v. 11b), and disaster has been the result. Verse 12 announces that God's judgment is already at work, and the images Hosea uses to announce this are vile indeed. Ephraim and Judah are already suffering from "maggots" and "rottenness." These are terms elsewhere associated with the decay of dead bodies. These two kingdoms, who should have behaved as covenant brothers, are corpses already. We should remember that only a few short years later (721 B.C.) the Northern Kingdom was permanently destroyed. Hosea was right; they were as good as dead already.

In verse 13, Hosea continues his indictment of both kingdoms and seems to move to the next stage in the sequence of events. His images shift to those of bodily illness and injury. The metaphors are medical in character. The prophet suggests that both kingdoms come to see how serious their plight is. Ephraim is sick, and Judah is wounded (v. 13a). What does Israel do? It goes to Assyria and its great king (v. 13b). No doubt this refers to Pekah's appeal for mercy to Assyria and his willingness to become an Assyrian vassal in order to save what was left of the Northern Kingdom. Hosea is scornful of this action. (Judah had already accepted Assyrian vassal status in return for help. Isaiah was also scornful of this action by Ahaz of Judah.) Israel has turned to "Dr. Assyria," but Assyria cannot "cure" or "heal" (v. 13b). Indeed, instead of healing, Israel will experience the wrath of God as if a raging lion had torn and carried them off (see also 13:7 and Amos 1:2). This is descriptive of what those who experience Assyria's conquest suffer. Hosea says their fate at the hands of Assyria should be understood as the judgment of the Lord on their folly. Again, this seems to foreshadow the final fate of the nation in 721.

As a final pronouncement in this section, Hosea announces God's word of divine withdrawal. God will "return again to my place" and wait for Israel to acknowledge guilt and seek God's presence once again (v. 15). This is similar to the theme we saw in the preceding section (see 5:6) and may account for the editor's placement of these sections together. God cannot endure to witness the sin of God's people. God will not be present in the face of the frantic and violent politics of Northern and Southern Kingdoms. God will withdraw to wait, but God has not abandoned the people forever. God clearly hopes for their return.

This entire section (5:8–15) is filled with graphic images of the sickness and brokenness that war represents. Hosea saw clearly that the supposed noble purposes behind such violence were merely vanity—the puffed-up self-importance of nations whose leaders imagine that they are in control of history and their own destiny. For twentieth-century readers of these verses we can only shudder at the implications. These nations brought catastrophe on themselves, and God would not save them from their sin and folly. Indeed, God's judgment is in those catastrophes. The twentieth century has been the most violent in human history—holocaust, nuclear devastation, world war, racial violence, drug wars, ethnic cleansing, apartheid, iron curtain, paranoid vigilante militias, armed citizenry, the bombing of public buildings, declared jihad, terrorists of all stripes. Could a more violent chronicle of the sickness and wounds of the peoples of our time possibly be imagined? Could we possibly be any further from the reality of community as brothers and sisters than this listing suggests? Where is God in all this? The asking of this question often implies that it is somehow God's responsibility to get us off the hook from the consequences of our own human folly. Hosea suggests that in the face of such violence and folly God is indeed absent—not unconcerned, but unwilling to be present and party to the sinful ways that sicken and wound us. God cannot miraculously turn us from our own folly. Wholeness and the healing presence of God require returning and acknowledgment of sin and folly. As long as we imagine and act as though we control our own destinies and refuse to acknowledge God's sovereignty over nations and history, then God will be shut from our midst. Former United States Secretary of Defense Robert McNamara has published a book in which he acknowledges his own awareness of the folly of policies he helped shape and carry out in the Vietnam War, and yet, he writes that in spite of this knowledge he felt almost compelled to carry them through to what became a disastrous end. We can be grateful for the frankness of this public confession; we can wish it had been possible at the time of the Vietnam War.

The People Respond to God (6:1–3)

In 6:1–3 the speaker changes. The people seem to be speaking, and their speech initially looks like a welcome development. These verses are a song of penitence, probably intended for recital in a liturgical context for repentance. There are two possible ways of understanding this speech of the people. The first is that Hosea may be reporting the actual response of some among the people to his preaching of God's judgment and the catastrophic events that had befallen the nation. The second is that Hosea is engaging in a parody of the people's response in order to make the message of God's true desire clear in the section that follows. In either case we will see that, although the response says many of the right words, the spirit behind the people's response falls far short of God's true desire for the people.

In 6:1–3 unidentified speakers issue two summons to the people. At first glance this seems promising, for these summons take up two of the central themes in Hosea's preaching. "Let us *return* to the LORD," says the first (v. 1a); "let us *know* . . . the LORD," says the second (v. 3a). In Hosea's message, "return" means to give up the idolatrous practices of Baal worship and reestablish relationship with the covenant God, the Lord (see 2:7; 3:5). To "know" God is to recognize God's sovereignty and to acknowledge God's claim to Israel's obedience in covenant relationship (see the fuller discussion in connection with 4:1–3). In 5:4, Hosea had accused Israel of unwillingness to return and lack of the knowledge of God. The song of penitence in 6:1–3 appears to be a response to the prophet's challenge.

In keeping with the medical imagery of 5:13, those who summon Israel to penitence express confidence in God as the one who truly can "heal" and "bind up" (v. 1b). They are confident that their death is only an experience of short duration; after two or three days God will "revive" and "raise up" (v. 2). The whole song of penitence concludes with expressions of confidence in God, comparing the divine nature to the certain rhythms of nature—"the dawn, the showers, the spring rains" (v. 3b).

Many will have heard the expression, "They can talk the talk, but can they walk the walk?" Here the representatives of Israel have used many of the right words, but something is still missing. Is this really the repentance for which God waits (5:15)? There are no expressions of acknowledged sin or guilt. There is no resolve to new life as the content of returning and knowing. The assumption is that God can fix things, but there is little indication of what might change in the lives of the people. As God's response in 6:6 and the previous note in 5:6 suggest, the people assume that returning to and knowing God is accomplished by acts of sacrifice and ritual—by increased religiosity. "With their flocks and herds they shall go to seek the LORD" (5:6). Even the attempt here at the praise of God can do no better than attribute to the Lord the same presence in nature (dawn and rain) that is so closely connected to the worship of Baal. It is God's lordship over history that needs acknowledgment. The people seem to assume that an increase in religious activity will compel God to rescue them from the plight to which sin has brought them. The assumption is that God can change things, but there is no indication that this might also require a change of the nation's own tendency to policies that promote violent and self-serving behavior. God's response in verses 4–6 makes clear that the people fall far short of genuine repentance.

The Response God Desired (6:4–6)

If we had any doubt about the inadequacy of the people's response in 6:1–3, it is removed by hearing the words of the Lord announced by Hosea in 6:4–6. It is a wearied and frustrated God who begins to address the kingdoms in verse 4a. The exasperated question "What shall I do with you?" is repeated for Ephraim and Judah. This frustration is caused by the inconstancy of the people. The people had desired a constancy of care from the Lord that was as reliable as the dawn or the spring rains (6:3). God now uses metaphors from nature to express the unreliability of the people's covenant love. Their love is like a morning cloud or the dew that disappears before the day has barely begun (v. 4b).

The word for *love* here is a Hebrew word often translated as "steadfast love" and it indicates the faithful, loyal commitment required of those joined in covenant (see the discussion of covenant love in 2:19 and 4:1). It is trustworthy and reliable love in covenant partnership with God that is called for, but what the people have offered is as unreliable and transitory as the morning dew. The people's song of penitence is seen by God for what it is—expedient religiosity in time of crisis. This is what used to be called "foxhole religion"—when we're hunkered down in the foxhole in the midst of a battle or a crisis, then we might think of God. But otherwise, it's business as usual, on our terms, not God's. The words of penitence sound beautiful, the right vocabulary is there, but God knows no fundamental changes have been made in the people's way of life. Their love is but a sometime thing. In the spring of 1995, the federal office building in Oklahoma City was bombed in the most tragic and destructive act of domestic violence in U.S. history. In the wake of this tragedy, rhetoric flowed freely in concern for the climate of distrust, hatred, suspicion, and fear that seems to have fed those who saw violence as an appropriate response. Many voiced the need for changes and initiatives toward building new trust in our national life. Only a few months later, some of those same voices were supporting congressional initiatives to repeal controls on ownership of assault weapons and light artillery and to allow citizens to carry concealed weapons. Is this the way of steadfast love? Has commitment to fundamental change proved no more lasting than the morning dew?

Because of the people's inconstancy, God has sent prophets to warn the people of the consequences of their path (6:5). In judgment, they have heard their own doom pronounced. The people desired God as the dawn (6:3). What has come through the prophets is God's judgment as certain as the "light" (v. 5b) if the people will only see it.

In 6:6, we come to the climactic statement of God's true desire—what God really wants from the people. This entire section has been building to this central verse, and much of the next section looks back to it. It is a key statement in Hosea's message. What God wants is not sacrifices and burnt offerings. What God truly desires is steadfast love and the knowledge of God. It is the committed love of covenant partnership with God and the knowledge that comes from experienced relationship with God that truly make a difference (see the fuller discussion of these concepts in connection with 4:1–3). Such love and knowledge of God have been made available to Israel and Judah in ongoing relationship to the God revealed in the exodus, in the wilderness wandering, and in giving of the covenant and law. But the people have focused on religious rituals and practices rather than on relationship to the God those practices were intended to honor.

It is clear that hypocritical religion must have been an important issue in Hosea's time. All the prophets of the eighth century B.C. in Israel and Judah single out this issue for special concern (Isa. 1:10–17; Amos 5:21–24; Mic. 6:6–8). For many in their time, religion was apparently defined by ritual practices and not by a quality of life defined by love, justice, righteousness, and knowledge of God—the marks of covenant life. What is at stake is the notion of true religion. Some have allowed religion to be defined by institutional practices, but the prophets proclaim that true religion is found only in relationship to God and the demands of that relationship.

Surely this is not just an issue confined to the eighth century of Hosea and his contemporaries. In Matthew 9:12–13 and 12:7, Jesus twice quotes this verse in Hosea against those in his time who would substitute institutionalized morality for the genuine love of God and neighbor. We in our time need the reminder and challenge of this verse no less than those of Hosea's or Jesus' time.

There is a constant tendency in the church to substitute loyalty to institutionalized needs (our congregation, our denomination) for the love and knowledge of God. When church attendance, church buildings, thriving programs, beautiful liturgies, and congenial communities become ends in themselves, then they are idolatrous. When our religious practices are separated from the fundamental ways we show loyalty to God's purposes in our lives, our communities, and our nation, then they are idolatrous. When the patterns of our religious life offer only the constancy of comfort without challenging us to self-examination and change, then they are idolatrous.

In the face of challenging and distressing patterns of violence and brokenness in our communities and nation, many voice the concern that God seems absent. Hosea's message suggests that God may indeed be waiting—for a return to relationship based on steadfast love and the knowledge of God. No outward show of religious practice will ensure God's presence in our midst if there is no sign of commitment to covenant faithfulness.

THEY CALL UPON EGYPT,
THEY GO TO ASSYRIA
Hosea 6:7–7:16

6:7 **But at Adam they transgressed the covenant;**
    there they dealt faithlessly with me.
  8**Gilead is a city of evildoers,**
    tracked with blood.
  9**As robbers lie in wait for someone,**
    so the priests are banded together;
  they murder on the road to Shechem,
    they commit a monstrous crime.
10 **In the house of Israel I have seen a horrible thing;**
    Ephraim's whoredom is there, Israel is defiled.

11 **For you also, O Judah, a harvest is appointed.**

When I would restore the fortunes of my people,
    7:1 **when I would heal Israel,**
    the corruption of Ephraim is revealed,
    and the wicked deeds of Samaria;
  for they deal falsely,
    the thief breaks in,
    and the bandits raid outside.
  2**But they do not consider**

that I remember all their wickedness.
Now their deeds surround them,
    they are before my face.
³ By their wickedness they make the king glad,
    and the officials by their treachery.
⁴ They are all adulterers;
    they are like a heated oven,
whose baker does not need to stir the fire,
    from the kneading of the dough until it is leavened.
⁵ On the day of our king the officials
    became sick with the heat of wine;
    he stretched out his hand with mockers.
⁶ For they are kindled like an oven, their heart burns within them;
    all night their anger smolders;
    in the morning it blazes like a flaming fire.
⁷ All of them are hot as an oven,
    and they devour their rulers.
All their kings have fallen;
    none of them calls upon me.

⁸ Ephraim mixes himself with the peoples;
    Ephraim is a cake not turned.
⁹ Foreigners devour his strength,
    but he does not know it;
gray hairs are sprinkled upon him,
    but he does not know it.
¹⁰ Israel's pride testifies against him;
    yet they do not return to the LORD their God,
    or seek him, for all this.

¹¹ Ephraim has become like a dove,
    silly and without sense;
    they call upon Egypt, they go to Assyria.
¹² As they go, I will cast my net over them;
    I will bring them down like birds of the air;
    I will discipline them according to the report made to their assembly.
¹³ Woe to them, for they have strayed from me!
    Destruction to them, for they have rebelled against me!
I would redeem them,
    but they speak lies against me.

¹⁴ They do not cry to me from the heart,
    but they wail upon their beds;
they gash themselves for grain and wine;

> they rebel against me.
> [15] It was I who trained and strengthened their arms,
>   yet they plot evil against me.
> [16] They turn to that which does not profit;
>   they have become like a defective bow;
>   their officials shall fall by the sword
>   because of the rage of their tongue.
> So much for their babbling in the land of Egypt.

The section that began with 5:8 builds to a climax in 6:6, which declares God's desire for steadfast love and knowledge of God rather than sacrifice and burnt offering. In 6:7–7:16, we find a series of four speeches by the prophet (6:7–7:2; 7:3–7; 7:8–12; 7:13–16) that appear to look back on 6:6. Hosea probably did not preach these oracles in this order. Those who collected his prophetic speeches have probably placed them here as evidence of the people's failure to give steadfast love and their lack of the knowledge of God. God's speech in 6:4–6 had charged that Israel's love was not reliable, and the four speeches in 6:7–7:16 document this unreliable love.

No new themes are taken up in these speeches. They add further evidence for Hosea's charges against Israel of unfaithful idolatrous behavior (harlotry/whoredom) and for the violence of Israel's ill-considered political life. However, these passages are a fine showcase for Hosea's special talent at verbal imagery. His ability to find apt and striking metaphors to illustrate his message is a significant part of what gives his prophetic preaching such enduring power. In these passages, he compares Israel to a "heated oven" (7:4), a "cake not turned" (7:8), a "silly dove" (7:11), and a "defective bow" (7:16). To see further how Hosea uses such unusual images, we can turn to brief comments on each of these four oracles.

Violence and Treachery (6:7–7:2)

The first section (6:7–7:2) is a chronicle of violence and treachery in Israel, complete with place-names and particulars that suggest Hosea was making reference to specific events that would be known to his audience. We, of course, no longer know the events to which he refers but the listing is grim nonetheless. At Adam (here used as a place-name and not as the Hebrew word for humankind), there was covenant breaking (6:7); at Gilead some sort of violence had left the city with a trail of bloody footprints (6:8); at Shechem robbers and even priests murdered people on the road (6:9). We are not certain of the circumstances that would allow us to understand what is happening in these places with any particularity. But the picture is one of general resort to violence and a kind of lawlessness in the land. Hosea characterizes the Israel of his time with terms such as "corruption" (7:1a), "wicked deeds" (7:1a), "false dealing" (7:1b), "thieves and bandits" (7:1b), and "wickedness" (7:2a). The picture here would fit the violent and chaotic final days of the Northern Kingdom when plots and counterplots were the order of the day for both domestic and international dealings (see the Introduction for historical background on this period).

What Hosea makes clear to the audience of his time and to us is that these matters are not "just politics" in the eyes of God. God takes these matters very personally. In doing these things, Israel has "dealt faithlessly *with me*" (6:7b). God "remembers all their wickedness" and such "deeds . . . are before my face" (7:2). Relationship to God is not simply a religious matter apart from the manner in which people live and act in the daily life of community or nation. Violence and treachery in Israel are related to their lack of faithfulness to God. Hosea even briefly uses the harlotry metaphor for Israel's unfaithfulness ("whoredom," 6:10b) to make clear that his message about Israel's idolatry and his message about Israel's violent political life are at root the same issue—failure to center their life in the love and knowledge of God (6:6). There are many in our time who believe that pursuit of their own individual religious practices will be sufficient, and the world with its brokenness can take care of itself. Hosea's message announces that God will not allow or recognize such a separation.

Hosea also makes clear that judgment is not the sum total of God's purpose for Israel (or God's people in any time). God wishes to "restore" and "heal" (6:11b), but God cannot ignore continued sin and violence when it arrogantly continues "before my face" (7:2b).

A Climate of Conspiracy and Assassination (7:3–7)

In 7:3–7, Hosea uses the image of a baking oven to represent the climate of conspiracy and assassination that consumed Israel in the period following the death of Jeroboam II (746 B.C.) and resulted in four different kings over a period of only twelve years. It may be the rise to power of a particular one of these kings that occasioned this oracle, since 7:3 seems to suggest the celebration of a new king, but Hosea knows this has come to pass through "wickedness" and "treachery." The key word "wickedness" appears also in 7:2 and links this speech of Hosea back to the previous one.

In verse 4, these conspirators are labeled "adulterers" (recalling Hosea's image of Israel as an adulterous wife, unfaithful to the Lord), and they are compared to a "heated oven." The type of oven to which the prophet refers was round with a stone or earthen floor and a dome of hardened clay. A fire was built inside the dome, and when it had burned down to a bed of coals, producing an even heat, flattened circles of bread dough were placed around the curved walls to bake. Hosea assumes a knowledge of this entire process for his image of Israel as a heated oven. In verse 4, the fire is already lit but does not yet need to be stirred into activity. The time has not yet come; the baker is only now mixing the dough, which must then rise overnight. The suggestion seems to be that the fires of rebellion already smolder in the hearts of the conspirators (v. 6a), but the time for action has not yet come. They wait for a day when the king is drunk from some festivity (v. 5) and is stretched out with the revelers ("mockers"). The conspirators have bided their time until the opportune moment (v. 6a), and when it comes, they blaze forth like the morning oven made hot by newly banked and refueled fire. But this fire is not under control. It consumes the rulers of Israel (v. 7a). "All their kings have fallen" (v. 7b), says Hosea, suggesting that he speaks after at least several of Israel's rulers have been deposed by assassination.

Perhaps the most crucial statement in this prophetic speech is its final line. "None of them calls upon me" (v. 7b). In the chaos of Israel's political life, it never occurred to any of these rulers that what was needed was trust and reliance on the Lord who alone truly governs all history. Each king and the conspirators who placed him on the throne through violence thought they had the answer. Appeal to Assyria. Oppose Assyria. Make alliance with Egypt. Make alliance with Syria. Force alliance with Judah. Get rid of those who oppose our policies; they are the enemy. Israel's kings and officials in this chaotic time made the mistake that those who hold power in any generation tend to make. They believed their authority and wisdom constituted ultimate authority and wisdom. They failed to recognize the sovereignty of God that goes beyond all human power and judges all rulers and nations. If they had recognized this, their policies would be tempered by humility, not inflamed by pride. Hosea's warning is no less pertinent today. Few who hold power in our nation or our world demonstrate the humility that comes from recognition of a power and wisdom beyond their own. Leaders in many different spheres of influence treat those who oppose their policies as enemies and engage in name-calling, accusation, and disrespect as legitimate political tactics. Increasingly, the climate in our nation fosters violence as a means of pursuing one's goals or settling one's grievance. For example, physical assaults on schoolteachers reached a new record high in 1994, and a significantly increased proportion of these assaults were by parents. A well-known radio personality suggested that listeners use the pictures of the President and First Lady for target practice. Hosea suggests that such inflamed passions, like the overheated oven, will not provide us with daily bread, but may well consume us.

Israel's Folly (7:8–12)

The theme of 7:8–12 is the folly of Israel's reliance on frantic alliances with the international powers of his day. In the final years of Israel's life, the kings and officials sought first one alliance and then another. Each succeeding group in power seemed to have a different idea about the coalitions that would give them security. Hosea reminds them that ultimate security lies not with any earthly power, but with return to the Lord whose power is ultimately behind their history and all history (7:10).

Hosea's ability to find striking images to reinforce his message is especially evident in this section. He begins with a quick series of images piled on one another. Israel (here addressed as Ephraim) has mixed itself with the peoples (v. 8a). The verb here is one used for mixing cakes by combining flour and oil, suggesting that Israel has combined its identity and fate with the nations as thoroughly as the mix of flour and oil for a cake. In verse 8b, however, Hosea says that Israel is a cake, but one unturned. Cakes baking on the hot sides of the oven without being turned are burned. They are thrown out and good for nothing. The batter formed by Israel's policy of seeking security among the nations ends in disaster. In fact, rather than nourishing Israel, this policy actually "devours" the strength of the nation as foreigners feed off of Israel, using this tiny kingdom to their own purposes without regard to Israel's fate (v. 9a). Israel is already gray-haired, reaching the end of its life span (v. 9b). Tragically, all this is true, says Hosea, and Israel "does not know it" (vv. 9a and 9b). The nation is blind to the reality of their situation.

It is pride that blinds them (v. 10a). It is returning to and seeking the Lord God that could remedy the situation (v. 10b). But the people have not done this. They unwittingly scheme their way toward their own end. How often have nations who thought they were at the center of human destiny in their time turned out instead to be near the end of their own destiny? Pride would not allow them to discern the reality of power in history beyond their human control. The list of nations that miscalculated their true reality is a long one: the Roman Empire in its final days, the aristocracy before the French Revolution, Nazi Germany, Emperor Hirohito's Japan, South Africa under apartheid. Our nation would do well to heed Hosea's warning that a nation's efforts to control its destiny by its own power cannot ultimately succeed.

Hosea has one last image on this theme. He pictures Israel as a silly and senseless dove (v. 11a) flitting back and forth between Egypt and Assyria (v. 11b). These were the two great powers of the day, vying with one another for influence and control among the smaller nations like Israel. And Israel had been drawn into the game, first seeking alliance with one and then with the other. The prospects for such a flighty bird are not good. Suddenly, Hosea pictures God as the fowler who casts the net and brings Israel down like "birds of the air" (v. 12a), a judgment to be understood as God's discipline for Israel's foolish and faithless ways (v. 12b).

God Cries Out (7:13–16)

The final segment of this section (7:13–16) begins with a cry of woe and seems to be a deeply personal cry out of the heart of God. God is deeply and personally wounded by Israel's faithless ways. This section is dominated by the references God makes to God's own personal stake in these matters. "They have strayed from *me*" (v. 13a); "they have rebelled against *me*" (v. 13a); "they speak lies against *me*" (v. 13b); "they do not cry to *me* from the heart" (v. 14a); "they rebel against *me*" (v. 14b); "they plot evil against *me*" (v. 15b). This is all in spite of the fact that "*I* would redeem them" (v. 13b), and "*I* . . . trained and strengthened their arms" (v. 15a). This is a remarkably personal testimony to the stake that God has in Israel. History is never just human history; it is God's history. Any nation, Israel or our own, that seeks to grasp control of its own fate is engaging in rebellion against God. Any nation, ancient or modern, that seeks only to advance its own ends is rejecting the purposes of God.

In a final image, Hosea says that Israel, seeking its own gain, has actually turned to that which profits them not at all and have become like a defective bow, that is, a useless implement (v. 16a). They sought their own gain and gained only worthlessness. The leaders (the officials constantly plotting to place a new king and a new alliance on the throne) will fall by the sword.

Hosea ends this speech with what almost amounts to a punchline. "So much for their babbling in the land of Egypt" (v. 16b). What has all Israel's violence and political maneuvering gained them? Nothing but their own destruction.

THEY HAVE BROKEN MY COVENANT
Hosea 8:1–14

8:1 Set the trumpet to your lips!
>One like a vulture is over the house of the LORD,
because they have broken my covenant,
>and transgressed my law.
²Israel cries to me,
>"My God, we—Israel—know you!"
³Israel has spurned the good;
>the enemy shall pursue him.

⁴They made kings, but not through me;
>they set up princes, but without my knowledge.
With their silver and gold they made idols
>for their own destruction.
⁵Your calf is rejected, O Samaria.
>My anger burns against them.
>How long will they be incapable of innocence?
6   For it is from Israel,
an artisan made it;
>it is not God.
The calf of Samaria
>shall be broken to pieces.

⁷For they sow the wind,
>and they shall reap the whirlwind.
The standing grain has no heads,
>it shall yield no meal;
if it were to yield,
>foreigners would devour it.
⁸Israel is swallowed up;
>now they are among the nations
>as a useless vessel.
⁹For they have gone up to Assyria,
>a wild ass wandering alone;
>Ephraim has bargained for lovers.
¹⁰Though they bargain with the nations,
>I will now gather them up.
They shall soon writhe
>under the burden of kings and princes.

¹¹When Ephraim multipled altars to expiate sin,
>they became to him altars for sinning.

¹² **Though I write for him the multitude of my instructions,**
      they are regarded as a strange thing.
¹³ **Though they offer choice sacrifices,**
      though they eat flesh,
      the LORD does not accept them.
   Now he will remember their iniquity,
      and punish their sins;
      they shall return to Egypt.
¹⁴ **Israel has forgotten his Maker,**
      and built palaces;
   and Judah has multiplied fortified cities;
      but I will send a fire upon his cities,
      and it shall devour his strongholds.

This chapter begins with a cry of warning and an incisive statement of Israel's sin (v. 1) followed by a series of short speeches giving specific illustration of this sin.

A Cry of Warning (8:1–3)

Verses 1–3 clearly set the theme for this chapter. What follows is illustration, perhaps arranged here by the editor rather than spoken by Hosea in this order. In these verses, the Lord is speaking and, in quick succession, voices an alarm, an indictment, an appeal, and a judgment.

The alarm (v. 1a) is a call for warning at the approach of an enemy. It is similar to the outcry of alarm in 5:8 that began an earlier section of oracles dealing with war. The trumpet is to sound and warn of an enemy, here characterized as a vulture hovering over "the house of the LORD" (a phrase to indicate the land and the nation together as God's possession). In light of later references in this chapter (v. 9), this enemy is most likely Assyria, and this speech comes from the time just before or after 733 B.C. when Assyria was threatening and actually annexed much of Israel's northern territory.

Why did this happen? God announces, "Because they have broken my covenant, and transgressed my law" (v. 1b). This is a succinct statement of Israel's sin that would cover all the specific indictments made by Hosea throughout his message. At root, Israel has simply failed to honor the covenant, the basic agreement and understanding of relationship established between God and Israel. In particular, Israel has violated God's law. The Hebrew word here is *torah*, a word more accurately translated as "instruction." Israel has paid no heed to the body of instruction, probably preserved by the priests, which spelled out their obligations to God in covenant relationship. In 4:6, Hosea charges that the priests have neglected this instruction or law; therefore, the people have no knowledge of God.

But remarkably, Israel, faced with this indictment, makes appeal to God (v. 2). Almost incredulous at God's charge, Israel cries out, "My God, we—Israel—know you!" Hosea ironically pictures Israel as falsely claiming to possess the very thing he has charged that they lack—the knowledge of God (4:1, 6; 6:6). Perhaps Israel mistakenly imagines they can "know God" without attention to God's covenant instruction or law.

God rejects the appeal. "Israel has spurned the good" (v. 3a). Judgment can be the only fate for those who reject the good that God makes available in covenant relationship. For Israel, judgment will take the form of the enemy (v. 3b), which is already upon them and occasions the cry of alarm (v. 1a).

Israel's Political and Cultic Sins (8:4–13)

In several short oracles, Hosea gives specific illustration to the broken covenant of verse 1. In 8:4–6, Hosea sets Israel's political and cultic sins side by side. First, he charges that Israel has chosen kings and elevated princes, but not with any knowledge or consultation with God (v. 4a). From the days of Saul and David, God, through the prophets, had participated in the designation of kings for Israel. The king was God's anointed one. In the latter days of Israel, during the time of Hosea, usurpers seized the throne by assassination, only to be deposed by violence themselves. God has nothing to do with this process of greed for power.

But the people dared to make not only kings on their own authority but gods as well (v. 4b). Out of silver and gold, Israel has fashioned idols. In particular, Hosea, speaking for God, singles out the calf of Samaria (vv. 5a, 6b). Here Samaria, as the capital city, probably refers to all of Israel. The calf is probably the bull image erected by Jeroboam I (1 Kings 12:26–33) as the pedestal for an invisibly enthroned Lord similar to the ark in Jerusalem. These were placed in royal sanctuaries at Bethel and Dan. It is probably the calf at Bethel to which Hosea refers, since Dan had already fallen to Assyria at this time. Whatever Jeroboam's intent, however, it is clear in Hosea's message here that the bull has itself become regarded as a god. Indeed, the bull is a chief symbol for the Canaanite god Baal. Hosea's speech for God is blunt. Such a thing is the work of human art; it is not God (v. 6a). In such a thing, royal power and idolatrous practice are intertwined in sin. The human making of kings and the human making of idols are both a "spurning of the good" (v. 3), and a "breaking of covenant" (v. 1b). Such sin leads only to "destruction" (v. 4b), God's anger (v. 5b), and the breaking of false gods (v. 6b) much as the golden calf was destroyed at Sinai.

Verse 7 consists of two proverbial sayings. It is hard to know whether they are intended as a comment in the passage just completed or as an introduction to what follows. Perhaps they are here as a transitional comment on both passages. The first (v. 7a) has become a familiar saying in our own time even among those who have no idea of its source. It basically reminds Israel and us that there is often a relationship between what we do and what later comes as a consequence of our action. These particular images add further meaning. In the wisdom tradition associated with Proverbs, wind symbolizes something foolish or insignificant. A whirlwind, of course, is an image of destruction. The suggestion here is that those who engage in foolishness risk their own destruction.

The second proverbial saying (v. 7b) draws on the agricultural world for its images. Grain that does not grow and develop properly cannot produce grain for flour, and, even if it did, foreigners would eat it anyway. Looking back, we are reminded of Israel's failure to develop under the instruction of covenant (v. 1b). Looking ahead, we find the next section beginning with Israel swallowed up ("devoured"?) by the nations (v. 8a). It would seem that Hosea intends us to understand Israel as the unproductive grain from which no good can come.

Political Sins

Verses 8–10 further elaborate on Israel's frantic political dealings. This time the focus is not on the unfaithful making of kings (v. 4a), but on the unfaithful making of international treaties and conspiracies. Coupled with the frequent overthrow of kings in Israel was a frantic vacillation from one alliance to another, largely in submission or opposition to Assyria. Hosea saw this as a frantic attempt to control the nation's destiny rather than to submit to God's sovereignty over history. Israel has lost its own identity by pandering to the nations—they are "swallowed up" and "among the nations"—and they are now "useless" (v. 8; see the similar theme in 7:8–10). In particular, Israel has chosen to bargain with the dreaded Assyrian empire, dealings that Hosea bitterly compares to an ass wandering in the desert, and a prostitute bargaining for lovers (v. 9). Such dealings can only end in disaster. God will gather up such a faithless people for judgment. They will writhe, not under the weight of a lover, but under the oppressive burden of kings and princes (v. 10; the Hebrew text actually reads "the king of princes," which is cited in some ancient texts as a title for the king of Assyria).

Cultic Sins

Just as verse 4 set the political and cultic sins of Israel side by side, now the elaboration of Israel's political faithlessness in verses 8–10 is matched by further words on Israel's cultic sin in verses 11–13. Israel seems to have been in a period of institutional growth ("multiplied altars," 11a), but for Hosea such "church growth" is to no avail if these are places that ignore the written instruction of the Lord (v. 12). If these places revel in the vigor of their services and rituals (v. 13a) but disregard God's law, then their rituals are unacceptable to God (v. 13a; see 6:6). Altars where such hypocritical worship is conducted may be intended to lift the burden of sin ("expiate sin," 11a), but in reality they are only "altars for sinning" (v. 11b). God will "remember their iniquity," and "punish their sins" (v. 13b). Indeed, "they shall return to Egypt" (v. 13b), a reference to the bondage in Egypt from which God had delivered them. The exodus will be reversed.

God's Judgment (8:14)

A final verse (14) concludes this chapter with the blunt announcement that "Israel has forgotten his Maker." Judah is also included in this indictment in the next phrase of this verse. And if God has been forgotten, where has the attention of Israel and Judah been? It has been in building palaces and forti-fied cities—in the false security of kings and military might. The judgment of fire that destroys city and fortress alike is pronounced in a pattern identi-cal to a recurring refrain of judgment on the nations used by Amos in his great speech against the nations (Amos 1–2). This may show some contact and influence among the prophets of this period.

Now that we have looked at the several parts of this chapter it is well to step back and take a look at the overall pattern and message of this chapter. What leads to broken covenant and transgression of God's law? Hosea seems to say that it is reliance alone on what humans can make or do, and not on God the Maker and what God has done. The question at stake is "Whose works really matter in the world?" Consider Hosea's list. Israel has:

made kings (v. 4a)
made idols of gold and silver (v. 4b)
made treaties with Assyria (v. 9)
made altars and sacrifices (vv. 11, 13)
made palaces and fortresses (v. 14)
but they have forgotten their *Maker* (v. 14a)

Trust has been placed in what humans make and not in the God who made us. What humans make, if cut off from the instruction or law of God (vv. 8b, 12), can only lead to disaster. Israel sought security in its own frantic political and religious actions, but Hosea suggests that true security lies in covenant partnership with God and the wisdom that comes from God's instruction (similar to his theme of the knowledge of God).

What an important word for those who would be God's people in the world of our time. We live in an age of information explosion and technological accomplishment, an age of geopolitics and sophisticated military capabilities. It is tempting for many to believe that we are the makers of our own destiny and to disparage or limit the need to remember our Maker. Hosea reminds us that we are not the makers of our own political or religious destiny. The list of twentieth-century wars is ample testimony to the futility and destruction wrought by those who thought human power could shape the world's political destiny—World War I, World War II, Korea, Vietnam, Afghanistan, and the Persian Gulf. In the age of the megachurch and the televangelist, there are those who believe human capabilities can market and control the religious destiny of the nation. But the public fall of figures like Jim Bakker and Jimmy Swaggart testify that God will confront and judge sin and faithlessness even when it wraps itself in religious garb. Those who see growth in church numbers, church dollars, and church influence as ends in themselves should heed Hosea's words in this chapter. In the political or the religious sphere, the Maker has no patience with "self-made men or women."

THE PROPHET IS A SENTINEL
Hosea 9:1–17

9:1 **Do not rejoice, O Israel!**
    Do not exult as other nations do;
  for you have played the whore, departing from your God.
    You have loved a prostitute's pay
    on all threshing floors.

²Threshing floor and winevat shall not feed them,
   and the new wine shall fail them.
³They shall not remain in the land of the LORD;
   but Ephraim shall return to Egypt,
   and in Assyria they shall eat unclean food.

⁴They shall not pour drink offerings of wine to the LORD,
   and their sacrifices shall not please him.
Such sacrifices shall be like mourners' bread;
   all who eat of it shall be defiled;
for their bread shall be for their hunger only;
   it shall not come to the house of the LORD.

⁵What will you do on the day of appointed festival,
   and on the day of the festival of the LORD?
⁶For even if they escape destruction,
   Egypt shall gather them,
   Memphis shall bury them.
Nettles shall possess their precious things of silver;
   thorns shall be in their tents.

⁷The days of punishment have come,
   the days of recompense have come;
   Israel cries,
"The prophet is a fool,
   the man of the spirit is mad!"
Because of your great iniquity,
   your hostility is great.
⁸The prophet is a sentinel for my God over Ephraim,
   yet a fowler's snare is on all his ways,
   and hostility in the house of his God.
⁹They have deeply corrupted themselves
   as in the days of Gibeah;
he will remember their iniquity,
   he will punish their sins.

¹⁰Like grapes in the wilderness,
   I found Israel.
Like the first fruit on the fig tree,
   in its first season,
   I saw your ancestors.
But they come to Baal-peor,
   and consecrated themselves to a thing of shame,
   and became detestable like the thing they loved.

[11] Ephraim's glory shall fly away like a bird—
    no birth, no pregnancy, no conception!
[12] Even if they bring up children
    I will bereave them until no one is left.
Woe to them indeed
    when I depart from them!
[13] Once I saw Ephraim as a young palm planted in a lovely meadow,
    but now Ephraim must lead out his children for slaughter.
[14] Give them, O LORD—
    what will you give?
Give them a miscarrying womb
    and dry breasts.

[15] Every evil of theirs began at Gilgal;
    there I came to hate them.
Because of the wickedness of their deeds
    I will drive them out of my house.
I will love them no more;
    all their officials are rebels.
[16] Ephraim is stricken,
    their root is dried up,
    they shall bear no fruit.
Even though they give birth,
    I will kill the cherished offspring of their womb.
[17] Because they have not listened to him,
    my God will reject them;
    they shall become wanderers among the nations.

This chapter begins with the prophet Hosea apparently showing up at a great festival celebration and denouncing what he perceives to be going on there (9:1–6) only to have the people turn and denounce the prophet himself (9:7), which provokes yet further comment from Hosea (9:8–9). It is in this section of the chapter that we see some unusual and new aspects of Hosea's message, and it is here we will focus. The last half of the chapter contains two speeches that recall God's history with Israel (vv. 10–14 and 15–17), and I will comment on these only briefly.

Hosea Denounces Israel's Behavior (9:1–6)

Imagine the shock of the celebrants when Hosea cries out in the midst of the festival proceedings that they are not to rejoice or exult (v. 1a). Joy and celebration are the purpose of Israel's festivals, and especially this one. The setting is the observance of Sukkoth or Booths, the great fall festival that remembered God's time with Israel in the wilderness, renewed the covenant with the Lord, and gave thanks for the bounty of the fall harvest. This feast was called the "festival of the LORD" (as here in v. 5; see also Deut. 16:13–15; Lev. 23:39–43; Judg. 21:19–21). Hosea negates the festival mood by commanding that they cease their celebration—at least they should not celebrate "as other nations do" (v. 1a).

Hosea follows his command with an indictment of the celebration he sees going on. The Festival of Booths was to be a special honoring of the Lord, but Hosea suggests that their celebration has become the behavior of a whore or a prostitute (v. 1b). They worship the Lord as if worshiping Baal. Their love is not for the Lord but for the grain and the wine as if they were the people's due from a god of fertility like Baal. When the people's celebration focuses more on the products of their material well-being than on the God who gives these gifts, these products become little more than "prostitute's pay" (v. 1b). Perhaps the rituals Hosea observes "on all threshing floors" (v. 1b) are more appropriate to the cult of Baal than that of the Lord.

Hosea announces that the very things the people of Israel celebrate and take for granted in their festival will fail them as a consequence of their sin. The grain and the wine will not be available to feed them (v. 2). They will not even continue to dwell in the land (v. 3a) that is characterized as the "land of the LORD" to counter the notion that the land and its produce are the province of Baal. Instead, they will find themselves in Egypt or Assyria where they will be forced to eat unclean food (v. 3b). It is probable that this oracle was preached after 733 B.C. when some had already been carried off into captivity by Assyria and others had already become refugees in Egypt. There will be no worship life in these places. Sacrifices and offerings of the land's produce will not take place; there will be no "house of the LORD" and no festival meals. The people will eat only to survive because of their hunger (v. 4). When Israel is gone from the land, what then will happen on the day of festival, asks Hosea (v. 5). Those who escape destruction will live as aliens in Egypt, perhaps even in Memphis, the funeral city of Egypt's dead (v. 6a). The shrine of Israel's celebration and its precious vessels of silver will lie abandoned and choked with weeds (v. 6b).

Here we can pause a moment to reflect on how frequently, in the churches of our time, material prosperity has been mistaken as a substitute for and even a sign of authentic relationship to God. Prosperous churches are most often judged to be successful churches. People search for churches to join not because they find a sense of God's presence but because the programs and practices of the church make them feel good. Marketing language and strategies suggest that religion is in danger of becoming a commodity. The celebration of our worship is sometimes reduced to an experience for our benefit rather than a gift to a God worthy of our worship. Would Hosea be tempted to stand up in one of our festivals and suggest that what he saw looked more like idolatry than authentic worship?

The People of Israel
Respond to Hosea (9:7–9)

In verses 7–9, Hosea gives us a rare glimpse of the reception he received among the people. It is not an attractive portrait. Hosea seems to be responding to critics of his message and citing their slanderous remarks about him. He begins by claiming that the days of judgment may already have started (v. 7a). The people may deny the reality of the consequences Hosea announces for their sin, but the prophet responds that such denial is already too late. The days of punishment and recompense have already come. He may be referring to the Assyrian conquest of considerable Israelite territory in 733. The people may have been rejoicing that the main part of the kingdom was spared, but Hosea says that God's judgment was in these events and they were only a beginning.

It is, of course, an age-old strategy of those who do not like the message to attack the messenger. Hosea mockingly quotes the people's attacks on him. "The prophet is a fool, the man of the spirit is mad!" (v. 7b). The term *fool* often appears as the opposite of the wise. The people think themselves wise, so they disparage Hosea as a fool. Even worse, they claim he is insane. If the messenger is discredited, surely the message has no validity. But Hosea suggests they are only hostile because he has struck close to home; the people know they are guilty of "great iniquity" (v. 7b).

Hosea redefines his role. No, he is not a fool or a madman. He is a sentry, a watchman (v. 8a). That is what the role of prophet is all about. Like a watchman, the prophet only warns of danger. To discount the watchman's warning is truly to act the fool. But a prophet is a watchman in the service of God, not of the nation. It is because God's sentry cannot be controlled in the national interest that the people have set out to ensnare him and greet him with hostility even in the sanctuary (v. 8b).

Thus, God will remember and punish Israel's sins (v. 9b). The sentinel warns them once more. Their sin is great as in the "days of Gibeah" (v. 9a). This is probably a reference to the violent and shameful events recounted in Judges 19—21. Because the tribe of Benjamin did violence against the Levite and his concubine in Gibeah, Benjamin was almost exterminated as a punishment. Perhaps Hosea is suggesting that Israel's sin similarly risks the end of the kingdom.

The image of the sentry or the watchman is one that was applied to other prophets personally (Jer. 6:17; Ezek. 3:17; Isa. 56:10) and was used by them in their preaching (see esp. Ezek. 33:1–6). It is an image worth thinking about again in the modern church. In the various institutional forums of the church, from congregation to national bodies, there is overwhelming pressure put toward a positive institutional image. In this climate, the church has often disbelieved and even discredited those who try to warn of dangers and point to problems. "Team players" are more often given institutional rewards than those who voice critical opinions. Teresa of Avila, Francis of Assisi, Martin Luther, John Wesley, Dietrich Bonhoeffer, and Martin Luther King, Jr. are but a few in the history of the church who have been labeled foolish and mad when they spoke the truth as sentinels in their times. We live in a culture that likewise treats public image for political figures as more important than honesty and candor. A well-known campaign publicist recently declared, "People want to hear that everything is all right or can easily be made all right, whether this is true or not." We have a federal law protecting whistle-blowers because without it, they usually lose their jobs, and the public perception of those who expose abuse or corruption is often that they are disloyal. Hosea would not have been any more welcome in our time than in his own.

God's Relationship with Israel: A Remembrance (9:10–14)

In 9:10–14 is the first of two speeches in which God speaks through the prophet in the first person. Both of these speeches give voice to the divine anguish over Israel's sin and look back to key moments in the story of God's relationship to Israel.

Verse 10 begins with divine nostalgia. God remembers with affection and pleasure the beginning of relationship between God and Israel in the wilderness. This speech uses agricultural images to express this. Israel is like grapes in the wilderness (a rare and pleasing discovery) or the first fruit on the fig tree (the pleasant taste that promises more to come). Later in this same speech God remembers thinking of Ephraim as a "young

palm, planted in a lovely meadow" (v. 13a). These are all images of pleasure and promise. They are also in keeping with Hosea's view of the
wilderness period as a kind of "honeymoon" period in Israel's relationship
with God (see 2:14–15; also Jer. 2:2–3).

But the idyllic days do not last. At Baal-peor the relationship was broken. The story of Israel's sin at Baal-peor is found in Numbers 25:1–9. It
was one of the last stops before entry into the promised land, and Israel
became involved in the worship of a Moabite fertility god known as the
Baal of Peor. This seems to have included sexual rites related to the cult
of Baal. God, speaking through Hosea, remembers this as a moment that
introduced the same issue of idolatry and unfaithfulness to the Lord that
now plagues Israel. The word *shame* is often used to replace the name of
Baal in a pejorative way, and now by yoking themselves to shame Israel
has become detestable (v. 10b).

God announces that for those who sought fertility through Baal the fitting penalty should be the reversal of fertility—"no birth, no pregnancy,
no conception" (v. 11). But even if children are born, they will not live (v.
12). The history of fruitful images in the wilderness time with the Lord
becomes a history of loss and death. God will depart this sinful people (v.
12b) and Ephraim's children will be led out to slaughter (v. 13b). It is a
grim reversal of images.

In verse 14, God is no longer speaking. It is Hosea who speaks, and he
seems to be trying to intercede. He begins a petition, "Give them, O LORD—
" but he can't finish it. He seems to puzzle over what he could possibly ask,
and seems to settle for asking that Israel have no children at all, rather than
to suffer such loss of their children. The miscarrying womb and the dry
breasts are better than to see one's children perish. It is the bleakest of hopes.

God Remembers Israel's Sin
(9:15–17)

In a final speech for this chapter, verses 15–17 again begin as a speech of
God, but this speech moves immediately to God's memory of Israel's sin.
God speaks of the people's ways as evil and wicked (v. 15a) and of Israel's
leaders as rebels (v. 15b). God says this began at Gilgal (v. 15a). It is not
certain what this means. Gilgal is one of the first places to which Israel
comes after crossing the Jordan and entering the promised land, so there
is a certain balance with the preceding Baal-peor speech in verses 10–14.
Gilgal was also where Saul was made king (1 Sam. 11:14–15). Hosea's attitude toward the kingship is generally very negative; it is the source of re-

bellion and sin (see Hos. 7:3–7; 8:4; 10:3, 7, 15). But Gilgal is also the location of a shrine that seems to be condemned elsewhere by Hosea as involved in idolatrous practices (4:15; 12:11). Perhaps kingship and idolatry are part of the sin that God sees emanating from Gilgal. In any case, the penalty God announces is similar to the preceding speech: Israel is to suffer loss of fertility. The images of the root drying up and the plant that bears no fruit are both images of barrenness. But if children are born, here again the bleak prospect is that they will perish (v. 16).

The final verse of this speech again shifts from God's speaking to the speech of Hosea himself. He no longer seeks to intercede as in verse 14. In verse 17, Hosea announces that Israel's rejection of God will result in their rejection and their fate is exile. Only too soon, this does in fact become Israel's fate.

ISRAEL IS A LUXURIANT VINE
Hosea 10:1–8

10:1 **Israel is a luxuriant vine**
    that yields its fruit.
The more his fruit increased
    the more altars he built;
as his country improved,
    he improved his pillars.
2 **Their heart is false;**
    now they must bear their guilt.
The LORD will break down their altars,
    and destroy their pillars.

3 **For now they will say:**
    "We have no king,
for we do not fear the LORD,
    and a king—what could he do for us?"
4 **They utter mere words;**
    with empty oaths they make covenants;
so litigation springs up like poisonous weeds
    in the furrows of the field.
5 **The inhabitants of Samaria tremble**
    for the calf of Beth-aven.
Its people shall mourn for it,
    and its idolatrous priests shall wail over it,
    over its glory that has departed from it.

> ⁶The thing itself shall be carried to Assyria
>   as tribute to the great king.
> Ephraim shall be put to shame,
>   and Israel shall be ashamed of his idol.
>
> ⁷Samaria's king shall perish
>   like a chip on the face of the waters.
> ⁸The high places of Aven, the sin of Israel,
>   shall be destroyed.
> Thorn and thistle shall grow up
>   on their altars.
> They shall say to the mountains, Cover us,
>   and to the hills, Fall on us.

The tenth chapter of Hosea is divided into two sections: Verses 1–8 are the prophet speaking in the third person and seem to represent a single connected speech, but verses 9–15 are posed as the speech of Yahweh in the first person and seem to consist of three separate speeches. We will look at verses 1–8 in this section and turn to verses 9–15 in the next section.

In 10:1–8, Israel is first celebrated as a "luxuriant vine" but then subjected to a prophetic speech of judgment in which Hosea claims that they will suffer the loss of all the institutions, cultic and national, on which they have come to rely. Altar, pillar, king, calf at Bethel, and high places are to be destroyed. In this indictment, Hosea seems to begin with worship and its apparatus (vv. 1–2), turn to kingship (vv. 3–4), and return to worship again (vv. 5–8).

Israel's Worship
with Altars and Pillars (10:1–2)

In the image of the luxuriant vine (v. 1), Hosea seems to be characterizing Israel's prosperous past. The vine yielding fruit remembers days of economic well-being, perhaps during the long reign of Jeroboam II (786–746 B.C.). Such prosperity yielded material results not simply for the economy but for the cult as well. Hosea tells us that as the "fruit increased" and the "country improved" Israel has built more altars and improved pillars. These were the furnishings for worship life in the shrines of ancient Israel. Although the pillars were later condemned as connected with Baal worship (especially in Deuteronomy; see Deut. 16:22) such monuments to memorialize elements of Israel's faith story were not uncommon (for example, Exod. 24:4; Gen. 28:18; 2 Sam. 18:18). Altars were, of course, the central focus of sacrificial worship.

Although the setting is rather different from ours, the tendency is one we know. Hosea is telling us that in prosperous times church building programs flourished. It is easy to be materially generous toward our religious institutions when things are going well. The North American landscape is covered with church buildings proudly erected during the times of relative peace and prosperity in the 1950s and early 1960s. Such buildings in our time, or altars and pillars in Hosea's time, are not in themselves unfaithful, although the timing suggests that the national economy is a more important factor in institutional well-being than the work of God's spirit. Such buildings and furnishings can serve God's faithful purposes and serve as signs of gratitude to God. The potential problem lies deeper.

In verse 2, Hosea names the real issue. "Their heart is false. . . . " Lavish and numerous places for worship are to no avail if the heart is not turned toward God. The word translated here as "false" has the connotation of "smooth" or "slippery." It conjures up a picture of religion as smooth talk, mouthing words with no real orientation of the heart to God. Lavish buildings and false hearts are the stuff of hypocrisy, and Hosea condemns it. The Lord will not allow such false altars and pillars to endure; they are brought down by Israel's own guilt (v. 2).

We, in the modern church, should tremble at such an indictment. It is so easy to serve the material needs of our buildings and institutions to the neglect of serving God's purposes. As I recently watched a well-known televangelist, he proudly announced, "If you could see our new, four-and-a-half-million-dollar tabernacle for yourself, it would be evident how God has blessed this ministry." Shouldn't the evidence of God's blessing on our ministries be in lives changed, brokenness made whole, reconciliation made possible, hearts opened, needs met, and woundedness healed? How many great buildings erected with pride in the fifties stand largely empty because the needs of the community changed and the ministry of the church did not? How many of our church buildings are more the focus of pride than the ministries those buildings might enable? How often do our denominational structures focus on recovery of material well-being to the detriment of a heart truly aligned to God's purposes? Hosea's warning of the dangers of the false heart is a timeless one.

Israel's Lament over the Loss of a King (10:3–4)

Verses 3–4 are difficult to translate and interpret. The subject clearly shifts to Israel's king. Some believe that Hosea is reflecting the people's fears in a time when assassination has struck down Israel's king: "We have no king" (v. 3a). Others believe Hosea is holding this out as a future possibility of God's judgment. Not only altar and pillar will perish but also king; religious and national institutions will fail. In any case, such threat to the stability of Israel's rulers is due to a failure to fear the Lord. The people cry out with a despairing question, "What could he [a king] do for us?" They then give answer to the question from their own sorrowful experience of kings (v. 4). Kings only give "mere words" and "empty oaths," and the result is the opposite of Israel as luxuriant vine. It is Israel covered with "poisonous weeds."

Israel's Worship of a Calf Image (10:5–8)

In verses 5–8, Hosea shifts focus back to Israel's worship life but this time to an object of special pride and veneration in Israel—the calf image at Bethel. Jeroboam I had set up calf images in Bethel and Dan (1 Kings 12:26–33). They were intended as pedestals for the enthroned Lord (much like the ark of the covenant in Jerusalem) and not as idols. But Hosea indicates that under the influence of Baal worship, which depicted Baal as a bull, the calves themselves became objects of worship and devotion and thus idolatrous (see our comment on 8:5). The calf at Dan had probably already been taken by the Assyrians in 733 so Hosea's focus here is on the calf at Bethel, which he scornfully refers to as Beth-aven (v. 5, "house of evil" rather than "house of God").

Like the altars, the pillars, and the king, the calf also will perish. In verses 5–6, Hosea pictures the lamentation over the calf. He describes the priest of Bethel as idolatrous and mentions their lament over glory already departed from the calf (v. 5b). This may reflect the stripping of wealth from the shrine, perhaps even the gold overlay on the calf, in the frantic effort to pay tribute to Assyria and avoid the total conquest of the land. We know that such efforts managed a temporary reprieve for Samaria and the central cities of Israel (such as Bethel) in the last years of the kingdom. But Hosea says their lamentation will come to nothing. The calf will eventually be carried to Assyria as tribute to the Assyrian king (v. 6a), and its idolatry with the calf will have brought only shame (v. 6b). Once again we might reflect on the idolatry of well-intended things. Objects meant to serve in praise and devotion to God become idolatrous themselves. I know a large city church with a fabulous organ, but it is not played for weekly worship. It is played only twice a year when concerts are given by invited organ masters who can play it to the "masterful level it deserves."

In a final, doleful pronouncement of judgment, Hosea declares that Samaria's king will perish (v. 7); the high places of Bethel will be destroyed (v. 8a); the altars shall be covered with thorn and thistle. Thus, the proud building days of Israel, the luxuriant vine, will have been totally reversed through Israel's false heart turned to idolatry. In such a day, Hosea predicts that the people will wish for death and hope that the mountains and hills will bury them (v. 8b).

SINCE THE DAYS OF GIBEAH
YOU HAVE SINNED
Hosea 10:9–15

10:9 Since the days of Gibeah you have sinned, O Israel;
      there they have continued.
      Shall not war overtake them in Gibeah?
10 I will come against the wayward people to punish them;
      and nations shall be gathered against them
      when they are punished for their double iniquity.

11 Ephraim was a trained heifer
      that loved to thresh,
      and I spared her fair neck;
   but I will make Ephraim break the ground;
      Judah must plow;
      Jacob must harrow for himself.
12 Sow for yourselves righteousness;
      reap steadfast love;
      break up your fallow ground;
   for it is time to seek the LORD,
      that he may come and rain righteousness upon you.

13 You have plowed wickedness,
      you have reaped injustice,
      you have eaten the fruit of lies.
   Because you have trusted in your power
      and in the multitude of your warriors,
14 therefore the tumult of war shall rise against your people,
      and all your fortresses shall be destroyed,
   as Shalman destroyed Beth-arbel on the day of battle
      when mothers were dashed in pieces with their children.
15 Thus it shall be done to you, O Bethel,
      because of your great wickedness.

> At dawn the king of Israel
> shall be utterly cut off.

The first half of chapter 10 was prophetic speech by Hosea, but in verses 9–15 the Lord speaks directly in the first person through Hosea. There seem to be three separate speeches here (9–10; 11–13a; 13b–15), but they are linked by key words that probably led to their position together when Hosea's preaching was collected and edited.

Gibeah's Violence Leads to Violence against Gibeah (10:9–10)

In verses 9–10, Hosea once again recalls the history of Gibeah as a sign of Israel's violent past (see also comment on 9:9). The prophet's reference is probably to the unspeakable violence committed by the Benjaminites at Gibeah against the Levite's concubine (Judges 19—21). This shameful act led to a tribal judgment against Benjamin that almost ended that tribe. Later, Gibeah became the capital of Saul, Israel's first king. Considering Hosea's rather negative view of Israel's kings, this connection with Saul may be a further reason to choose Gibeah as a sign and source for Israel's sinful behavior. For Hosea, Gibeah set a pattern of sin that Israel has not left, and, as a result, Gibeah shall not escape judgment by war (v. 9b). Israel as a "wayward" people shall be opposed by the nations (v. 10a). The "double iniquity" mentioned in verse 10b may refer simply to the past sin of Gibeah and the present sin of Israel. God's judgment comes a scond time.

The Heifer Israel Reaps What It Sows (10:11–13a)

Hosea's rich imagination turns in verses 11–13a to the agricultural life of Israel for images to enliven his message. He pictures Israel as a young heifer and God as the proud owner who trained her. In her youth (perhaps in the wilderness time about which Hosea speaks, e.g., 2:14) the heifer learned to thresh, but was spared from the yoke (v. 11a). But in verse 11b God indicates that the time came when the heifer must do the work of plowing and planting. Perhaps this indicates the time after the wilderness when Israel came into the land and had to care for it. The reference to Judah in verse 11b may be an editorial change by later editors since all the surrounding references and images are to the Northern Kingdom of Israel.

In verse 12, we see what the prophet intends behind his metaphor of the heifer. The service of Israel, the young heifer, is the service of covenant obedience. God characterizes the sowing as the planting of righteousness, and the reaping as the harvest of steadfast love. It is the fruits of covenant toward which Israel was to bend its labor, and to bring the growth they were to seek the Lord as the rain of righteousness upon them. These images take on additional meaning because Hosea is struggling against idolatry to the agricultural god Baal, who was seen as the lord of the rainstorm. The fertility here is not of land but of covenant.

The bucolic mood is broken by verse 13a. Israel has not plowed righteousness but wickedness; they have not reaped steadfast love but injustice. The fruit is not the issue of God's righteous rain but the "fruit of lies," and Israel has eaten it.

The Machinery of War
Brings War (10:13b–15)

The images and the focus change in verse 13b from agriculture to war, but in the present arrangement verses 13b–15 serve as the announcement of judgment on Israel who failed as the covenant heifer of verses 11–12.

The brief indictment in verse 13b accuses Israel of trusting in its own power, specifically its own military power ("multitude of your warriors") rather than in the Lord. What follows in verses 14–15 is a judgment of war destroying Israel. It is a graphic statement of that old saying "Those who live by the sword shall die by the sword." Israel's trust in its own military power only invites the reality of war and its destruction. Verse 14b uses as an example an event no doubt well known to Hosea's listeners, but there are no other references known to us beyond this mention of Shalman's conquest of Beth-arbel so we can say no more about it. That it was an event that included the slaughter of women and children says enough for the purpose of illustrating the atrocities of war.

Verse 15 refers to Bethel as subject to this fate of judgment by war and states that the king will be cut off. These references to Bethel and kingship may explain the placement of this material in the chapter with 10:1–8. The mention that it was due to Bethel's "wickedness" links back to the heifer who "plowed wickedness" in verse 13a. This kind of arrangement through the linking of key words was common in the prophetic books.

We cannot but observe that although the three separate pieces of prophetic speech in 10:9–15 are very different in imagery they do share a central idea. Each speaks of consequences for sin that fit the nature of the sin. In verses 9–10, the history of Gibeah's violence unchanged leads to violence against Gibeah. In verses 11–13a, the heifer Israel reaps what it sows. In verses 13b–15, trust in the machinery of war brings the reality of war. It is food for thought in our time. A significant segment of our nation's population believes that the violence of crime can best be met by an increasingly armed populace prepared for counterviolence. Hosea's message would suggest that increased violence can only lead to violent consequences. In Oklahoma City in the spring of 1995 those who chose violence to protest government policy took the lives of innocent men, women, and children in a bombing in which the target may have been a government office but, instead, the entire building was destroyed. Hosea's message tells us that if we desire righteousness and steadfast love, then these must be sought in righteousness and steadfast love.

WHEN ISRAEL WAS A CHILD,
I LOVED HIM
Hosea 11:1–11

11:1 **When Israel was a child, I loved him,**
      and out of Egypt I called my son.
     2 The more I called them,
         the more they went from me;
      they kept sacrificing to the Baals,
         and offering incense to idols.

     3 Yet it was I who taught Ephraim to walk,
         I took them up in my arms;
         but they did not know that I healed them.
     4 I led them with cords of human kindness,
         with bands of love.
      I was to them like those
         who lift infants to their cheeks.
         I bent down to them and fed them.

     5 They shall return to the land of Egypt,
         and Assyria shall be their king,
         because they have refused to return to me.
     6 The sword rages in their cities,
         it consumes their oracle-priests,
         and devours because of their schemes.
     7 My people are bent on turning away from me.

To the Most High they call,
  but he does not raise them up at all.

⁸How can I give you up, Ephraim?
  How can I hand you over, O Israel?
How can I make you like Admah?
  How can I treat you like Zeboiim?
My heart recoils within me;
  my compassion grows warm and tender.
⁹I will not execute my fierce anger;
  I will not again destroy Ephraim;
for I am God and no mortal,
  the Holy One in your midst,
  and I will not come in wrath.

¹⁰ They shall go after the LORD,
  who roars like a lion;
when he roars,
  his children shall come trembling from the west.
¹¹ They shall come trembling like birds from Egypt,
  and like doves from the land of Assyria;
  and I will return them to their homes, says the LORD.

This chapter is widely regarded as one of the most moving and eloquent chapters in all prophetic literature. It presents a remarkable portrait of God as a loving parent in relationship to Israel as a rebellious child. The language is unusually personal and intimate. In Hosea's portrayal, God's relationship to Israel is not motivated simply out of covenant partnership but out of love. It is not simply the "steadfast love" of covenant that is important to Hosea's message, but love analogous to the human love of a parent that goes beyond the obligations of covenant.

There are two matters of structure that should be observed for this chapter. The first is that it concludes the second major segment of the book of Hosea. Chapters 4—11 began with the phrase, "Hear the word of the LORD" (4:1a) and end in 11:11b with the concluding formula, "says the LORD." (Verse 11:12 in English translations appears as 12:1 in the Hebrew text.) Each major section of the book of Hosea ends with a speech of hope and renewal. Chapter 3 serves this function for chapters 1—3, and chapter 11 plays this role for the long central section in chapters 4—11. The final segment, chapters 12—14, also ends with a speech of hope in 14:4–9. In Hosea, there is a strong and confronting message of judgment, but hope and renewal always have the final word.

Within the chapter, there are four distinct sections. Verses 1–4 portray the *past of God and Israel* as one of parent and child. Verses 5–7 speak of *Israel's present* as marked by the consequences of rebellion. Verses 8–9 speak of *God's present*, in which God refuses to give up on the rebellious child, and verses 10–11 speak of a *future for God and Israel* when reunion and restoration can take place.

God and Israel as Parent and Child (11:1–4)

Hosea moves to a new metaphor for relationship between God and Israel; it is the metaphor of parent and child (v. 1). This relationship began with Israel as a child, and it began in Egypt. It was in the exodus experience, the bringing of Israel "out of Egypt," that Israel was "called." The verb "called" (used again in v. 2) indicates that Israel's bond is not so much a matter of biology as a matter of divine initiative—God chooses to make Israel God's son. Some have used the language of adoption for this.

The motive for God's deliverance of Israel out of Egypt and God's calling of Israel as a son is clear. "I loved him." From its opening lines, this chapter is established as a testimony to divine love—the love of parent to child, given freely long before the child can reciprocate with any understanding, and as we shall see, given continuously even when it is rejected. Hosea should be regarded as the first to base God's relationship to God's people on love—freely given love prior to any reciprocal relationship like covenant. Deuteronomy follows him in this and makes God's love a major theme. For Christians, this theme receives its climactic expression in the New Testament witness to Jesus as the gift of God's love.

In this chapter, Israel is clearly identified as a son; but because God speaks entirely in the first person, the gender of God is left unclear. It is perhaps best to think of God as divine parent, rather than as father or mother. Indeed the range of caring, parental actions seems to cover tasks traditionally carried out by fathers and by mothers. What is remarkable here is the intense personal language of parenting that God uses to speak of divine love for the child, Israel. The language is dominated by direct, personal I-statements: "I love . . . I called . . . I taught Ephraim to walk . . . I took them up in my arms . . . I healed . . . I led . . . I lifted them like infants to the cheek . . . I bent down . . . I fed."

The parent-child image allows for the development of the history of God's relationship with Israel through the lens of that image. The statement of God's love and calling out of Egypt is followed in verse 2 by the statement of Israel's rebellion. The more God desired relationship as parent to child, the more Israel rejected God in favor of idolatry, particularly with the Baals. The sense of the verse is of a continuing process of estrangement. God continues to call, desiring relationship, but Israel continues to turn to other gods—the Baals, idols.

Verses 3–4 are remarkable for the pathos of God's response. It is not the angry God who responds to rejection with wrath. It is the wounded God who responds by recalling with tenderness the care that God, the parent, had given Israel, the child. This is not the lofty, transcendent God of power. Portrayed here is a God of intimate relationship, involved from Israel's infancy in nurturing and enabling its life. God taught them to walk, and held them in arms (v. 3a; could this be the wilderness time to which Hosea elsewhere refers?). God healed them without thought to acknowledgment: "they did not know" (v. 3b). Hosea elsewhere uses the verb "to heal" to indicate redemption from enemies (5:13; 6:1; 7:1). God led them, and the leading was out of kindness and love (v. 4a). Verse 4b is difficult to translate, but the NRSV rendering fits well with the portrait of parental tenderness. God lifts them like an infant to the cheek, bends, and feeds them. This passage has no parallel for its portrait of divine tenderness, care, and love. By the same token, coming immediately after the statement in verse 2 of Israel's continuous rebellion, the effect is to portray divine woundedness, the God whose tender love has been rejected.

Israel as Rebellious Child
(11:5–7)

From tender beginnings, the text turns abruptly to tragic present. Israel has refused to return to God (v. 5b). Instead they have brought themselves into desperate circumstances that will bring a return to Egypt and a submission to Assyrian rule (v. 5a). The return to Egypt is ironic in light of the deliverance from Egypt that established God's love for Israel (v. 1). It is a theme that Hosea uses often to indicate the coming judgment against Israel (7:16; 8:13; 9:6). The threat of Assyrian rule has shadowed Israel's life for much of Hosea's ministry, and verse 6 seems to indicate that the violence of the Assyrian sword is already being felt in the land, perhaps reflecting the bitter Assyrian invasion of 733 B.C. that took most of the land by the sword. At that time many fled as refugees to Egypt while many others were forced to submit to Assyrian rule. The double bondage to Egypt and Assyria of verse 5a is not just Hosea's vision for the future but also a present reality already happening to Israel. Yet, the people remain stubbornly "bent on turning away from me" (v. 7a). They call on the "Most High" (probably a title for some other deity; some scholars with a slight emendation of the text read "Baal" here), but no false god can save them (v. 7b).

God Refuses to Give Up on Israel (11:8–9)

Elsewhere in Hosea, the fate of Israel reflected in verses 5–7 would seem a perfectly appropriate expression of God's judgment on Israel's apostasy. But in verses 8–9 of this speech we find, not a portrait of divine wrath and judgment, but a remarkable and impassioned divine self-questioning that leads to compassion and mercy as God's response to Israel's sin.

Verse 8 opens with a dramatic glimpse into the internal life of God. God engages in an intense self-questioning. Four rhetorical questions suggest the fate that Israel's behavior deserves: They are to be given up (the end of relationship) and handed over (to captivity), and totally destroyed like Admah and Zeboiim (cities destroyed with Sodom and Gomorrah, Gen. 10:19; 14:2, 8). But when God asks "Can I do or allow these things?" the implied answer is "I cannot!" God's internal inventory finds not the expected final execution of divine judgment. Instead God reports, "My heart recoils within me" (v. 8b). In Hebrew the heart is the seat of will and understanding. God's will rejects the execution of Israel's punishment. God further reports, "My compassion grows warm and tender" (v. 8b). Justice may demand Israel's judgment, but God's compassion is growing, not God's wrath. The Hebrew phrase here refers to the arousing of tender desires to console and treat with affection.

The divine self-reflection leads to divine resolve in verse 9. In three emphatic negative statements, God thunders, "I will not. . . . " God declares against anger and destruction and wrath. These will not be. The judgment against Israel need not be the final word. The relationship need not be finally ended. The future of Israel need not be utterly ended. God will not do these things. As a parent, God cannot leave Israel to its chosen fate.

In the midst of these declarations, God appeals for justification to the divine character, "for I am God and no mortal, the Holy One in your midst . . . " (v. 9b). God has acted in love like a human parent, but God retains sovereign freedom and chooses to use that freedom for mercy. God is both "the Holy One" and "in your midst." As the "Holy One," no fate is irreversible; as the one "in your midst," God refuses to end the relationship in spite of Israel's sin. This does not mean there are no consequences for Israel's sin. As verse 11 makes clear, Egypt and Assyria remain part of the fate Israel has chosen in its sin. But Israel's sin will not end the relationship because God's love will not allow it, and God's divine power will enable a future where human powers alone could not prevail.

Reunion and Restoration in the Future (11:10–11)

This future for God and Israel is the focus of verses 10–11. If the present has seen God and Israel, parent and child, on a divided path, then the divine speech through Hosea ends by envisioning a future of reunion. Verse 10 is somewhat enigmatic. The Lord is portrayed as a roaring lion in a manner reminiscent of Amos 1:2, and the future is seen as one when Israel will "go after the LORD." The future is also one of return as God's children come "trembling from the west." It is not clear where this envisions Israel having been. Many believe this verse is a later Judean addition to the speech.

Verse 11 is considerably less enigmatic. It envisions Israel's return from Egypt and Assyria, reversing the exile implied in verse 5. It seems very much in character with Hosea, using the image of trembling birds and doves to picture the anxious, tentative return of Israel. But the ending is clear. In a final, first-person declaration, God declares, "I will return them to their homes." God brings them home—to the land, to the relationship. The child will return.

Christians who read this chapter are reminded of Jesus' parable of the prodigal son (Luke 15). The loving father—the self-indulgent son—the consequences of alienation in a distant land—the persistence of the father's love—the return to forgiveness and love in spite of rebellion: These are all elements of the parable that clearly echo the passionate speech of the Lord in Hosea 11. One cannot but wonder if Jesus had this tradition in mind as he narrated the parable. It reminds us that the history of God's grace is one that extends back to Egypt in the childhood of our faith story. It is both reassuring and humbling to recognize that from the beginning of our story as the people of God we have been dependent on the graceful love of God that perseveres in spite of our sin and enables our homecoming no matter how distant we have strayed. God's parental love, as Hosea expresses it so eloquently in this chapter, is the gift of God's grace that allows us to hope in the future even when we know we have acted in ways that seem destructive of hopeful possibility.

One gift of Hosea is that he gives us concrete images not only for sin but for hope. The prophet's critique of Israel's sin and its relevance to our sin are what we know best in the church, but Hosea, especially in chapters like this one, will not allow us to end with indictment and judgment. We must claim the hope and the promise as well.

In Hosea, and in many other prophetic books, Israel in its sin helps us to understand how often we too are those who have been the rebellious children. Often the church's effort to be prophetic settles for engaging in indictment and judgment on the failures of our communities, social and religious. Hosea's picture of God in chapter 11 suggests a message beyond judgment that is also the church's responsibility to communicate. God in relationship to us models what we are to be in relationship to one another. We are to love as God has loved. When we recognize the sins of idolatry, injustice, lack of the knowledge of God in our society and ourselves, we are called, nevertheless, to love and compassion, even as disappointment and anger at the consequences of sin rise within us. The church that takes to heart this portrait of God's persevering love will be prepared to look for possibility where others surrender to hopelessness. It will be prepared to couple the demands of justice with the tenderness of compassion. It will be prepared to be as concrete in articulating the promises as in voicing the judgments of God.

If God refused to give up on relationship to rebellious Israel, perhaps the church should look again at its role in a society that has increasingly given up on criminal offenders, settling for incarceration at the expense of rehabilitation. Perhaps we should persevere in the hope for a less racially polarized society even when there are signs of backsliding on the progress that has been made. Perhaps the church must steadfastly hold visible the divine promises of peace and community even when new nationalisms seem to fracture the human family. The perseverance of God's love and compassion encourages the church to turn toward a broken and rebellious world with the hope of a promise and not the finality of a judgment.

THE LORD WILL PUNISH JACOB
Hosea 11:12–12:14

11:12 **Ephraim has surrounded me with lies,**
  and the house of Israel with deceit;
 but Judah still walks with God,
  and is faithful to the Holy One.
 12:1 **Ephraim herds the wind,**
  and pursues the east wind all day long;

they multiply falsehood and violence;
        they make a treaty with Assyria,
        and oil is carried to Egypt.

² The LORD has an indictment against Judah,
        and will punish Jacob according to his ways,
        and repay him according to his deeds.
³ In the womb he tried to supplant his brother,
        and in his manhood he strove with God.
⁴ He strove with the angel and prevailed,
        he wept and sought his favor;
    he met him at Bethel,
        and there he spoke with him.
⁵ The LORD the God of hosts,
        the LORD is his name!
⁶ But as for you, return to your God,
        hold fast to love and justice,
        and wait continually for your God.

⁷ A trader, in whose hands are false balances,
        he loves to oppress.
⁸ Ephraim has said, "Ah, I am rich,
        I have gained wealth for myself;
    in all of my gain
        no offense has been found in me
        that would be sin."
⁹ I am the LORD your God
        from the land of Egypt;
    I will make you live in tents again,
        as in the days of the appointed festival.

¹⁰ I spoke to the prophets;
        it was I who multipled visions,
        and through the prophets I will bring destruction.
¹¹ In Gilead there is iniquity,
        they shall surely come to nothing.
    In Gilgal they sacrifice bulls,
        so their altars shall be like stone heaps
        on the furrows of the field.
¹² Jacob fled to the land of Aram,
        there Israel served for a wife,
        and for a wife he guarded sheep.
¹³ By a prophet the LORD brought Israel up from Egypt,
        and by a prophet he was guarded.

¹⁴ **Ephraim has given bitter offense,**
    so his LORD will bring his crimes down on him
    and pay him back for his insults.

In the Hebrew text of Hosea, chapter 12 begins with what is 11:12 in our English translations. This is important because 11:12a could serve as a topic sentence for the whole of chapter 12. Israel is charged with lies and deceit before God in this opening sentence. Most of the rest of the chapter serves as examples of this lying and deceitful behavior. (In 11:12b Judah is held up as a contrasting example of faithfulness. This is probably an addition by a later Judean editor suggesting why Judah still survives when the Northern Kingdom of Israel perished.)

Israel Charged with Lying
and Deceit (11:12–12:1)

The immediate example Hosea couples with the charge of lying and deceit is composed of an image followed by a political charge. First, he says that Ephraim, the Northern Kingdom, is herding the wind and pursuing the east wind (12:1a). This is an image intended to suggest futile and useless pursuits. Who can capture or control the wind? But, 12:1b goes on to suggest that what Ephraim is actually doing is futile and senseless. They multiply violence and falsehood, and they think they can enter a treaty with Assyria (2 Kings 17:3) and then deal with Egypt in breaking it (2 Kings 17:4). This is foolish, deceitful, and dangerous behavior.

The remainder of the chapter develops further evidence of Israel's duplicitous character, first, through a lengthy illustration using Jacob's story (12:2–6, 12–14) and also through two shorter speeches on Israel's deceitful behavior (12:7–9, 10–11).

Israel's Duplicity Illustrated
by the Jacob Story (12:2–6, 12–14)

Verse 2 opens with an announcement of the lawsuit of God, thus beginning this last segment of Hosea (chaps. 12—14) in the same way as the second segment (chaps. 4—11; see 4:1). God calls Israel to account as the plaintiff in a covenant lawsuit. Israel has violated the terms of the covenant and must face the penalties (v. 2). Although verse 2 names Judah in the present Hebrew text, most scholars believe that Hosea's words were addressed to Israel since the next line uses Jacob as the parallel. *Israel* is the customary poetic parallel word to *Jacob* in the prophets. A later editor has probably tried to make Hosea's preaching pertinent to Judah after Israel has been destroyed, a practice that we see fairly frequently in the prophets.

This lawsuit by God is developed in an unusual way. It is directed to the Israel of Hosea's time by means of comment on the story of Israel's ancestor, Jacob. Hosea, as we have seen, makes frequent use of Israel's earlier history in his message, but he usually goes to the stories of the exodus or wilderness. This is his first use of ancestor stories of the promise from the book of Genesis. Hosea's speech is almost like a sermon to Israel with the story of Jacob as his text. The implication is that Israel is like Jacob and should learn from the comparison. Perhaps Jacob seemed a likely story to use because of Jacob's special connection with Bethel and the central role Bethel plays in Hosea's preaching of judgment for Israel's idolatry (see 4:15; 10:5–8, 15). Hosea draws on three episodes from Jacob's life in verses 2–6 and makes use of another in verse 12.

Jacob at Birth

In verse 3a, Hosea refers to the story of the birth of Jacob and his twin brother, Esau, in Genesis 25:24–26. Hosea claims that even in the womb Jacob tried to "supplant" his brother. This word (Hebrew, *'aqab*) means "to deceive or trick." At birth Esau was born first, but Jacob was delivered grasping the heel (Hebrew, *'aqeb*) of Esau as if trying to hold him back. For that reason Genesis 25:26 says he was named Jacob (Hebrew, *ya'aqob*). Later, when Jacob has tricked his brother out of his birthright and then deceived his father, Isaac, while cheating Esau out of his rightful blessing, Esau bitterly cries that Jacob (*ya'aqob*) is rightly named because he has "supplanted (*'aqab*) me these two times" (Gen. 27:36). Jacob's very name means "supplanting by deception." Hosea seems to be implying that Israel's very beginnings as a people are in deception and self-centeredness.

Jacob at Jabbok

In verses 3b–4a, Hosea draws on the episode of Jacob's wrestling with the night visitor at the fords of the Jabbok River when he is returning to face his alienated brother, Esau (Gen. 32:22–32). Hosea seems to have a different version of this story than the one found in Genesis, or at least he chooses to interpret it differently. Verse 3b seems to refer to Jacob's change of name to Israel, which is part of this story. The name Israel is a play on the words for *struggle* and *God*, meaning perhaps "one who struggles with God." The Genesis story takes this as a positive naming, but Hosea seems to imply that Jacob was born struggling with his brother and in manhood even struggles with God. It is for Hosea evidence of Jacob's trying to have his way with and manipulate even God.

Verse 4a names Jacob's night visitor as an angel, which is not the case in Genesis 32 where the assailant is called a man, but Jacob comes to believe that God is present in the encounter with this man. The NRSV translates the verb *prevailed* with the suggestion of Jacob as the subject. This is consistent with Genesis 32:28, but it is not in harmony with Jacob's weeping and seeking of favor in verse 4a of our text. The text says literally "and he prevailed" so that the one who prevailed for Hosea could be the angel. In any case, it is clear that in Hosea's use of the episode, Jacob's struggle with God did not lead to his triumph, but to his tears and entreaty. Hosea's point seems to be that self-will cannot prevail against God. Like Jacob, Israel's only chance in the present was to recognize the futility of struggle with God and to seek God's favor in tears (of repentance?).

Jacob at Bethel

In verse 4b Hosea remembers the story of Jacob's encounter with God at Bethel (Gen. 28:10–22). Jacob is running for his life because Esau has vowed to kill him. On his way out of the land, headed for Haran, he sleeps with a stone as a pillow and God appears to him in the dream of the ladder or stairway from heaven. The promise to the ancestors is given to Jacob, and, on awakening, Jacob names the place Bethel ("house of God") and vows to build a shrine there if God will only return him safely to the land.

The order of events in Hosea 12:2–4 is different from the story in Genesis. Bethel comes long before the wrestling at the Jabbok. But, for Hosea, Bethel is the climactic Jacob memory. There are two factors about the Bethel experience of Jacob that seem to make it significant for Hosea's message to eighth-century B.C. Israel. First, in the Bethel story Jacob is on the way out of the land. He is headed into exile because of his deceitful ways. Second, in spite of Jacob's sinful past God appears to him (this is called theophany), and, further, God has a promise for him that involves a future in relationship to God and a return to the land.

Both of these elements are involved in the climax of Hosea's Jacob sermon in verses 5–6. The name of the Lord as the God of hosts is announced in verse 5. It is the presence and character of God, the Lord, that will make a difference for Israel, even as God's promise enfolded sinful Jacob. Israel is like sinful, self-centered Jacob in its deceptions and lies. As a consequence, they are about to leave the land. Hosea knows that destruction and exile are the inevitable result of the path Israel is on. But, as with Jacob, God will not allow this to be the end. In the power of God's name, Israel can still have a future, with the land and with God.

God desires relationship in spite of sin. But what does this require? Verse 6 makes clear the response needed from Israel. Return to the land requires "return to your God." Israel must "hold fast to love and justice, and wait continually for your God." In these qualities of relationship, there can be a future for Israel in God's promise (see also the discussion on 2:19 and 4:1). The love here is the steadfast and loyal love of covenant relationship. Justice is a concern for the just order of God in relation to the neighbor. To wait for God is to trust that relationship as sufficient and to do so continually. This verse is reminiscent of the great text in Micah 6:8, often used to summarize the message of the eighth-century prophets: "What does the LORD require of you but to do justice, and to love kindness, and to walk humbly with your God?" Those who would be the community of God's people would do well to ask what these verses in Hosea 12:6 and Micah 6:8 demand of them in their own times and contexts.

Jacob in Haran

In verses 12–14, Hosea refers again to the story of Jacob. This is not part of the sermonlike composition on Jacob in the earlier part of the chapter, but its use of the Jacob story probably led the editors to include it in this chapter. Verses 12 and 13 draw a contrast between Jacob and the Lord. The Jacob in view here is the one who tended sheep for his father-in-law, Laban, in order to marry his daughters Leah and Rachel (Genesis 29—31). The God in this contrast is the Lord who brought Israel out of Egypt.

The contrast is not intended to be favorable to Jacob or to Jacob's descendants, Israel. Jacob fled from the land because of his own deceptions. The Lord brought Israel up from Egypt and back to the land. Jacob became bound in service with his father-in-law. The Lord released Israel from bondage and servitude to the pharaoh. Jacob kept ("guarded") sheep. The Lord kept ("guarded") Israel. Jacob did this for a wife. The Lord did it by a prophet. In this last pairing the prophet is undoubtedly a reference to Moses, but with some implication that Hosea himself now stands in that role. The wife referred to for Jacob may have overtones of sexual relationship determining Jacob's actions, a possible reference to the sexual imagery Hosea uses for Israel's idolatry.

Verse 14 pronounces judgment on Israel for giving offense, committing crimes and giving insults against the Lord. These terms are often related to idolatry. The implication is that Israel has acted like its ancestor Jacob, looking out for himself. They have not paid attention to God's action in their behalf but have offended God, and these offenses will be judged.

The uses of the Jacob story by Hosea in chapter 12 are quite remarkable. In general, we must imagine that Israel pointed proudly to its ancestor Jacob. Hosea, in effect, says, "Look again." Apart from God's grace, what would Jacob have been? Nations and churches are always tempted to think they are self-made in their successes because of their own gifts and virtues. We conveniently forget the sins and blemishes that appear in our story, the places where only the grace of God could have brought us through. What would a prophet such as Hosea remind us of in our nation's history? What could we gain from a reading of our true history, warts and all? Some of this is now happening, but it can be painful. Women and minorities are reminding us they are often absent altogether in our "official" histories. It is painful but important to remember our struggles over slavery and racism, our treatment of native populations, the rugged individualism that sometimes undercuts our efforts at community. And what is demanded when we dare to hear our true histories? The prophet's answer is still a good one: "Hold fast to love and justice, and wait continually for your God" (12:6).

Other Evidence of Israel's Deceitful Behavior (12:7–11)

Two small speeches in verses 7–9 and 10–11 contribute further to the examples of Israel's deceitful and lying behavior. Verses 7–9 portray Israel as a Canaanite trader. The word translated *trader* is actually the word *Canaan*, but because of the Canaanite reputation as merchants the word has come to mean a trader in that area no matter what ethnic or cultural background. This is an ironic way for Hosea to speak. In effect, it says that Israel has lost its identity and has adopted the character of its Canaanite neighbors. The character portrayed by Hosea is not attractive. Israel as Canaanite trader is dishonest, oppressive, boastful, rich, and deluded. Wealth is gained by deception and injustice (v. 7), but such wealth is then taken as evidence of the favor of God and the absence of sin (v. 8).

But God is not deceived. God's identity as one who delivered the oppressed from Egypt is set over against the false identity of Israel (v. 9a).

The God of exodus can deal with the boastful and deceitful trader. God can return them to tents and to the wilderness days that are remembered in the Festival of Booths or Tabernacles.

In verses 10–11, God speaks of the prophets who have brought vision to Israel in the past. Through prophets, God can now also bring destruction (v. 10; Hosea may be speaking of his own sense of his task). Verse 11 specifically speaks of punishment to Gilead and Gilgal, two of the centers of worship in Israel that Hosea names as places of idolatry and evildoing (see 6:8 and 9:15).

Unfortunately, the boastful, self-centered trader is not really an unknown figure to us in our nation and churches. Many believe that success vindicates their methods of reaching it. Many confuse the traits and values of contemporary culture for God's values. A man recently attempted to justify to me why he did not want to give money to the church when the church used that money to help poor people. He said, "I believe what it says in the Bible, 'God helps those who help themselves.'" This, of course, is not in the Bible, but it is a definite part of the individualistic ethos adopted by many in our culture. And it certainly helps justify keeping all one's resources for oneself. Hosea tells us that God intends a quite different set of values than the self-centered values of Jacob or of the Canaanite trader. God has shown us love and justice in God's own acts toward us, and God expects no less in our dealings with one another.

I WILL DESTROY YOU, O ISRAEL
Hosea 13:1–16

13:1 **When Ephraim spoke, there was trembling;**
        he was exalted in Israel;
        but he incurred guilt through Baal and died.
    2 **And now they keep on sinning**
        and make a cast image for themselves,
    idols of silver made according to their understanding,
        all of them the work of artisans.
    "Sacrifice to these," they say.
        People are kissing calves!
    3 **Therefore they shall be like the morning mist**
        or like the dew that goes away early,
    like chaff that swirls from the threshing floor
        or like smoke from a window.

⁴Yet I have been the LORD your God
     ever since the land of Egypt;
  you know no God but me,
     and besides me there is no savior.
⁵It was I who fed you in the wilderness,
     in the land of drought.
⁶When I fed them, they were satisfied;
     they were satisfied, and their heart was proud;
     therefore they forgot me.
⁷So I will become like a lion to them,
     like a leopard I will lurk beside the way.
⁸I will fall upon them like a bear robbed of her cubs,
     and will tear open the covering of their heart;
  there I will devour them like a lion,
     as a wild animal would mangle them.

⁹I will destroy you, O Israel;
     who can help you?
¹⁰Where now is your king, that he may save you?
     Where in all your cities are your rulers,
  of whom you said,
     "Give me a king and rulers"?
¹¹I gave you a king in my anger,
     and I took him away in my wrath.

¹²Ephraim's iniquity is bound up;
     his sin is kept in store.
¹³The pangs of childbirth come for him,
     but he is an unwise son;
  for at the proper time he does not present himself
     at the mouth of the womb.

¹⁴Shall I ransom them from the power of Sheol?
     Shall I redeem them from Death?
  O Death, where are your plagues?
     O Sheol, where is your destruction?
     Compassion is hidden from my eyes.

¹⁵Although he may flourish among rushes,
     the east wind shall come, a blast from the LORD,
     rising from the wilderness;
  and his fountain shall dry up,
     his spring shall be parched.
  It shall strip his treasury
     of every precious thing.

¹⁶ **Samaria shall bear her guilt,**
   because she has rebelled against her God;
they shall fall by the sword,
   their little ones shall be dashed in pieces,
   and their pregnant women ripped open.

This is a chapter permeated with death. It is composed of four separate oracles (vv. 1–3, 4–8, 9–11, 12–16) all of which pronounce Israel's end in the starkest terms. Chapter 12 began with the announcement of God's lawsuit (12:2) and in effect stated an indictment against Israel. Chapter 13 is the announcement of judgment in this lawsuit. The verdict is death!

These oracles may well come from the final years of the Northern Kingdom when the catastrophic end of Israel begins to become evident under the inept policies of King Hoshea. Indeed, verses 10–11 may indicate the time after King Hoshea was captured and the total collapse of the country by Assyrian conquest is but weeks away. In any case, these speeches by the prophet Hosea make clear his understanding that the end is near.

By itself, this chapter would be an overwhelming and devastating portrait of a God of anger and wrath. As we will see, the images are powerful and searing. But chapter 13 is part of a larger closing structure to the book of Hosea. The movement in the three-chapter sequence from 12 to 14 is from major emphasis first on indictment (chap. 12), then on judgment (chap. 13), and finally on salvation (chap. 14). This is a general pattern of movement that some also find in the other two sections of the book of Hosea (chaps. 1—3 and chaps. 4—11). Certainly it is true that each major section ends with emphasis on salvation, renewal, and hope.

Chapter 13 is a harsh portrait of God's anger and judgment on Israel. But this chapter looks back to chapter 12 and its testimony to Israel's entire history of rebellion and sin. God is not arbitrarily angry; Israel has sealed its own fate. Even more important, this chapter looks ahead to chapter 14, which gives testimony to a God unwilling to allow a final end in relationship to Israel. God's mercy and grace supersede God's anger and speak the final word.

God's ultimate grace does not, however, soften the need for Israel (and us) to face the reality of the death sin has brought. This is the function of chapter 13. It is analogous to the Christian understanding that the full meaning of resurrection in the gospel story can only be understood by facing the full reality of the cross and the power of sin that leads to death. For Israel, for the early church, for us, the verdict of death must be heard before the depth of God's mercy can be understood.

Ephraim Singled Out
for Death (13:1–3)

The chapter opens with a speech of judgment that reviews the past (v. 1), present (v. 2), and future (v. 3) of Ephraim. The name *Ephraim* singles out the most important and influential tribe in Israel. Ephraim means "to be fruitful," and Hosea may have intended use of this name as a contrast to the death that is in prospect instead of fruitfulness.

In the past, Ephraim was feared and respected among the tribes of Israel (v. 1a). But Ephraim squandered this promising reputation by the worship of the Baals, which led to guilt and death (v. 1b). Yet, they persist in this foolish path to death. In the present, they "keep on sinning" by making cast images and idols of silver, gods who are but the work of human hands (v. 2a). These are not gods, but the people call for sacrifices to honor them (v. 2b). Why, they even kiss calves! This is undoubtedly a reference to veneration of the golden calf or bull at Bethel (see 8:5–6 and 10:5–6). Although it may have been intended originally as a pedestal for the Lord's throne, Hosea is clear that the calf itself has now become an object of veneration and probably mixed with devotion to Baal whose image was a bull. Kissing the image is said to indicate devotion to Baal in 1 Kings 19:18.

Hosea uses his skill with images to chilling effect in verse 3. Because of Ephraim's idolatry, its death will be final. Ephraim will be no more. They will pass from the scene as easily as "morning mist," or the early "dew." They will be blown and scattered like the "chaff . . . from the threshing floor" or the "smoke from a window." There will be no future. They will be utterly gone. The images are of the chilling silence of finality. The verdict is death!

Indictment and Punishment
for Israel (13:4–8)

Another speech of indictment and punishment appears in verses 4–8. Here the indictment begins with the historical memory of exodus (v. 4; see also 11:1). God speaks in the first person, and verse 4 seems almost like a confession of faith for Hosea. It expresses the foundation of the prophet's theology as a statement by God of God's own character. This remarkable statement also seems like a paraphrase of the first commandment of the Decalogue. God reminds Israel that God has been "the LORD your God ever since [they were in] the land of Egypt." Exodus was the beginning of relationship in covenant. Further, Israel has known no gods but the Lord. For Hosea, knowledge of God is crucial (see 4:1, 6). To know is to experience relationship, and Israel's history since Egypt has been of the Lord and no other. It was the Lord who saved them from bondage in Egypt and Israel has no other savior. The hope of any other who might save is futile. This makes loyalties to any other gods false loyalties.

Further, this same Lord fed Israel in the wilderness (v. 5) with all its hardships and continued to provide for their needs until they were satisfied in the land (v. 6a). But satisfaction did not bring gratitude and praise to the Lord. Instead, Israel became proud of heart (v. 6b). This phrase indicates arrogance and self-exultation. The result was "they forgot me" (v. 6b). This is the key to the indictment. Pride has displaced the Lord, and Israel no longer remembers who saved them, led them, fed them, and satisfied them. Instead of knowledge there is forgetfulness. Instead of gratitude there is self-congratulation.

In prophetic speeches like this, we have become accustomed to judgment following indictment, but this announcement of God's angry judgment is terrible to contemplate. Hosea turns from the quietly final images of verse 3 to images of savage violence in verses 7–8. Death is announced for Israel in the brutal images of wild beasts who tear and mangle the body of the nation. God's wrath descends as a lion and as a leopard (v. 7) and as an angry mother bear robbed of her cubs (v. 8a). The prideful heart will be ripped open. The body of the nation will be devoured, leaving only mangled remains (v. 8b). The verdict is death!

God Questions Israel (13:9–11)

Verses 9–11 pick up on the theme of verse 4 that Israel has no other savior. God now enters into a taunting disputation with Israel, hurling questions that can only be answered in despair. "I will destroy you, O Israel"—the divine resolve is clear. "Who can help you?"—the clearly implied answer is no one (v. 9)! Israel has no other savior (v. 4). Baal or other idols could not save them, bringing only death (vv. 1–3). Israel's own prideful heart could not save them (v. 6). Hosea now turns God's harsh questioning toward Israel's kings. "Where now is your king, that he may save you?" (v. 10a). The question is mocking and seems to imply that the kingship has already ended in Israel. There are no rulers left in the city. This oracle may reflect the final days of the Northern Kingdom after its last king, Hoshea, had already been taken (2 Kings 17:4–5). In any case, the kings had been dramatically ineffectual as a source of salvation in Israel. During the last half of the eighth century, Israel had seven different rulers and most of these were assassinated in the petty political turmoils of Israel. Hosea's negative attitude toward the kingship in general has been well evidenced thus far in the book (7:3–7; 8:4–10; 10:3–4, 7, 15).

God's speech recalls the request for a king by the elders of Israel (1 Samuel 8) and says that God only allowed kings in Israel out of anger, and now God takes them away in anger (v. 11). God seems to say that kingship was a bad idea that predictably turned out bad. Sinful lack of trust in the Lord's kingship (see 1 Sam. 8:7–8) has brought kingship to a sinful end and with it the end of the nation.

Ephraim Refuses New Life and Rebirth (13:12–16)

In verses 12–16, we come to Hosea's final and perhaps most brutal announcement of Israel's end. These verses are bracketed by a reference in verse 12 to Ephraim (the most prominent tribe) and in verse 16 to Samaria (the royal capital). Both Israel's tribal past and its royal present are caught up in judgment. The particulars of the indictment have been given in other speeches of Hosea. Here are simply named the iniquity and sin of Ephraim, kept on record and waiting God's response (v. 12), and the guilt and rebellion of Samaria, leading to the final violent images of the end (v. 16).

Hosea has two last images of Israel's predicament (vv. 13 and 15) flanking a final internal dialogue of God over Israel's fate (v. 14).

First, in verse 13, Hosea says Israel is like an unborn child that refuses to come forth from the womb when the opportunity for life presents itself. Israel cannot stay in its sinful ways. It is a false security. The time has come. Crisis could lead to new life and rebirth. But Israel unwisely refuses. There is no future for such a child. The verdict is death.

Second, in verse 15, Hosea pictures God's judgment as a hot, east wind that dries up all water and withers all plants before its blast. Israel thinks itself safe as a reed planted in the waters of the marsh, but its safety is an illusion. God's judging wind will strip Israel bare. Especially since the last phrase of verse 15 speaks of Israel's treasury and precious things, one can imagine that the wind of judgment from the east is Assyria, who by this time had already stripped the kingdom of much of its wealth. Hosea's message is clear once again. There is no safety for the guilty and the rebellious. The verdict is death!

The final images of death in this chapter are terrible ones. They are the images of conquest, made all the more horrible by the realization that this was indeed the fate suffered by the Northern Kingdom of Israel in 722 B.C. Men fall by the sword; children are dashed to death; pregnant women are ripped open. Death!

A Glimpse into the Heart of God over Israel's Death (13:14)

In this chapter of pervasive death, we have left verse 14 to a final discussion, both because of its role in the chapter and its unusual use in the letter of Paul to the church at Corinth in 1 Corinthians 15:55.

Verse 14 is a gripping glimpse into the heart of God in the midst of the death images of this chapter. God raises within the divine self questions of redemption or ransom, both words that suggest actions in behalf of those helpless to help themselves. "Shall I ransom them from the power of Sheol? Shall I redeem them from Death?" (v. 14a). Sheol is the shadowy realm to which the dead are consigned in Hebrew thought. The internal questioning of God suggests that God is not without regard and sympathy for Israel's fate. God considers a stay of sentence.

But God must decide that Israel stands convicted and shows no sign of moving from its course of death (v. 14b). The opportunity for new life, rebirth was refused (v. 13). Along with the NRSV translation and most scholars, we believe that verse 14b must be read as God's call for Death and Sheol to take Israel. "O Death, where are your plagues?" (Unleash them!) "O Sheol, where is your destruction?" (Let it happen!) God refuses to look with compassion. "Compassion is hidden from my eyes."

(There has been some debate over the translation and interpretation of this verse. The word translated as "compassion" is a rare Hebrew word, and some have translated it as "vengeance." This would make the final phrase a refusal of vengeance rather than a refusal of compassion. This in turn makes the preceding questions a mocking of Death and Sheol rather than a summons for them to execute the verdict against Israel. This is not our view. The NRSV and most recent comment on this verse have translated the word as "compassion" and see here a refusal of God to take Israel off the hook of its own guilt. This is not yet the time for mercy.)

The apostle Paul quotes Hosea 13:14 in his letter to the Corinthian church (1 Cor. 15:55). He used the Greek translation of Hosea (the Septuagint), which, in contrast to our discussion, took this verse as an announcement of salvation rather than a giving up of Israel to death. Paul writes, "Death has been swallowed up in victory." "Where, O death, is your victory? Where, O death, is your sting?" (1 Cor. 15:54b–55; Paul takes the first quote of this passage from Isaiah 25:7). Paul is using this quote from Hosea in a discussion of Jesus' death and resurrection. For him the context is one of God's victory over death. For Hosea, the context was one of God's anger and discouragement. Yet even for Paul sin and death had to be faced in all their power. Only then could the word of God's grace be heard in its full power. The cross is the necessary prelude to resurrection. For Paul this facing of death and revealing of new life take place in Jesus Christ.

In Hosea 13:14, God is angry and the power of death is given its full course. But as Paul later sees clearly in Jesus Christ, God's character is not exhausted in anger. Death does not have the final word. For Hosea, too, the final word is not of anger and death, but of grace, hope, and renewal. This is the subject of 14:1–9. This final word of life is not to remove Israel from its chosen course of death. Chapter 13 makes this clear. It is to say that in God's grace this choice will not be allowed to say the final word about God's relationship to God's sinful people. God has a word of life to speak to Israel beyond the reality of the death they have chosen.

In a way, Hosea foreshadows the relationship between cross and resurrection. Too many want to bypass the cross. Paul knew this could not be done. Jesus actually died as a result of our sin. The power of death is real. The lure of the deathly powers is real. Israel chose them. People still choose them. The verdict is still death! But in God's grace, there is yet another reality. Hosea knew it. Paul knew it. For Christians, Jesus Christ embodied it. The text that gives us up to death in Hosea 13:14 is transformed in Jesus Christ into Paul's victory cry.

I WILL LOVE THEM FREELY
Hosea 14:1–9

14:1 **Return, O Israel, to the LORD your God,**
    for you have stumbled because of your iniquity.
  ²**Take words with you**
    and return to the LORD;
  say to him,
    "Take away all guilt;
  accept that which is good,
    and we will offer
    the fruit of our lips.

³Assyria shall not save us;
   we will not ride upon horses;
we will say no more, 'Our God,'
   to the work of our hands.
In you the orphan finds mercy."

⁴I will heal their disloyalty;
   I will love them freely,
   for my anger has turned from them.
⁵I will be like the dew to Israel;
   he shall blossom like the lily,
   he shall strike root like the forests of Lebanon.
⁶His shoots shall spread out;
   his beauty shall be like the olive tree,
   and his fragrance like that of Lebanon.
⁷They shall again live beneath my shadow,
   they shall flourish as a garden;
they shall blossom like the vine,
   their fragrance shall be like the wine of Lebanon.

⁸O Ephraim, what have I to do with idols?
   It is I who answer and look after you.
I am like an evergreen cypress;
   your faithfulness comes from me.
⁹Those who are wise understand these things;
   those who are discerning know them.
For the ways of the LORD are right,
   and the upright walk in them,
   but transgressors stumble in them.

The book of Hosea ends not in judgment and death (chap. 13) but in hope and healing, forgiveness and new life. Each major section of Hosea ends in hope (chaps. 3, 11, 14). Chapter 14, which also ends the entire book, is the most lavish in its imagery of salvation and life.

There are three parts to the chapter. First, there is a summons by the prophet for Israel to return to the Lord, which actually offers them words of penitence for the occasion (vv. 1–3). This is followed by the joyous response of the Lord, offering salvation in full measure to returning Israel (vv. 4–8). Finally, there is a single verse offered by the collectors of Hosea's preaching as an admonition and word of advice to readers (v. 9). The pattern of confession and repentance followed by an announcement of salvation is very reminiscent of the liturgies of penitence that may have been used at shrines and holy places where petitioners came to offer penitential sacrifices. Hosea may have had this model in mind.

A Summons to Confession and Repentance (14:1–3)

It is Hosea, the prophet, who speaks in 14:1–3, and he summons Israel to new possibility for its life. The life of the nation may have ended as they had known it, but relationship to God has not ended, and in God there is hope for new life beyond judgment. Hosea calls, "Return, O Israel, to the LORD your God" (v. 1a). Returning is for Hosea the basic movement that can reverse the separation from God through sin. He has called for Israel's return before, but Israel's sin has prevented it (see 3:5; 5:4; 7:10; 11:5). Perhaps the collapse of the kingdom had to come before return was possible. In 5:5 the prophet had warned that "Ephraim stumbles in his guilt" (Hebrew, 'awon), but now 14:1b acknowledges that Israel has indeed "stumbled because of your iniquity" (also Hebrew, 'awon). The guilt/iniquity of Israel has brought its end; Israel lies fallen. But the prophet offers return to the Lord as hope to fallen Israel. Such a return can signal a new beginning.

Those seeking forgiveness in ancient Israel normally came to the sanctuary with a sacrifice of penitence, but Hosea has a different piece of advice to penitent Israel. Hosea had already spoken God's word in 6:6, "I desire steadfast love and not sacrifice, the knowledge of God rather than burnt offerings." Hosea tells returning Israel to bring words not sacrifices (v. 3a)—words of confession and commitment to turn from sin.

Remarkably, Hosea, who could speak the fiery words of God's judgment, becomes the patient teacher. He offers returning Israel a script for repentance; he tutors them in penitent response. Verses 2b–3 are a prayer of repentance offered as a model for Israel to follow. Israel is to begin with a humble seeking of forgiveness: "Take away all guilt." God is asked to accept only what is good. Israel offers restitution not with sacrifices but with the "fruit of our lips." It is confession of sin and commitment to turn from paths of sin that Israel offers. Verse 3 gives this substance in a series of vows. They acknowledge that Assyria cannot save them and, thus, give up the frantic international maneuvering that sought advantage but brought disaster. They renounce the riding of horses and give up the military machinery that they falsely believed would give them security. They refuse to consider as a god any object made by human hands and they give up the practice of idolatry, which falsely offered the good life but instead led away from the true source of life in the Lord. The nations, military might, idols—none of these can save (see 13:4). Only God can save. Thus, the prayer ends with an appeal to the mercy of this God who can save. "In you the orphan finds mercy" (v. 3b). One cannot but remember the moving portrait of loving parent and child in chapter 11. But Israel rejected that loving parent God. They chose to become as orphans. But Israel's God has always shown special compassion to the helpless. Helpless Israel needs the mercy of such a God.

An Announcement of Salvation
(14:4–8)

In verses 4–8, the Lord speaks in response to this prayer of penitence. There is no hesitation in the divine response. It is almost as if God has longed for the occasion to speak of salvation rather than judgment. Verse 4 begins with a declaration of God's healing and love and an announcement that anger has passed. "I will heal their disloyalty; I will love them freely, for my anger has turned from them." Healing has been part of Hosea's vocabulary of God's salvation (5:13; 6:1; 7:1). Disloyalty has been Israel's illness. Now God's healing will make the relationship broken by disloyalty whole again. Love is poured forth freely like salve over a healing wound. Love can now displace anger as God's word for Israel's life. God's love was always available (see chap. 11), but Israel had turned away. God's love can be reclaimed by a returning Israel; it has never ceased.

Hosea turns again to rich and imaginative images from nature as God describes new life springing from restored relationship to Israel. God will be like the dew to Israel (v. 5a). Here the image is not of passing quickly (as in 13:3a), but of the moisture in desert climates that is essential for the flourishing of life. In response to God as the dew that brings life, Israel "shall flourish as a garden" (v. 7a). Verses 5–7 abound in plant images to describe Israel's new life in restored relationship to God. This choice of images may be an intentional rebuff to the worship of Baal, which promised fertility but brought death. A crucial difference in these images is that the people flourish and not the land. The images for flourishing Israel tumble out one after another (vv. 5–7). Israel shall experience:

growth like the lily.
rootedness like the forests of Lebanon.
beauty like the olive tree.

fragrance like the hills of Lebanon.
fruitfulness like the vines that produce the wines of Lebanon.

In the midst of this flourishing garden, Israel, God's protection is envisioned as the shade under which Israel rests (v. 7a). The final image of this divine speech pictures God as an evergreen cypress (v. 8b), protecting Israel in the divine shade. The NRSV reads "your faithfulness comes from me," but as the NRSV footnote tells us, the Hebrew reads "your fruit comes from me." This seems more in keeping with the garden imagery of the speech, and it suggests that God's final word to returning Israel is that life and sustenance ("fruit") are to be found in God.

Before this final image of the evergreen cypress, God seems to give a climactic, exuberant cry. "O Ephraim, what have I to do with idols? It is I who answer and look after you" (v. 8a). It is God's joyous statement of what has been true all along, but only in return and new life can Israel come to know. God is the source of healing, love, and protection. "It is I," says the Lord.

It is the grace of God in healing love that speaks the final word from the prophet Hosea. And it is spoken to sinners. It is spoken to "stumbling" Israel, asking forgiveness with the prophet's tutored words. But it is enough. "Forgive us our trespasses . . . give us this day our daily bread," Jesus taught us to pray in our stumbling need for God's forgiveness and care. And it is enough.

In the end the book of Hosea is about God's refusal to overlook our sins:

our loyalties given to false gods
our attraction to the lure of cultural accommodation
our forgetfulness of our own religious traditions
our trust in human institutions and maneuverings that cannot save us

But it is further a book about God's love in spite of our sin. The book is addressed not to the whole but to the wounded, not to the righteous but to the sinner. Which means that the word of Hosea is one of hope and healing for all of us.

An Admonition and Word of Advice (14:9)

The truth of Hosea's message and our need for his words were recognized by those who collected and edited his book, and they gave us the final verse

(14:9). It is filled with the vocabulary of the wisdom tradition (for example, the book of Proverbs or Psalm 1). The wise and the perceptive, they tell us, will recognize the ways of the Lord in Hosea's preaching. The righteous will find here a path to life, but those who are transgressors (the word has the connotation of rebelliousness) and reject the truth of Hosea's teaching will return to the stumbling with which this chapter began (14:1).

Joel

Introduction

The book of Joel has not always been held in high esteem among the prophets. In fact, even church people who have done some significant Bible study would be hard-pressed to tell you anything about Joel's message. But even among those who have studied the prophets and dutifully read the three chapters of Joel, tucked unobtrusively between Hosea and Amos, there has been a lack of regard for this prophet. Many have felt that the crisis of an invasion by a swarm of locusts, which occasions Joel's prophecy, was not really as significant as the great historical and political events with which many of the prophets were occupied. The book of Joel contains no social critique and does not show the passion for social justice we have come to associate with the Hebrew prophets. Joel's final vision of God's future for Israel strikes many as unnecessarily exclusive, and the picture of God as the divine warrior vanquishing the nations is not a popular divine image.

These problematic issues are not to be minimized, and I hope the comments that follow this brief introduction will be helpful in understanding the context in which these issues can be understood. Let me simply say at this point that the book of Joel contains three brief chapters devoted almost entirely to the theme of God as our source of help in time of trouble. Initially, the prophet focuses on an immediate crisis (a plague of locusts), but when he celebrates the end of this crisis as God's salvation, his thoughts turn to the future salvation of God when all enemies and dangers are vanquished and an age of harmony and well-being is established. It is not a complex, multifaceted message, but it is one of perennial interest to those who seek help in time of trouble.

JOEL'S HISTORICAL CONTEXT

Some elements of the context within which the message of Joel is to be understood are obvious. The trouble that initially prompts the prophet to speak and urge the community to turn to God for aid is a massive invasion by swarms of locusts (1:4). Judah and Jerusalem are devastated by this horde that leaves the land desolate and without resources, food and water supplies destroyed, and livestock dying. This may have gone on for years (2:25). But when the crisis of the locusts does end, Joel includes the celebration of this deliverance as God's salvation for which they had prayed (2:18–27).

Dating these events to a time in Israel's story is more difficult. It is clear that Joel speaks only to Judah and Jerusalem, although the title Israel is used when referring to God's people. This would imply a date sometime after the destruction of the Northern Kingdom in 722 B.C. when the term *Israel* no longer refers to a political kingdom. The list of atrocities committed against Judah and Jerusalem in 3:2–8, 19 seems to reflect the experience of the destruction of Jerusalem in 587 B.C. and the Babylonian exile that followed. At this time many of the surrounding nations exploited the vulnerability of Judah and plundered its land and resources. But Joel also refers to the temple in Jerusalem several times (1:14, 16; 3:18) yet there is no mention of a king. Appeals by Joel to the leadership seem to be addressed to priests (1:13–16). This would suggest a time after the exile and after the temple had been rebuilt (515 B.C.). It is not possible to single out a more precise date. It is probably best to think of Joel's prophecy somewhere between the late sixth and the early fourth centuries B.C. Some think that chapter 3 was written later than chapters 1 and 2. Even if this is the case, the two stages of the writing of Joel should be dated in this postexilic second-temple period.

THE BOOK OF JOEL

The book of Joel falls naturally into two parts. The first part is in 1:1–2:17 and focuses on the invasion of locusts that the prophet Joel sees as a sign of God's judgment. He fears they indicate the onset of the day of the Lord, and he warns of the judgment of God that may be directed at Israel on that day. He counsels lamentation and repentance. Abruptly the focus shifts in 2:18–3:21 to God's salvation. The infestation of locusts is ended, and the prophet understands this as God's salvation in response to the people's prayers and lamentations. In this section, the day of the Lord is a day of deliverance for Israel, and a vision of that future day is announced by the prophet.

This twofold division of the book is misleading. While it is true that a shift is made from judgment to salvation, there are other dynamics in the structure of the book. Verses 2:18–27 are the natural conclusion of the locust crisis. God responds in deliverance, and the prophet summons the people to celebration and joy in God's salvation. These verses are the natural conclusion of the story that occasioned Joel's preaching. Something quite different begins in 2:28–32 and continues in 3:1–21. The prophet Joel now shares a vision of God's future day of salvation when an egalitarian community will be formed by the pouring out of God's spirit (2:28–29), enemies of Judah will be vanquished (3:1–13), and the people of God will dwell in well-being with the Lord in their midst (3:16–21). Some have thought this material was added to the book at a time later than the locust crisis, and this is a possibility. But it may also be that the experience of God's salvation in a present crisis (the locusts) prompted him to envision God's final day of salvation. In any case, seen as present experience and future vision the two sections of the book of Joel are 1:1–2:27 and 2:28–3:21.

THE MESSAGE OF JOEL

The preaching of Joel is occasioned entirely by a single crisis. The land of Judah has been invaded by swarms of locusts. Massive clouds of these grasshopper-like insects migrate across the landscape, eating all vegetation in their path, fouling the water sources, and leaving humans and animals without food. When the environmental conditions are right for hatching and creating such a swarm of locusts, the result is one of the most feared catastrophes in many parts of the world. These plagues of insects have continued down to modern times and are difficult to control even with modern technological methods. Such a locust invasion in postexilic Judah was a matter of life or death. The community in Jerusalem in that period struggled on the brink of survival. The locusts must have seemed like the final crisis.

The prophet Joel raises his voice in the midst of this crisis. He interprets the crisis in keeping with Israel's faith tradition and prophetic themes with which he is in continuity. But beyond interpretation, he offers a plan of response that is based on trust that God is our help in time of trouble. We can look at his message more closely as it finds expression around major themes.

The Day of the Lord

As early as Amos in the eighth century the prophets refer to a coming day of the Lord when God will decisively intervene in human history. On that day, God's enemies will be vanquished (usually in battle) and a new age of peace and well-being will begin. In Amos 5:18–20, the prophet rebukes the people of Israel for their enthusiasm for the day of the Lord. He claims that for them it will be a day of judgment and disaster because of their sinful behavior, especially their failure to embody justice and righteousness. His message of this day as one of judgment implies, however, that most in Israel thought of that day as a day of their own salvation. Thus, from its first appearance the concept of the day of the Lord is seen by some in Israel as involving Israel's judgment and by others as bringing Israel's salvation. Some prophets follow Amos in seeing the day of the Lord as judgment (Ezek. 7:1–20; Zephaniah 1). In the period following exile, however, several prophetic voices revive the notion of the day of the Lord as a day of Israel's salvation (Isa. 63:1–4; Obadiah; Zech. 14:1–9), perhaps because in exile they believed they had already experienced God's judgment.

The book of Joel refers to the day of the Lord five times: Three of these speak of it as a feared day of judgment (1:15; 2:1, 11), and two speak of it as a time of salvation for Judah and Jerusalem (2:31; 3:14). Some have said this is evidence for two different voices in the book of Joel, but it may simply reflect changed circumstances for the prophet's speaking. He had both perspectives on the day of the Lord in earlier prophetic tradition to influence him. Perhaps he was influenced by both.

As a Day of Judgment

In the life-threatening crisis of the locusts, Joel sees the threat of God's judgment. He compares the locust invasion to the invasion of a divine army accompanied by cosmic signs such as darkened skies and trembling earth (2:1–11), both elements associated with the day of the Lord. In the tradition of Amos and Zephaniah, Joel fears that Judah is being judged as among God's enemies and is experiencing the divine wrath of that final day of judgment (1:15).

It is striking that Joel sees the fate of the people and the fate of the land so intertwined. As we will see in the commentary, Joel often uses the same vocabulary to describe the anguished suffering of the people and of nature in the crisis of the locusts (e.g., as the vine withers so does the joy of the people wither, 1:12). Wholeness and well-being depend on harmonious relationship between people and environment, a theme that sounds quite modern in our day of ecological concern. For Joel the failure of that harmony and wholeness has theological meaning. Judah may well be out of harmony with God. Harmony between the people and creation is not possible for Joel apart from harmonious relationship with God.

Thus, for Joel there is only one avenue of response. They are to lament ("wail," 1:5, 11, 13) the crisis that has befallen them, but more important, they are to turn to God as the only possible help in this time of need. All the people (2:16) are to assemble at the temple and "cry out to the LORD" (1:14). They are to declare a fast (1:14; 2:15) and make petition ("Spare your people, O LORD . . . , " 2:17). Above all else they are to "return" to the Lord (2:12–13), a word that means repentance in the Hebrew prophets. Such repentance, Joel warns, must be more than external words and show. It must be a turning of the heart rooted in trust that God is "gracious and merciful" (2:12–13). Unlike earlier prophets, Joel never details the specifics of the sins from which he believes the people must turn. It is to a general repentance and renewal of relationship to God that he calls the people.

As a Day of Salvation

In 2:17–27, the threat of judgment is transformed by God's deliverance into the joy of salvation. The crisis of the locusts is over, and the Lord is restoring people and land. Joel's fear that the day of the Lord would be the day of Judah's judgment has proven groundless. It is God's mercy and the people's repentance that have prevailed.

This experience of salvation in a present crisis leads to the prophet's vision of God's future salvation, when the day of the Lord does come (2:31; 3:14). The prophet dares hope that this will not be a day of judgment for Judah. With relationship restored between God and God's people that future day will be a day of salvation in all its fullness. Such a day of salvation includes, in Joel's vision, a pouring out of God's spirit on all people in a way that overcomes differences of gender and age and social status; men and women, young and old, slave and free alike shall be linked to God by the mutual empowerment of God's spirit (2:25–29). This is the text and the vision that formed the basis of Peter's sermon following the Pentecost experience.

Further, this coming day of salvation will include cosmic signs (2:30–31; 3:15). The neighboring nations who have oppressed and exploited Judah and Jerusalem will be judged by the Lord for their crimes (3:2–8, 12), and God as divine warrior will vanquish them in battle for their wickedness (3:9–13). God will then establish a new day in which the earth will flourish (3:18), and the people of Judah and Jerusalem will dwell in peace and well-being while God dwells in their midst on Mount Zion (3:17, 20–21).

The Presence of God

A central theme for Joel, whether in the time of the locust invasion or in the visions of God's future salvation, is confidence that God is present in the midst of the people. God is not absent or removed. Even when the locust swarms cause Joel to fear God's judgment, the prophet's response is to appeal to God for help. Even in his call for the people's repentance, he assumes that God is present and responsive. This trust grows out of his confidence that God is one and sovereign over all the earth. The whole meaning of the locust plague and God's deliverance from its terrors is summed up by the prophet in 2:27: "You shall know that I am in the midst of Israel, and that I, the LORD, am your God and there is no other." Even when the prophet envisions the final day of judgment on oppressive nations and the tumult of final battle with wickedness (3:13) is great, there comes the word of comfort to those who choose life as God's people. "But the LORD is a refuge for his people, a stronghold for the people of Israel" (3:16b).

It is here that we might find an important and enduring word for the modern church from this brief and often neglected book. God is in our midst and is the only real source of help in the troubles that most deeply afflict our world. In our well-meaning efforts to find solutions to the serious problems of our communities and our world, we sometimes forget that there is a spiritual dimension to our struggles and fail to seek spiritual resources alongside our practical programs. The repentance of the heart, of which Joel speaks, could do much in helping to alleviate some of our most serious societal conflicts.

If we have problems with aspects of Joel's message, we should take seriously the desperation of the community for which that message was meant. His words were addressed to a people who had already suffered much and were now put in danger of perishing.

Is a swarm of locusts a trivial matter for prophetic attention? A failure of crops and a shortage of food (such as the locusts caused in Judah) represents little more than an inconvenience or higher prices for most citizens of the United States, but for the poorest families of our nation it means malnutrition and hopelessness. In the poorest countries of our world, it means death for thousands, as we have seen in places like Ethiopia or Somalia.

Is the hostility of Joel to neighboring nations and the invoking of God as divine warrior against them an unacceptable theme for us? It will always be a difficult theme. But it is one that looks different for people who have suffered grievously at the hands of those who should have been neighbors and not enemies. For many such peoples throughout history, God's judging power has been their only hope in the face of impotence and hopelessness. These texts would be received differently by those who have been subjected to "ethnic cleansing" in Bosnia, by those who struggled through years of apartheid in South Africa, by those whose families have been slaughtered by the "death squads" of El Salvador, or by those whose children have been cut down as bystanders in the drug wars of our cities.

Joel's confidence is that in times of trouble when human solutions seem impossible, there is help from the Lord. Even if our circumstances and troubles are very different from his, we can take courage and hope from his confidence. "The LORD is a refuge for his people" (3:16b).

Commentary

Before we begin to discuss individual portions of the book of Joel there are some larger structures within the organization of the book I should point out. The first section is 1:1–2:17 and is dominated by the prophet's description of a plague of locusts. He sees the judgment of God in the locusts and the crisis they bring, and he associates this judgment with the day of the Lord as a day of judgment calling for the people's lamentation and repentance. The section in 2:18–3:21 shifts its focus to the salvation of God, first from the plague of locusts but also in the future coming of the day of the Lord as a day when the enemies of God and of Judah will be destroyed and a time of blessing will begin for Judah and Jerusalem. This movement from judgment to salvation is known in the arrangement of earlier prophetic books as well, especially Hosea.

The first section, focusing on the plague of locusts and God's judgment, also shows a definite structure in the arrangement of its parts. Verses 1:1–4 are an opening announcement of a dramatic crisis in Judah that has come in the form of a plague of locusts. The sections of the following material in 1:5–2:17 are arranged in a symmetrical pattern that can be depicted as follows:

> 1:5–14 Call to the people for lamentation, fasting, and prayer
>> 1:15–20 Announcement that the coming day of the Lord can be seen in the plague of locusts; prophet appeals to God
>> 2:1–11 Announcement that the locusts are like an invading army on the coming day of the Lord
> 2:12–17 Call to the people for repentance, fasting, and prayer

Calls for the people's response to the plague of locusts are used to bracket two oracles that speak of the relationship the prophet sees between the crisis of the locusts and the coming of the day of the Lord. We will discuss all these concepts further as we take up the individual segments of this symmetrically structured section.

TELL YOUR CHILDREN OF IT
Joel 1:1–4

1:1 The word of the LORD that came to Joel son of Pethuel:
²Hear this, O elders,
    give ear, all inhabitants of the land!
Has such a thing happened in your days,
    or in the days of your ancestors?
³Tell your children of it,
    and let your children tell their children,
    and their children another generation.

⁴What the cutting locust left,
    the swarming locust has eaten.
What the swarming locust left,
    the hopping locust has eaten,
and what the hopping locust left,
    the destroying locust has eaten.

The opening verse gives us a bare minimum of information about the prophet Joel. Only his name and that of his father are given, along with the statement of prophetic vocation—the word of the Lord came to him. Unlike many of the prophetic books, no kings or other historical indicators are mentioned, making it difficult to date Joel's prophecy with any certainty (see the discussion in the Introduction). The name Joel itself means "Yahweh is God," and it is unusually common in ancient Israel, appearing as the name for fourteen other individuals mentioned in the Old Testament. It is clear that Joel is to be considered a prophet because of the common phrase indicating prophetic vocation, "The word of the LORD that came to Joel . . . " (1:1).

The words of Joel as God's prophet begin with a summons to hear, directed first to the elders and then to all the "inhabitants of the land." Something unprecedented has happened, something beyond the experience of the people's lifetime or of their ancestors (v. 2). This is so important that Joel instructs them to tell of it to subsequent generations. In fact, he mentions four generations specifically, although he surely intends the progression to indicate a telling of this event for all ongoing generations of the community (v. 3).

By this time, the reader is anxiously waiting to learn what could have happened to justify such a breathless summons. What could be of such magnitude? Finally, in verse 4, we hear what the crisis is. A plague of locusts has descended on the land. We are introduced to this scourge in verse 4 with a piling up of terms that itself evokes the piling up of these insect bodies as they swarm across the land eating everything in sight. Cutting locust, swarming locust, hopping locust, destroying locust—what one has left the other eats until there is nothing they could possibly eat left at all in their wake. The terms may describe stages in the life cycle of the locust although the order here is different from that in 2:25. The terms, nevertheless, suggest the chaos of devouring activity they bring.

The desert locust is an insect related to the grasshopper family that, when environmental conditions are conducive, can mass in huge migratory swarms that destroy everything in their wake. This was one of the most feared catastrophes in the ancient world. For Israel, the onslaught of such a swarm must have seemed like the visitation on Israel of the plague sent against the Egyptians in the exodus confrontation with the pharaoh in Exodus 10:2, 14. The book of Joel has sometimes been criticized for focusing on insignificant matters when compared with other prophets. They spoke of God's judgment in terms of political and military upheavals and conquests and spoke of the suffering that resulted from social injustice. Here is Joel preoccupied with an infestation of insects. Such comments do not appreciate the magnitude of the catastrophe that a plague of locusts can represent. Starvation, poverty, and disease come in the wake of these swarms. As the life cycle of the locust repeats itself, the plague can continue for repeated assaults over a period of time. Verse 2:25 uses the term *years*, which suggests that the crisis referred to by Joel is of some duration.

The danger of such migratory plagues of desert locusts continues to exist today in North Africa and the Middle East. When conditions of moisture and temperature favor a large hatch of these grasshopper-related insects, the crowding conditions of the hatched nymphs lead to gregarious behavior and actual bodily changes in the insect, and they begin to migrate on the winds as a swarm in search of food. International agencies and multinational efforts try to destroy such swarms as they hatch and before they swarm because efforts to control a fully developed swarm are ineffective even today. In 1988, a civil war in Chad prevented efforts to keep a swarm from forming and a large portion of North Africa was devastated. A swarm in Somalia in 1957 was estimated at 1.6×10^{10} insects and weighed 50,000 tons. Since each insect eats up to three times its weight in green food each day, the potential devastation of such a swarm is obvious.

When a swarm dies at the end of its life cycle, the desiccation of the millions of dead insect bodies becomes a breeding ground for diseases such as typhus so that a plague of locusts is often followed by a pestilence of disease. In light of such information, one begins to appreciate the urgency in Joel's words and the unprecedented and catastrophic crisis that led him to speak.

CRY OUT TO THE LORD
Joel 1:5–14

1:5 Wake up, you drunkards, and weep;
    and wail, all you wine-drinkers,
  over the sweet wine,
    for it is cut off from your mouth.
  ⁶For a nation has invaded my land,
    powerful and innumerable;
  its teeth are lions' teeth,
    and it has the fangs of a lioness.
  ⁷It has laid waste my vines,
    and splintered my fig trees;
  it has stripped off their bark and thrown it down;
    their branches have turned white.

  ⁸Lament like a virgin dressed in sackcloth
    for the husband of her youth.
  ⁹The grain offering and the drink offering are cut off
    from the house of the LORD.
  The priests mourn,
    the ministers of the LORD.
  ¹⁰The fields are devastated,
    the ground mourns;
  for the grain is destroyed,
    the wine dries up,
    the oil fails.

  ¹¹Be dismayed, you farmers,
    wail, you vinedressers,
  over the wheat and the barley;
    for the crops of the field are ruined.
  ¹²The vine withers,
    the fig tree droops.

Pomegranate, palm, and apple—
  all the trees of the field are dried up;
surely, joy withers away
  among the people.

13 Put on sackcloth and lament, you priests;
  wail, you ministers of the altar.
Come, pass the night in sackcloth,
  you ministers of my God!
Grain offering and drink offering
  are withheld from the house of your God.

14 Sanctify a fast,
  call a solemn assembly.
Gather the elders
  and all the inhabitants of the land
to the house of the LORD your God,
  and cry out to the LORD.

This section contains a series of calls to lamentation directed to different groups in the community: drinkers of wine (1:5), farmers (1:11), and priests (1:13). Each of these groups has a special interest in the crops that have been devastated by the invasion of the locusts. The first group is sometimes seen as "drunkards" (thus in NRSV), but the terms used here have also been seen merely to indicate consumers of wine, a staple of the ancient diet. These groups are summoned to the activities associated with lamentation in ancient Israel. The drinkers are to "wake up" and "weep," the farmers to "be dismayed," the priests to "put on sackcloth" and "lament." In the second phrase addressed to each group, Joel calls on them to "wail," a verb associated with the formal voicing of lamentation and grief.

As he summons the community to lamentation, Joel also continues to build a fuller picture of the terror and devastation brought by the locusts. He compares their arrival to the invasion of a powerful and numberless nation in verse 6a, an image that plays an important role later in Joel when he begins to reflect on the locusts as an image of the day of the Lord (see esp. 2:1–11). He further compares the locusts to the teeth of a lion or lioness in their power to destroy (v. 6b). Then he lets go of such images in order to give explicit descriptions of the damage the insects inflict (vv. 7–13). They destroy the vines and the fig trees, even eating the bark off the branches so that only the white inner core is left (vv. 7, 12a). The fields of wheat and barley are ruined; the ground itself seems to mourn (vv. 10, 11b). The groves of olive, pomegranate, palm, and apple are left bare (v. 12b). There will be neither grain nor wine to bring as offerings to the temple (vv. 9, 13b). With the loss of food, economic well-being, and even the means to make sacrifices at the temple, the spirit of the people itself is destroyed; "joy withers away among the people" (v. 12b).

It is difficult for us to imagine the terror and devastation that a plague of locusts brings. Due to use of pesticides that prevent such insect attacks, we no longer experience this particular assault by nature, but such assaults were known by settlers in earlier times in this country. As a schoolboy growing up on the plains of Kansas, I have a vivid memory of reading O. E. Rölvaag's *Giants in the Earth*, the story of Norwegian immigrants struggling to make new homes on the Dakota plains. Rölvaag's description of a plague of locusts (grasshoppers) captures the terror of such an event. I can remember standing on the edge of a wheat field near my house after we had read this section of the book in school and shuddering as I envisioned the clouds of insects approaching.

> Tonseten turned in his seat, to face a sight such as he had never seen or heard before. From out of the west layers of clouds came rolling—thin layers that rose and sank on the breeze; they had none of the look or manner of ordinary clouds; they came in waves, like the surges of the sea, and cast a glittering sheen before them as they came; they seemed to be made of some solid murky substance that threw out small sparks along its face.
>
> The three men stood spellbound, watching the oncoming terror; their voices died in their throats; their minds were blank. . . . The ominous waves of cloud seemed to advance with terrific speed, breaking now and then like a huge surf, and with the deep, dull roaring sound as of a heavy undertow rolling into caverns in a mountainside. . . .
>
> The next moment the first wave of the weird cloud engulfed them, spewing over them its hideous, unearthly contents. The horses became uncontrollable. . . . And now from out the sky gushed down with cruel force a living, pulsating stream, striking the backs of the helpless folk like pebbles thrown by an unseen hand; but that which fell out of the heavens was not pebbles, nor raindrops, nor hail, for then it would have lain inanimate where it fell; this substance had no sooner fallen than it popped up again, crackling, and snapping—rose up and disappeared in the twinkling of an eye; it flared and flittered around them like light gone mad; it chirped and buzzed through the air, it snapped and hopped along the ground; the whole place was a weltering turmoil of raging little demons; if one looked for a moment into the wind, one saw nothing but glittering, lightninglike flashes—flashes that came and went, in the heart of a cloud made up of

innumerable dark-brown clicking bodies! All the while the roaring sound continued. . . .

They whizzed by in the air; they literally covered the ground; they lit on the heads of grain, on the stubble, on everything in sight—popping and glittering, millions on millions of them. . . . The people watched it stricken with fear and awe. . . . [Tonseten] spoke slowly and solemnly: "This must be one of the plagues mentioned in the Bible!"

. . . They would swoop down, dashing and spreading out like an angry flood, slicing and shearing, cutting with greedy teeth, laying waste every foot of the field they lighted in. (331–33, 341)

Such an attacking insect horde must be terrifying indeed, and as devastating in its effects as any invading army, an analogy Joel develops in 2:1–11. From Joel's summons to lamentation and his description of the crisis emerges a profound portrait of the interrelatedness of people and crops and animals and land. The wholeness of this interrelated chain is crucial to human survival and well-being. As the priests mourn, the ground mourns (vv. 9–10); as the crops wither, so does the joy of the people wither (v. 12). In using the same verbs for people and environment, Joel stresses the closeness of relationship.

There is nothing in human power to do in the face of such crisis, so finally Joel summons the people to the only action that makes sense in the face of such unspeakable threat. He calls them to "sanctify a fast," to gather in "solemn assembly" at the temple, and to "cry out to the LORD" (v. 14). This call to action, repeated in similar words also in 2:15–17, recognizes God as the only source of hope in such a crisis. Fasting and prayer are both acts of devotion that recognize in humility the power of God that holds possibilities for the future beyond those that seem within human power. Joel will have more to say on the proper way to approach God (2:12–14). For now, this is his first admonition to turn to the Lord. It is worth noting that this is to take place at the temple in Jerusalem and with the priests as those who lead the people in gathering, praying, and fasting. Joel does not reflect the sharp conflict between priest and prophet seen in other prophetic books.

THE DAY OF THE LORD IS NEAR
Joel 1:15–20

1:15 **Alas for the day!**
> **For the day of the LORD is near,**
>> **and as destruction from the Almighty it comes.**

¹⁶ Is not the food cut off
    before our eyes,
joy and gladness
    from the house of our God?

¹⁷ The seed shrivels under the clods,
    the storehouses are desolate;
the granaries are ruined
    because the grain has failed.
¹⁸ How the animals groan!
    The herds of cattle wander about
because there is no pasture for them;
    even the flocks of sheep are dazed.

¹⁹ To you, O LORD, I cry.
    For fire has devoured
        the pastures of the wilderness,
and flames have burned
    all the trees of the field.
²⁰ Even the wild animals cry to you
    because the watercourses are dried up,
and fire has devoured
    the pastures of the wilderness.

In 1:15–20, Joel turns from his summons to community lamentation and expresses his own distress over the crisis, ending in a personal plea to God in verses 19–20. The prophet joins his own voice with the community in lamentation.

The prophet adds additional details to the portrait of devastation from the locust plague. The crisis is one of material and spiritual dimensions; the locusts rob them of food for sustenance and of joy for praise of God in the temple (v. 16). The storehouses stand empty (v. 17), and the animals are dazed and starving, robbed of pasture and assaulted in their senses (v. 18). Some have treated the imagery of fire in verses 19–20 as Joel's reference to yet a different crisis—some kind of fire in the fields. This does not seem supported by any other clues in the book. More likely, Joel is using fire as an image for the consuming, onrushing wave of locusts. They leave the pastures and trees barren, the animals bereft of food and water, as surely as if a fire had consumed it all.

But to this picture of devastation, the prophet Joel also adds a theological evaluation. In verse 15 he cries out that the day of the Lord is near and states that the destruction must come from the Almighty. In the locusts, Joel sees the hand of God.

The concept of the day of the Lord was used by earlier prophets. It referred to an expected time when God would intervene in history in a decisive way. Both Amos (5:18–20) and Zephaniah (1:4, 7, 14) saw this as a day of judgment for Israel when the Lord would judge Israel for its sin and breaking of covenant. But Amos, in particular, makes clear that this was a reversal of the normal expectation in Israel. Most looked to the day of the Lord as when God would decisively defeat the enemies of the divine purpose and Israel would experience the full joy of God's salvation and peace. This view of the day of the Lord as a day of salvation became used again after the exile by prophets who stressed God's ultimate defeat of Israel's enemies (presumed to also be God's enemies) and the full restoration of Jerusalem and Judah (Isa. 63:1–4; Obad. 15—21; Zech. 14:1–9).

In the midst of the crisis of the locust plague, Joel seems to believe that the day of the Lord is at hand in the form of judgment on Judah and Jerusalem. Such destruction must be from the Almighty (v. 15b). This understanding leads the prophet first simply to cry out to the Lord (v. 19a) in intercession and appeal for mercy as people and land lie devastated. Later this sense of the crisis as God's judgment leads Joel to call for repentance—return to the Lord—in an effort to turn aside God's wrath (2:12–17). When the day of the Lord is at hand, God's people must ensure that they are not among those who oppose God's purposes in the world or they too will be judged.

In the second half of the book of Joel, after God's deliverance from the locusts is celebrated, Joel will share his vision for the future. That future will include the coming day of the Lord as the day of salvation, once again to be hoped for and not feared. Thus, Joel uses the day of the Lord in both ways suggested above, as a feared day of Judah's own judgment and as a hoped-for, final experiencing of God's salvation. It is Judah's repentance and obedience that will turn aside the day of judgment and assure the experience of God's eventual day of salvation. Both are the day of the Lord for Joel.

In 1:15, Joel is fearful that God's judgment is on them in the form of the locusts. In 2:1–11, he continues to develop this theme of the day of the Lord as God's judgment in the devastation of the locust horde.

THE DAY OF THE LORD . . .
WHO CAN ENDURE IT?
Joel 2:1–11

2:1 **Blow the trumpet in Zion;**
    sound the alarm on my holy mountain!

Let all the inhabitants of the land tremble,
    for the day of the LORD is coming, it is near—
2 a day of darkness and gloom,
    a day of clouds and thick darkness!
Like blackness spread upon the mountains
    a great and powerful army comes;
their like has never been from of old,
    nor will be again after them
    in ages to come.

3 Fire devours in front of them,
    and behind them a flame burns.
Before them the land is like the garden of Eden,
    but after them a desolate wilderness,
    and nothing escapes them.

4 They have the appearance of horses,
    and like war-horses they charge.
5 As with the rumbling of chariots,
    they leap on the tops of the mountains,
like the crackling of a flame of fire
    devouring the stubble,
like a powerful army drawn up for battle.

6 Before them peoples are in anguish,
    all faces grow pale.
7 Like warriors they charge,
    like soldiers they scale the wall.
Each keeps to its own course,
    they do not swerve from their paths.
8 They do not jostle one another,
    each keeps to its own track;
they burst through the weapons
    and are not halted.
9 They leap upon the city,
    they run upon the walls;
they climb up into the houses,
    they enter through the windows like a thief.

10 The earth quakes before them,
    the heavens tremble.
The sun and the moon are darkened,
    and the stars withdraw their shining.
11 The LORD utters his voice
    at the head of his army;

> how vast is his host!
>   Numberless are those who obey his command.
> Truly the day of the LORD is great;
>   terrible indeed—who can endure it?

In a longer poem, the prophet here describes the infestation of locusts using a number of images, but most prominently the likening of the locusts to an invading army (2:3–9). This poetic description is bracketed by references to the day of the Lord as a day of darkness bringing God's judgment. As we have seen, Joel has already directly associated the crisis of the locusts with the approach of the day of the Lord in 1:15.

The invading locusts and the terror they bring have made Joel fear that the day of the Lord is upon them. Some have treated the locusts only as a forerunner or sign of the eventual coming of the day when God will judge the enemies of divine purpose and defeat them. It is true that when Judah experiences God's deliverance from the locusts (2:18–27), then Joel's preaching shifts to this expected future day of salvation. But in the midst of the locust invasion, Joel fears that the day of the Lord is on them as God's immediate judgment. The urgency of Joel's cry to the Lord (1:19a), his summons of the people first to lamentation (1:5–14) and then to repentance (2:12–17), coupled with his cries that the day of the Lord is *near* (1:15a; 2:1b), make clear that Joel is not thinking of the locusts as the sign of some distant final day of reckoning. The alarm is to be sounded on Zion now (2:1a), and the inhabitants are to tremble at the prospect of God's coming in judgment now (2:1b). The language is reminiscent of Amos's description of the coming day of the Lord (Amos 5:18–20). It is a day of darkness, gloom, clouds, and blackness (2:2) so great that sun, moon, and stars are blotted out (2:10). Perhaps it is this imagery that suggests a connection between the locusts and the day of the Lord, since an invasion of these insect hordes covers and darkens the sky with massive clouds of insect bodies.

The most prominent image Joel uses to describe the coming of the locusts is the comparison he makes of their coming to the invasion of "a great and powerful army" (2:2), although nothing like this crisis has ever been experienced or will be again, in the prophet's view (2:2b). This imagery of locusts as invading enemy dominates the description in verses 4–9. Some have wanted to reverse this comparison. They suggest that Joel perhaps speaks of a threat from human armies or the armies of the Lord that will come in a future time to defeat God's enemies (a theme that does appear in Joel, chapter 3). But the language of the comparison in 2:4–9 is clear. It is the locusts that are like an invading army. They have the "appearance of horses" and charge "like war-horses."

The images of Joel speak of an army, but it is an insect army. They are like war-horses, chariots, warriors, soldiers, and a powerful army drawn up for battle. These terms suggest overwhelming force, attack, ferocity, power, and invasion. But the verbs are not of human clashes with sword and shield, combat, siege, wounding, and death. The verbs are appropriate to the terrors of an insect army. They leap on the tops of mountains, devour the stubble, scale walls, keep to their own track not jostling one another, burst through, and cannot be halted (2:9).

Coupled with the invading army imagery, Joel twice uses the image of raging brush fire for the locusts (2:3, 5b; see also 1:19). In the literature on locust invasions, eyewitnesses often comment on the similarity of the sound from an onrushing cloud of locusts to a forest fire or brush fire. The sound is a roar with constant popping and cracking noises. Of course, a fire leaves nothing living in its wake. This was also the case with the locusts who leave paradise-like landscapes as only "desolate wilderness" (v. 3b).

Joel returns to the day of the Lord image in verse 11b. The crisis of the locust plague must be from God. The whole of creation quakes and trembles before them (v. 10a); the sun, moon, and stars are blotted out (v. 10b); the numbers are vast and overwhelming (v. 11a); the sound is like the thunder associated with God's voice (v. 11a). Surely God is at the head of this army (v. 11a). Such a day is "terrible indeed—who can endure it?" (v. 11b). In the face of such a threat, and faced with the possibility that it is the advent of God's judgment in the day of the Lord, Joel can only call for repentance in hope of God's mercy.

REND YOUR HEARTS AND
NOT YOUR GARMENTS
Joel 2:12–17

2:12 **Yet even now, says the LORD,**
  return to me with all your heart,
with fasting, with weeping, and with mourning;
  ¹³ rend your hearts and not your clothing.
Return to the LORD, your God,
  for he is gracious and merciful,
slow to anger, and abounding in steadfast love,
  and relents from punishing.

[14] Who knows whether he will not turn and relent,
    and leave a blessing behind him,
a grain offering and a drink offering
    for the LORD, your God?

[15] Blow the trumpet in Zion;
    sanctify a fast;
call a solemn assembly;
    [16] gather the people.
Sanctify the congregation;
    assemble the aged;
gather the children,
    even infants at the breast.
Let the bridegroom leave his room,
    and the bride her canopy.

[17] Between the vestibule and the altar
    let the priests, the ministers of the LORD, weep.
Let them say, "Spare your people, O LORD,
    do not make your heritage a mockery,
    a byword among the nations.
Why should it be said among the peoples,
    'Where is their God?'"

In the midst of devastating crisis and the prophet's fear that it represents the day of God's judgment, Joel now announces a prophetic word from the Lord. The formula for the announcing of God's word ("says the LORD," v. 12a) prefaces a call to "return to me with all your heart" (v. 12a), and "Return to the LORD, your God" (v. 13a). The people are summoned to repentance. The Hebrew word here is a verb that means "to turn or return." It signals a change of direction, and the direction of the new turning is to be toward God. Thus, repentance is always forward-looking in new directions of response, never guilt-stricken backward regret for sins already committed. The call to return is the summons to leave sin behind and turn toward God.

One of the great puzzles of Joel is that he never specifically names the reality of sin from which Judah is called in repentance. We really have no idea how the prophet understood the sin of his people, what was deserving of such judgment, what they were to turn from in returning to God. Some have suggested that Joel has been shaped by liturgical use, and this matter is intentionally left unspoken so that worshipers can see their own sins in this summons to return and repentance.

In any case, the prophet does offer some words about the nature of this returning. The traditional practices of lamentation and repentance are mentioned and affirmed: fasting, weeping, and mourning (v. 12b). But these are external practices. Joel goes beyond such externals to matters of the heart. "Rend your hearts and not your clothing" (v. 13a). Here Joel stands with others in the prophetic tradition (e.g., Isa. 1:11–17; Hos. 6:6; Amos 5:21–24) in proclaiming to the people that ritual observance will not be enough. There must be an inner reorientation to God. It was traditional to tear the clothing in rituals of lamentation and repentance. Joel, speaking figuratively, now asks for a tearing of the heart. True repentance does not simply change the outer appearance; it must change the inner person as well. Return to God must be "with all your heart" (v. 12a).

The great composer Felix Mendelssohn used this line from the prophet Joel in his oratorio *Elijah*. After years of drought a prophet sings, "Ye people, rend your hearts; rend your hearts and not your garments. For your transgressions the prophet Elijah has sealed up the heavens, through the word of God." Mendelssohn lets this introduce the famous aria that begins, "If with all your hearts, ye truly seek me, ye shall ever surely find me. Thus saith your God." What follows in the oratorio is the story of Elijah's victory over the priests of Baal on Mount Carmel and the ending of the drought. This sequence of reorienting the heart, trusting in God's mercy, and finding that trust was not in vain is a sequence very much in keeping with the message of Joel. He moves from his call to reorient the heart to a testimony about the trustworthy character of God.

Verse 13 follows the summons for return with a testimony on God's nature taken from an ancient formula of witness to the character of God. In its fullest and perhaps its earliest form it is found in the experience of encounter with God on Mount Sinai in Exodus 34:6–7. It is a listing of God's gracious attributes. Similar or partial lists are also found in Numbers 14:18; Nehemiah 9:17; Psalms 86:15; 103:8; 145:8; Jonah 4:2; and Nahum 1:3. This would appear to suggest that Joel is drawing on some well-known creed or recital of God's attributes as a way of urging the people to remember the character of the God to whom they must return. Their God is "gracious and merciful, slow to anger, and abounding in steadfast love, and relents from punishing." Surely, this is a God who will respond if Judah but returns by reorienting their hearts to God. These attributes are rooted in a covenant tradition of a God loyal to the covenant commitment even in the face of Israel's frequent sin. Joel sees hope in relying on the character of God and reminds his people of these trustworthy divine qualities.

Ultimately, however, the future lies in God's hands. Such a God will not be manipulated. It lies within the realm of God's freedom to grant mercy, and the people can only rest their hope with God; they cannot control the divine decision. "Who knows whether he will not turn and relent, and leave a blessing behind him" (v. 14a). The people can only leave offerings and trust in God's mercy (v. 14b). Jonah 4:2 is the listing of God's attributes most like the one used by Joel. In that story, it is the king of Nineveh who calls on his people to repent and says, "Who knows? God may relent" (3:9). And the Ninevites did receive God's mercy! Perhaps Joel knew that tradition and found hope there that none are beyond God's grace.

From a call to individual reorientation of the heart, the prophet suddenly calls for community response as well. Repeating language directing the actions of the priests in 1:14, Joel calls again for a solemn gathering of the people at the temple on Mount Zion (2:15). None are to be excluded or neglected; the aged, the children, even nursing infants are to be assembled (v. 16a). No excuse is acceptable; even the bridegroom and the bride must leave their ceremonies for the sake of this urgent moment of community need (v. 16b). Joel calls on the priests to stand between the people and God (vestibule or porch and altar) and to weep in appeal to God (v. 17a). The appeal they are to make asks for divine mercy and bases the appeal on God's own reputation among the nations. If Judah perishes, then Judah's God becomes a mockery as well: "Where is their God?" (v. 17b). The appeal is to have mercy, not for Judah's sake, but for God's sake. With this appeal to divine self-interest, Joel's impassioned response to the crisis of the locust invasion and the judgment of God he sees therein comes to an end. He has summoned the people to public lamentation and personal renewal of the heart. He has seen in the locusts the terror of the approach of God's judgment in the day of the Lord. He has made his own personal cry for mercy to God.

Before turning to the shift in Joel's preaching from judgment to salvation, we would do well to note the particular combination of response urged by the prophet on his people in 2:12–17. He calls for response of the heart and of communal solidarity. He bases response on individual trust in God's character and on corporate prayer and ritual. It would be well for the modern church to note this combination. Personal faith and corporate community are not an either/or choice. The religion of the heart and the gathered prayers of the community are both necessary for God's people. Too often in our churches, persons treat these necessary elements of our faith as opposing poles and feel compelled to choose between them. Joel is in agreement with earlier prophetic voices that the rituals, prayers, and praises of the gathered community become hypocritical when the heart is not oriented to God and all that covenant partnership with God implies. But Joel is clear that if the heart is oriented in return to God, then we will become part of a community of God's people and must join with that community in intercession for the well-being of all. The rituals, the prayers, and the praises of such a community are not superseded but enriched by the experience of the heart. In need of God's mercy, Joel knows that appeal must be made to the renewed heart and the gathered congregation.

THE LORD . . . HAD PITY
ON HIS PEOPLE
Joel 2:18–27

2:18 Then the LORD became jealous for his land,
        and had pity on his people.
  ¹⁹ In response to his people the LORD said:
  I am sending you
        grain, wine, and oil,
        and you will be satisfied;
  and I will no more make you
        a mockery among the nations.

  ²⁰ I will remove the northern army far from you,
        and drive it into a parched and desolate land,
    its front into the eastern sea,
        and its rear into the western sea;
    its stench and foul smell will rise up.
        Surely he has done great things!

  ²¹ Do not fear, O soil;
        be glad and rejoice,
        for the LORD has done great things!
  ²² Do not fear, you animals of the field,
        for the pastures of the wilderness are green;
    the tree bears its fruit,
        the fig tree and vine give their full yield.

  ²³ O children of Zion, be glad
        and rejoice in the LORD your God;
    for he has given the early rain for your vindication,
        he has poured down for you abundant rain,

the early and the later rain, as before.
²⁴ The threshing floors shall be full of grain,
   the vats shall overflow with wine and oil.

²⁵ I will repay you for the years
   that the swarming locust has eaten,
the hopper, the destroyer, and the cutter,
   my great army, which I sent against you.

²⁶ You shall eat in plenty and be satisfied,
   and praise the name of the LORD your God,
   who has dealt wondrously with you.
And my people shall never again be put to shame.
²⁷ You shall know that I am in the midst of Israel,
   and that I, the LORD, am your God and there is no other.
And my people shall never again
   be put to shame.

The message of Joel now shifts from the onset of crisis and God's judgment to crisis ended and God's salvation. In 2:18–27, Joel focuses on God's salvation from the immediate terrors and threats of the locust invasion. God has heard the cry of Joel and the people, removed the locust threat, and sent renewal in the wake of the crisis. With the immediate crisis over, Joel seems to turn his thoughts to God's salvation in the longer prospect. If the coming of the day of the Lord as judgment has been averted in the present crisis, Joel can dare hope for salvation in the eventual coming of the day of the Lord. In 2:28–32 and 3:1–21, Joel turns to visions of God's future, the judgment of the nations, and the final participation of Judah in the victory of God's salvation. We will return to these future visions at a later point.

In 2:18–27, the prayers, laments, and fasting of the people are answered by God's response. A brief narrative introduction in verse 18 makes clear that the Lord is the source of a dramatic reversal. God has become "jealous for his land" and has had "pity on his people." What follows is the direct speech of God announcing salvation (vv. 19–20; 25–27). It comes in two parts because it is interrupted by the voice of the people in verses 21–24.

Restoration and Renewal (2:18–20)

The theme of God's speech in verses 18–20 is the reversal of the locust threat. God announces restoration and renewal. The crisis is past. The disastrous effects of the locusts are now reversed. Where the grain had been destroyed, the wine dried up, and the oil failed (1:10; cf. also 1:11–12, 16), the Lord now promises to send grain, wine, and oil so that the people will be satisfied (2:19a). Where Judah has become "a mockery" and "a byword among the nations" (2:17b), God promises, "I will no more make you a mockery among the nations" (2:19b).

Perhaps most important of all, the army of locusts themselves God promises to drive into the desert and into the sea (2:20). There they will perish and the threat will be ended. It is reminiscent of the end of the eighth plague against Egypt at the time of the exodus when God drove the locusts into the Red Sea to end the threat (Exod. 10:19). Even in modern times, swarms of locust often meet their end when their path takes them into the desert or the sea where there is no food to maintain the swarm and they die. The death of these gigantic swarms of locusts creates a foul mess of dead and decaying insect bodies, and 2:20b notes the "stench and foul smell" associated with such dead and decaying swarms. Augustine writes of such an incident in his *City of God* (3.31):

> When Africa was a Roman province it was attacked by an immense number of locusts. Having eaten everything, leaves and fruits, a huge and formidable swarm of them were drowned in the sea. Thrown up dead upon the coast, the putrefaction of these insects so infected the air as to cause a pestilence.

With the prophet's use of the imagery of an army for this attack of locusts (v. 20; cf. also 2:2, 6–9), this death in the sea inevitably evokes images of God's salvation through destruction of the enemy in the sea at the time of the exodus deliverance from bondage in Egypt.

God Delivers the People (2:21–24)

At this point, God's speech of promise and salvation is interrupted by the voice of the people. It is almost as if the spontaneous joy and praise of the people breaks out in the midst of God's announced salvation. The effect is to make clear that God's promise is becoming actualized. Deliverance from the crisis of the locust plague is a reality. The people experience it and testify to it.

Their witness actually begins with the last phrase of verse 20, "Surely he has done great things!" Again the theme is the reversal of the crisis. The earlier imperative summons of the prophet to wail (1:5, 11, 13) are now answered by a series of imperatives summoning the people and the land to confidence and rejoicing. Several refrains are repeated, giving a dramatic forcefulness to this speech:

"Surely he/the LORD has done great things" (vv. 20b, 21b)
"Do not fear" (vv. 21a, 22a)
"Be glad and rejoice" (vv. 21a, 23a)

These calls to confidence and rejoicing are addressed to different parties. The first is to the land itself, the soil. Where once the fields were devastated and the soil mourned (1:10), it now can be called to rejoice in God's salvation (2:21). The second call is to the animals. They were once groaning in a desolate landscape (1:17–20), but now they can graze in a restored landscape of plenty and need not fear (2:22).

Finally, the people are addressed as the "children of Zion." They had been called to wail in the face of the locust threat (1:5, 11, 13), but they can now be glad and rejoice (2:23a). The focus of Judah's rejoicing is to be the "LORD your God," who has restored the parched and barren fields (1:10–12, 19–20) to abundance through the gift of early and abundant rain (2:23). Where there were no crops or food, grain will now cover the threshing floor and "the vats shall overflow with wine and oil" (2:24).

Salvation Comes to the People
(2:25–27)

God's speech resumes in verse 25. Many of the same elements from the first half of the divine speech are reiterated but with new details. Using some of the specific terminology for the "swarming locust" that was used in the announcement of the crisis in 1:4, "the hopper, the destroyer, and the cutter," note that God promises repayment for the "years" of this crisis. The plural here suggests that the crisis was of some duration with repeated infestations of the insect hordes. This is not an uncommon pattern in such locust threats even in recent times. Verse 25 makes explicit that the great army that came against Judah was the swarm of locusts.

Again God promises plenty and satisfaction and an end to shame in the eyes of the nations (2:26). But 2:27 concludes God's speech with an important witness to the divine character that can be discerned in this salvation event. Salvation has been given to the people. The locust plague is over. Presumably the day of the Lord as final judgment has been averted. The prophet's call to turn to the Lord has been effective. But the meaning of this event is to be found in its testimony to the character and commitment of God.

The climactic affirmations of verse 27 announce:

"You shall know that I am in the midst of Israel"
"I, the LORD, am your God"
"There is no other"

The salvation God has accomplished is for the sake of reaffirming the relationship between God and God's people and making clear the absolute sovereignty of God. In the joy of deliverance from crisis the people are not to focus on their own experience of salvation but on the one who gave this salvation. Joy is to be channeled into praise. "Praise the name of the LORD your God, who has dealt wondrously with you" (v. 26). The end of the locust crisis is not just a fortunate opportunity, but an occasion to witness and acknowledge the grace of God. It is an occasion to recognize that God "is in the midst of Israel" (v. 27a) even in such times of crisis. Hope lies with no other than the one who has committed to relationship with God's people.

There is an important witness here to the modern church. In our time, we too have known great crises but also the great joy of salvation and unexpected hope. The danger comes when we too often focus on human celebrating and renewed opportunity following crisis and do not focus on the God whose grace lies behind all such events. In recent years, our world has seen unexpected moments of salvation and hope: the fall of the Berlin wall and the restructuring of the Soviet Union, the end of South African apartheid, and peace agreements between Palestinians and Israelis. These have been great moments of hope that many thought they would not see in their lifetimes. But human struggle and opportunism have followed in the wake of these events. There have been not enough thanks or praise in recognition of what God has done and the grace we have experienced as God's gift. Freedom in the Balkans was used for ethnic cleansing; the end of communism in the Soviet Union saw the rise of nationalistic conflict; peace in the Middle East gave birth to the chauvinistic assassin of Prime Minister Rabin; and South Africa struggles with tribalism and factionalism. In our own experiences of God's grace and salvation as individuals and churches, we often become so busy resuming our post-crisis lives that we fail to give praise to the God who was in our midst, who is our God, and before whom there is no other. Let the witness of Joel in these verses remind us of the need for humility and praise when we experience the grace of God in our lives.

AFTERWARD I WILL
POUR OUT MY SPIRIT
Joel 2:28–32

2:28 **Then afterward**
    I will pour out my spirit on all flesh;
   your sons and your daughters shall prophesy,
      your old men shall dream dreams,
      and your young men shall see visions.
 ²⁹ **Even on the male and female slaves,**
      in those days, I will pour out my spirit.

³⁰ **I will show portents in the heavens and on the earth, blood and fire and columns of smoke.** ³¹ **The sun shall be turned to darkness, and the moon to blood, before the great and terrible day of the LORD comes.** ³² **Then everyone who calls on the name of the LORD shall be saved; for in Mount Zion and in Jerusalem there shall be those who escape, as the LORD has said, and among the survivors shall be those whom the LORD calls.**

Although 2:17 represented a shift in the book of Joel from judgment to salvation, the focus was still on the crisis brought by the swarms of locusts. The salvation in 2:17–27 was God's deliverance from this insect horde and the restoration of land and people. A further shift in Joel's prophecy takes place beginning with 2:28. The prophet's attention turns from the immediate salvation God has given to the future time when God's salvation will be complete. The remainder of the book (2:28–32; 3:1–21) has an eschatological focus, which means the focus is on the end times when God's purposes for history and for God's people will be brought to fruition and completion. When biblical texts focus on these end times, there are often phrases that signal this shift in perspective. In 2:28, the prophet begins with the words "Then afterward . . . , " and continues in verse 29 with "in those days." In 3:1, he says, "For then, in those days and at that time . . . ," and in 3:18 he uses the phrase "In that day. . . . " These words all signal that the prophet's experience of God's present salvation (from the locusts) has caused him now to reflect on God's future salvation (at the end of the age). There are three sections: 2:28–32 focuses on the fate of Israel in this future time; 3:1–17 speaks of the fate of the nations at that time; 3:18–21 mixes elements dealing with the fate of Israel and the nations in a final vision of God's future. Twice in this final section of Joel, the prophet uses the phrase "day of the Lord" (2:31; 3:14) to refer to this future time. We shall discuss further below the shift in the prophet's use of this phrase.

The Fate of Israel (2:28–32)

Signaled briefly by the words "Then afterward . . . ," the prophet moves in 2:28–32 from celebration of God's deliverance in the present (2:17–27) to a vision of God's future salvation as Israel will experience it. This coming time of salvation is called the day of the Lord by the prophet (v. 31). It is the same day of the Lord that the prophet had feared was on them as a day of judgment in the midst of the devastation of the locusts (1:15; 2:1, 11). But judgment has been averted by the people's prayers, laments, and sacrifices. The people of Jerusalem and Judah are not to be numbered among God's enemies. God has delivered them; judgment has become salvation. The crisis of locust invasion was not the onset of God's final judgment, but the day of the Lord will someday come. And the prophet Joel now dares hope for and envision that coming day as a day of salvation rather than of judgment for God's people.

Joel's vision for the coming day of salvation includes several elements. The first is a pouring out of God's spirit on all flesh (vv. 28–29). This portion of Joel's vision has had a rich history and influence in the Christian church and we will come back to it later in this section. A second element is the announcement of cosmic signs and portents that will accompany the "great and terrible day of the LORD" (vv. 30–31). Blood, fire, and smoke— elements often associated with the presence and power of God—will be in evidence. The sun will be darkened and the moon turned to blood. These signs all signal the cosmic proportions of the vision. The prophet envisions the climactic consummation of God's purposes for the cosmos. All cosmic reality will be affected. The third element is that in this time "everyone who calls on the name of the LORD shall be saved" (v. 32). This will explicitly include inhabitants of Mount Zion and Jerusalem. After all, Joel knows that in their recent crisis the people did call on the name of the Lord and they were saved. Should this not be true on the scale of God's final purposes for the cosmos? The prophet's vision becomes not only a hope but an admonition to those who have called on God's name in the present that they should not cease to do so. Their present salvation may then become but a foretaste of God's ultimate salvation. Those who call on the Lord's name become "those whom the LORD calls" (v. 32b). The early church picked up this image from Joel to emphasize the availability of salvation for all. In Romans 10:13, Paul quotes this phrase from Joel 2:32 to stress that everyone includes the Gentiles as well as the Jews. For him, calling on the name of the Lord signified acknowledgment of Jesus Christ. Confession of faith then cuts across other barriers.

God's Spirit Poured Out
on All Flesh (2:28–29)

It is Joel's vision of the pouring out of God's spirit that has made verses 28–29 the most well-known passage in the book of Joel. The section is framed by God's statement that in that future time "I will pour out my spirit" with the opening statement adding the words "on all flesh." Israel's tradition has known the gift of God's spirit before. The Hebrew word for spirit can also mean "wind" and the spirit of God is associated with the gift of power. Sometimes this power enabled mighty deeds. Many of the early judges and kings of Israel were said to receive God's spirit and to be enabled thereby to perform deeds of deliverance and leadership in times of crisis. Gideon, Samson, Saul, and David are among those who receive the spirit's power. The power of God's spirit also can enable prophecy. Micah declares, "But as for me, I am filled with power, with the spirit of the LORD, and with justice and might, to declare to Jacob his transgression and to Israel his sin" (Mic. 3:8). The spirit of God even has the power to bring new life as in Ezekiel's vision of the valley of dry bones, which yet can live through God's spirit.

What is remarkable about Joel's vision is not his mention of God's spirit but that this gift should be poured out "on all flesh." Verses 28b–29a testify to the inclusivity of this gift of spirit in Joel's vision. Six categories of people are included as recipients: sons and daughters, old and young, male and female slaves. God's gift of the spirit in this time of salvation is without regard to gender or age or social status. It is for all. And it enables all to prophesy, to dream dreams, to see visions. These are all modes of direct communication and revelation from God. What was true in the past for the remarkable leaders and prophets of the biblical story will now be true for all. Direct relationship to God will become the norm not the exceptional experience. All will know the empowerment of God's spirit.

For Christians, this text from Joel has special significance because Joel 2:28–32a became the text for the first Christian sermon by Peter at Pentecost. The book of Acts recounts Jesus promising his disciples in Acts 1:8, "But you will receive power when the Holy Spirit has come upon you." In Acts 2, the Spirit comes upon the assembled crowd with tongues of flame and a rush of wind, and they are enabled to speak with understanding in the various languages of the world. Peter then preaches (Acts 2:14–21) that what they have witnessed is the fulfillment of this prophetic vision in the book of Joel, and he quotes the entire text of these verses. The pouring out of God's spirit signaled the start of a new age for Peter and the early church, and the gift of the spirit broke down many of the barriers that separated and divided people from one another. The inclusive vision of God's gift of the spirit in Joel 2:28–29 inevitably reminds us of the inclusive community envisioned by the apostle Paul in Galatians 3:28: "There is no longer Jew or Greek, there is no longer slave or free, there is no longer male and female; for all of you are one in Christ Jesus." The inclusivity of Joel's text has been cited often by modern Christians who seek more inclusive patterns of participation in church and society. The text has been turned to for support especially by those who have advocated the ordination of women in this century.

In recent Christian history, this text from Joel and its use by Peter at Pentecost has become foundational for the development of Pentecostalism as a variety of Christian experience and expression. Pentecostal congregations and denominations make the gift of God's spirit and various manifestations of that gift central in their experience of the Christian faith. The inclusivity of Joel's vision for the pouring out of God's spirit has had a significant effect on Pentecostal communities although this has not always found wider social expression.

Joel's vision of the pouring out of God's spirit should continue to challenge all modern readers of this prophet to reflect on the ways in which God's spirit continually acts to make new in our time as in the prophet's or Peter's time. This text tells us that the spirit of God constantly breaks down the barriers we erect. The spirit of God constantly unites us in spite of our divisions. Our encounter with this text should always be an exercise in humility and self-examination. We must strive anew to open ourselves to the winds of God's spirit and allow our human barriers to that pouring out of God's spirit to be swept away.

I WILL RESTORE THE FORTUNES
OF JUDAH AND JERUSALEM
Joel 3:1–21

3:1 **For then, in those days and at that time, when I restore the fortunes of Judah and Jerusalem, 2 I will gather all the nations and bring them down to the valley of Jehoshaphat, and I will enter into judgment with them there, on account of my people and my heritage Israel, because they have scattered them among the nations. They have divided my land, 3 and cast lots for my people, and traded boys for prostitutes, and sold girls for wine, and drunk it down.**

⁴ What are you to me, O Tyre and Sidon, and all the regions of Philistia? Are you paying me back for something? If you are paying me back, I will turn your deeds back upon your own heads swiftly and speedily. ⁵ For you have taken my silver and my gold, and have carried my rich treasures into your temples. ⁶ You have sold the people of Judah and Jerusalem to the Greeks, removing them far from their own border. ⁷ But now I will rouse them to leave the places to which you have sold them, and I will turn your deeds back upon your own heads. ⁸ I will sell your sons and your daughters into the hand of the people of Judah, and they will sell them to the Sabeans, to a nation far away; for the LORD has spoken.

⁹Proclaim this among the nations:
Prepare war,
   stir up the warriors.
Let all the soldiers draw near,
   let them come up.
¹⁰ Beat your plowshares into swords
   and your pruning hooks into spears;
   let the weakling say, "I am a warrior."

¹¹ Come quickly,
   all you nations all around,
   gather yourselves there.
Bring down your warriors, O LORD.
¹² Let the nations rouse themselves,
   and come up to the valley of Jehoshaphat;
for there I will sit to judge
   all the neighboring nations.

¹³ Put in the sickle,
   for the harvest is ripe.
Go in, tread,
   for the wine press is full.
The vats overflow,
   for their wickedness is great.

¹⁴ Multitudes, multitudes,
   in the valley of decision!
For the day of the LORD is near
   in the valley of decision.
¹⁵ The sun and the moon are darkened,
   and the stars withdraw their shining.
¹⁶ The LORD roars from Zion,
   and utters his voice from Jerusalem,
   and the heavens and the earth shake.

But the LORD is a refuge for his people,
> a stronghold for the people of Israel.

¹⁷ So you shall know that I, the LORD your God,
> dwell in Zion, my holy mountain.
And Jerusalem shall be holy,
> and strangers shall never again pass through it.

¹⁸ In that day
the mountains shall drip sweet wine,
> the hills shall flow with milk,
and all the stream beds of Judah
> shall flow with water;
a fountain shall come forth from the house of the LORD
> and water the Wadi Shittim.

¹⁹ Egypt shall become a desolation
> and Edom a desolate wilderness,
because of the violence done to the people of Judah,
> in whose land they have shed innocent blood.
²⁰ But Judah shall be inhabited forever,
> and Jerusalem to all generations.
²¹ I will avenge their blood, and I will not clear the guilty,
> for the LORD dwells in Zion.

This chapter continues Joel's vision of the future day of the Lord (see v. 14) that was begun in 2:28–32. The chapter begins with the phrase "in those days and at that time . . . " (3:1a) and introduces its final section with "In that day . . . " (3:18a), both phrases that indicate visions of the future when God's purposes are consummated.

The chapter may be divided into three parts. Verses 1–8 introduce the theme of God's judgment against the nations and restoration of Judah and Jerusalem, but the focus is on identifying the crimes for which the nations are judged. Verses 9–17 speak of the actual coming of the day of the Lord as a day of war in judgment against the nations and to bring salvation to Israel. Verses 18–21 portray God's final blessing on Judah and Jerusalem.

The underlying image that unifies this chapter is the image of God as the divine warrior. Here, the prophet Joel seems to be using a common pattern in the ancient Near East to portray God's salvation to Judah. That pattern tells of a deity challenged by enemies who meet them in battle with cosmic proportions. The enemy is defeated and the deity is enthroned victoriously in his mountain abode. Then blessing is bestowed on the natural world, which overflows with abundant fertility and produce.

Joel 3 may be read as a hymn in which Joel pictures the Lord as a divine warrior in a manner similar to this pattern. The nations have committed atrocities against God's people (vv. 2–8), so God is roused as a warrior to bring judgment in the defeat of these nations (vv. 9–13). The sun, the moon, and the stars are darkened (v. 15) and the cosmos shakes at God's roar (v. 16). God's people are vindicated as God dwells again on Mount Zion (vv. 16b–17), the abundance of the earth is restored (v. 18), the enemies are defeated (v. 19), and God's people will dwell securely with the Lord in their midst (vv. 20–21). With this overview we can now look more closely at the parts.

The Restoration of Judah and Jerusalem (3:1–8)

Verses 1–8 open with the announcement of the theme for this entire chapter. Joel envisions a future day when God will "restore the fortunes of Judah and Jerusalem" (v. 1b) and will judge the nations for their atrocities against God's people (v. 2). Although Judah's salvation is announced first as God's goal, judgment will have to precede the reaching of that goal. Thus, the text focuses on God's judgment and the detailing of the nations' crimes against Judah. This will take place in the "valley of Jehoshaphat," which is a symbolic rather than an actual place. Jehoshaphat means "the Lord judges." It is God, the judge, who acts first in this vision by confronting the nations with the violence they have done to God's people.

The indictment gets very specific. The nations have scattered Israel among the nations, divided its land, sold its people, and used its young boys and girls as prostitutes (vv. 2b–3). There is no doubt that God takes this as a personal affront, for God speaks in these verses of "*my* people," "*my* heritage," and "*my* land." These crimes against Israel would seem to fit best with the experience of Judah and Jerusalem during and after the Babylonian exile (587–539 B.C.), which leads most scholars to date the book of Joel to the postexilic period (see the Introduction). These were difficult times in which the neighboring nations around Israel often took advantage of Israel's weakened condition. In verse 12, God speaks of sitting in judgment on the "neighboring nations."

In verse 4, the indictment becomes even more specific. The names of Tyre, Sidon, and Philistia are mentioned. Later, verse 19 names Egypt and Edom. These are traditional rivals and enemies of Israel. We are not dealing with a single occasion in which these nations acted together against Judah and Jerusalem. God's judgment looks back over occasions when these nations by their acts against God's people have made themselves the enemies of the Lord and, thus, now face God's judgment. It is not the great empires (such as Assyria or Babylon) who are listed here, but neighboring kingdoms who exploited Judah in times of weakness and vulnerability. They have plundered Judah's wealth and taken her treasures for their own temples (v. 5). They have sold Judeans into slavery with the Greeks (v. 6). Verse 19 speaks of Egypt and Edom as doing violence and shedding innocent blood. In verse 7, God announces the return of those who have been sold and scattered and the consequences that now fall on the nations. They will now be sold into the hand of the Sabeans to suffer the same fate they imposed on others (v. 8). The certainty of this judgment is signaled by the concluding formula "the LORD has spoken."

The Day of the Lord as a Day of War (3:9–17)

With the crimes of the nations detailed and God's intention to bring them to judgment announced, God must now act to subdue, vanquish, and judge the nations who have become God's enemies. Verses 9–17 speak of divine warfare against the rebellious nations, their final judgment, and the vindication of God's people in the midst of this tumult. This part of Joel's vision speaks of the fulfillment of God's intention to judge the nations announced in verses 1–8.

The section opens with a summons to war (vv. 9–10). As we discover in verse 14, this is the day of the Lord, and it will involve a battle of cosmic proportions (compare vv. 15–16a). Although the nations are summoned to war, the summons is probably also intended to be the call to arms for the divine armies. It is a time of God's conflict with "wickedness" (v. 13). In such a time, the well-known vision of peace in Isaiah 2:4 and Micah 4:3 is reversed. Plowshares are beaten into swords, and pruning hooks into spears (v. 10). These roused armies will meet at the "valley of Jehoshaphat," and God will sit in judgment on "all the neighboring nations" (v. 12). Verse 13 is a verdict of this judgment, but it is cast in the metaphor of a harvest ripe for reaping or a vineyard with grapes ready to crush. This reaping and crushing is to be of the nations' wickedness. The valley of judgment becomes a valley of decisions rendered (v. 14). The day of the Lord has arrived (v. 14). It is a day of cosmic proportions. The sun, moon, and stars are blotted out (v. 15). The heavens and the earth quake at the roar of the Lord from Zion like a raging lion (v. 16a). This same verse on God's roar from Zion appears in Amos 1:2 where it serves as a prologue to the entire book of Amos, which is given almost entirely to the announcement of God's judgment. It would seem that Joel knew this prophetic tradition and uses the image of God as the lion of judgment to add drama to his vision.

In the midst of the terrible, cosmic tumult of God's war of judgment against the nations, there suddenly comes a word of comfort to God's people. It is a promise of salvation in the midst of judgment. "But the LORD is a refuge for his people, a stronghold for the people of Israel" (v. 16b). For those in relationship to God, there is a "refuge" and a "stronghold" when the day of God's judgment comes. These are both words known elsewhere in the Hebrew tradition, especially in the Psalms and the prophets. "God is our refuge and strength, a very present help in trouble" (Psalm 46:1). "For you have been a refuge ["stronghold" in Joel] to the poor, a refuge to the needy in their distress, a shelter ["refuge" in Joel] from the rainstorm and a shade from the heat" (Isa. 25:4). In general, the Hebrew word used in 3:16 for refuge means a shelter from storm or danger in the wild, while the Hebrew word for stronghold indicates a military fortress. Joel's use of the two together gives assurance that in the Lord there is protection from all conceivable dangers. For Joel, God's war against the nations is not simply an expression of a wrathful God. God's purpose is salvation for those who have already suffered unspeakable atrocities at the hands of oppressive powers (vv. 2–8). God's people can trust in the protection of God.

Further, verse 17 affirms that these events are to make known that God dwells on Mount Zion in the midst of Israel. Jerusalem is God's holy city, and God does not intend it to fall into the hands of strangers again. This reassurance reminds us of Joel's affirmation at the conclusion of the section celebrating deliverance from the invasion of the locust army (2:27). With similar words in 3:17 Joel affirms that God's salvation is not just on the occasion of the locust plague but is God's intention for God's people to the end of the age. Israel can trust that God's delivering presence in their midst is constant for those who continue to understand themselves as God's people. Even when the nations are judged for their crimes, God will protect and care for the people of God and will continue to dwell in their midst on Mount Zion.

God's Final Blessing on Judah and Jerusalem (3:9–17)

This chapter and the entire book of Joel ends with a vision of blessing for Judah and Jerusalem in God's new age (vv. 18–21). The phrase "In that day . . . " (v. 18a) indicates that we are still in the prophet's vision of the future. In the preceding section, God's enemies, and Israel's, are vanquished in the day of the Lord. Now a new age of plenty and well-being can begin.

First, the blessings of the natural order become abundant and bountiful. These blessings sound like the reversal of the threat brought to nature by the invasion of locusts that began the book of Joel. The sweet wine that was cut off (1:5) now drips from the mountains (3:18). The cattle who had wandered desolate with no pasture (1:18) now give milk in such abundance that it flows from the hills (3:18). The stream beds of Judah that had dried up (1:20) now flow with water. The house of the Lord where there was no joy or gladness (1:16) is now the source of a fountain that waters even the wilderness (3:18). This latter image is reminiscent of Ezekiel's vision of the fountain that flows from the temple to bring blessing and abundance to the New Jerusalem (Ezek. 47:1–12; compare also Zech. 13:1; 14:8).

Verse 19 serves to remind us that this time of abundance and blessing has been made possible by the vanquishing of those enemies who have done violence to Judah in the past. Here Egypt and Edom are named, but as with the naming of Tyre, Sidon, and Philistia in 3:4 the impression is that these nations are symbolic of all who have exploited and oppressed Israel in the past. This pair may be especially symbolic since Egypt is the most ancient oppressor in Israel's story (bondage in Egypt) and Edom was one of the chief exploiters of fallen Judah and Jerusalem at the time of the Babylonian exile. From the beginning of Israel's story to its most recent chapter, those who have oppressed Judah and shed innocent blood will be left desolate in God's new age of blessing (v. 19).

If nature is restored, so too will God's people be restored. Verse 20 promises that Judah and Jerusalem will be inhabited forever. God will be the avenger of bloodguilt, and the final word of Joel and of this blessing is that "the Lord dwells in Zion" (v. 21). Again this is reminiscent of Ezekiel's vision of the New Jerusalem. The final word of the book of Ezekiel is the name of the new city, "The LORD is There" (Ezek. 48:35). One could well imagine that the prophet Joel has been influenced in his final vision by the final vision of that great prophet of the exile, Ezekiel.

We cannot leave the book of Joel and its final vision without a word about the problematic elements of this vision for many in the modern church. We are troubled by images of God as warrior and battles as the instrument of God's vengeance against enemies. We are further troubled that in Joel's vision the beneficiaries of God's final battle against evil appear to be only Judah and Jerusalem. It is an exclusive picture with no hint of more expansive visions of a time of peace that might encompass all peoples, such as appear in other prophets.

What is reflected in the book of Joel and especially in this final chapter is a prophet speaking to people who see themselves as marginalized and at the mercy of hostile powers beyond their control. In the period during and just after the experience of Babylonian exile, the community of Jews in Jerusalem suffered one crisis of survival after another. Indeed, the plague of locusts that occasioned the prophecy of Joel must have seemed like the final straw. It is not accidental that the locusts are compared to human armies, for Judah and Jerusalem have experienced the ravages of hostile armies, and they live as the restored community of exiles in the midst of hostile neighbors, some of whom plundered Jerusalem before the time of their exile. When appeals to God for help are heard in the crisis of the locusts it is little wonder that Joel dreams of the final time when all the powerful and violent forces that have threatened Judah and Jerusalem are met by God. It is only in God that such a beleaguered people can have hope, and it is only natural to picture God as a warrior capable of meeting worldly oppressive power and defeating it.

The new age Joel envisions is egalitarian in terms of men and women, old and young, slave and free (2:28–32). It is in harmony with nature (3:18). But it is not universal in its inclusion of the nations, for in this time Judah knows its neighboring nations only as threats to security and well-being.

In the end, the word of Joel is nevertheless the word for us as well. Joel articulates a vision, but at its heart is trust in God. God is their refuge and stronghold, and God is ours as well. Joel's fears and those of Judah to whom he speaks may have been locusts and hostile nations. Our fears may be nuclear holocaust or ideological terrorism or cycles of urban violence. In the face of the terrors over which we feel little control, before which we cower in fear and helplessness, Joel reminds us that God dwells in our midst and will not abandon God's faithful people. There is a power capable of meeting the hostile powers of this world. There is a refuge and a stronghold in time of crisis. The Lord dwells not only in Zion but also in Washington, in Bosnia, Israel/Palestine, in Moscow, in South Africa, in El Salvador, and in Oklahoma City.

Amos

Introduction

In a recent week it seemed as if I encountered the message of Amos at every turn. The sample for new Sunday bulletin covers was a striking graphic design of a plumb line with the words "I have set a plumb line in the midst of my people" (see Amos 7:8). A Christian singing group on tape in a local bookstore was singing, "Give me justice, justice, like free flowing waters!" (see Amos 5:24). A preacher at morning worship for a national conference paraphrased the prophet and placed his words in our context: "Woe to those who are at ease in Nashville, and to those who feel secure in any of the cities of our land" (Amos 6:1). An advocate for the homeless, testifying before a congressional committee, declared passionately that our policies were "trampling the head of the poor into the dust of the earth" (Amos 2:7).

In an age when many in the church are reexamining the importance of social conscience as a measure of faithfulness and claiming concern for the poor and oppressed as a primary arena for expression of Christian social conscience, the preaching of Amos to Israel in the eighth century B.C. has taken on new relevance. It becomes important to consider his message carefully in the context of ancient Israel while at the same time reflecting on the enduring message of Amos to our own time and place. After only a brief introduction to the book of Amos, we will turn to comment and reflect on the preserved words of Amos's preaching.

AMOS AMONG THE PROPHETS

Historically, the book of Amos is the first of the prophetic books, although in the canonical order of the minor prophets it is third. Amos was the earliest to preach of those prophets whose words have been collected, preserved, and passed on to future generations in the prophetic books of the

Old Testament. His message marks a distinct turning point in the history of our biblical faith. Amos, as a representative of God's word, announces that the nation Israel has been judged for its failures to be obedient to God's will and must perish as a consequence. This is a shocking message, but the actual conquest and end of Israel (the Northern Kingdom) a few years later commanded attention to Amos's words. Amos had no predecessors in this message. There were prophets before him, and they did boldly declare God's judgment at times, but never against the whole of God's people and never with the claim that "the end has come upon my people Israel" (8:2). Earlier prophets had confronted individuals (Samuel to Saul; Nathan to David; Elijah to Ahab) or even groups (Elijah and the priests of Baal), but it is Amos who first suggests that the covenant with God has been broken; therefore, the curses are invoked by the people's sin. God as judge must exact the penalty.

If Amos has no predecessors in this message, he certainly has successors. Hosea, Isaiah, Micah, Zephaniah, Jeremiah, and Ezekiel all take up this theme of judgment on God's people and develop it appropriately for their own settings. To be sure, most of these succeeding prophets also develop a message of hope and renewal beyond judgment, but not as a softening of God's opposition to sin, even in the midst of God's people. Except for the final verses of chapter 9, these themes of promise beyond judgment play little or no role in Amos. It was Amos's role to announce the theme of divine judgment that allowed the tradition to make sense of the conquest of the Northern Kingdom of Israel in 721 B.C. and the Babylonian captivity of Judah in 587 B.C. as part of God's will and work in the world.

AMOS'S HISTORICAL CONTEXT

The opening verse of the book dates Amos's preaching during the reigns of Uzziah (783–742 B.C.) in Jerusalem, the capital of the Southern Kingdom, Judah, and Jeroboam II (786–746 B.C.) in Samaria, the capital of the Northern Kingdom, Israel. The same verse tells us that Amos was from Tekoa, a village to the south of Jerusalem in Judah. But Amos's preaching was all in and to the Northern Kingdom of Israel. The only place we know this preaching to have taken place is in Bethel where the royal sanctuary was located and Amos was confronted by Amaziah, the priest of Bethel (7:10–17). Other sanctuaries are mentioned (Gilgal, Beersheba) as is the capital, Samaria, but there is no evidence that Amos visited or preached at these places.

Jeroboam II was descended from Jehu who overthrew the dynasty of Omri (2 Kings 9—10). Jehu and his immediate successors had been forced to pay tribute to Assyria and lost territory to the Aramaeans (2 Kings 10:32–33). Jeroboam II was the dynasty's most successful king. He restored territory to Israel and took the throne in a time when Assyria was weak and its threat seemed remote (2 Kings 14:23–29). Shortly after the death of Jeroboam II, Tiglath-pileser III took the Assyrian throne (745 B.C.) and vigorously reasserted Assyrian authority in the area. The preaching of Amos says nothing about the threat of Assyria and seems to be before the death of Jeroboam II, since Amos proclaimed he would die by the sword (7:11) and he did not. On the other hand, Amos seems to know of the territory Jeroboam II restored from Aramaean hands (6:13), and his preaching generally is addressed to a nation at the height of its self-confidence and prosperity. This would suggest a dating for the preaching of Amos between 760 and 750 B.C. after Jeroboam's expansion of Israel's borders but before the stirring of Tiglath-pileser in Assyria. Amos 1:1b also says his preaching was "two years before the earthquake." This earthquake is mentioned in Zechariah 14:5 and must have been of significant proportions. Excavators at Hazor found evidence of an earthquake in northern Israel in a layer of material that they dated circa 760 B.C. (considered accurate only within ten years). This could fit with other considerations placing Amos's preaching in the decade after 760 B.C. It also tells us his preaching was of short duration because it must have concluded before the earthquake actually occurred. Most would suggest a ministry for Amos of no more than a year, and many would make it of only a few weeks.

AMOS, THE MAN

There is little we can say about the person of Amos. He is not mentioned outside the collection of his own oracles. Within the book of Amos we have direct information about the person of Amos only from the superscription to the book (1:1), one narrative in which Amos speaks to Amaziah about his call to be a prophet (7:10–17), and an account of four visions that came to Amos (7:1–9; 8:1–3).

From these few references, we learn that Amos was a herdsman, and a dresser of sycamore trees (see comment on 1:1 and 7:14) from the village of Tekoa south of Jerusalem. He was called from these common vocations to be a prophet by the Lord (7:15). The visions in 7:1–9 and 8:1–3 may reflect the early shaping of Amos's message in response to God's call. They show Amos as inclined to intercede for Israel with God in asking for mercy. The picture is not of a harsh, forbidding man. Nor is Amos to be romantically pictured as a rustic, parochial man, as was the fashion earlier in the twentieth century. Although his occupations are rural and agricultural in character, Amos was probably a respected man of consequence in his community (see the discussion of the term for "herdsman" in 1:1). Furthermore, Tekoa is only a few short miles from Jerusalem on one of the main travel routes, not at all an isolated, uninformed, and parochial place. Amos's preaching shows him quite knowledgeable and well informed on the events of nations and kingdoms as well as the inner workings of Israelite society.

It should be stressed that, for Amos and those who collected his preaching, the emphasis was not on Amos the person but on the "words of Amos" (1:1), which came to him from God. Of his life, Amos speaks only of his call from common occupation to vocation as God's messenger. This undoubtedly was the only biography he would have thought important.

THE BOOK OF AMOS

The book of Amos has been widely admired and praised for the power and eloquence of its language. The book is largely a collection of poetic oracles, most of them only a few verses in length. The notable exception is the long oracle against the nations in chapters 1 and 2, which is composed of shorter stanzas for each nation but clearly is intended to gain its impact as a longer connected speech. There is one prose narrative in 7:10–15 and an account of Amos's visions that mixes prose and poetry (7:1–9; 8:1–3).

Amos is adept at using a wide variety of speech types and patterns to convey his message effectively. The most common pattern of speech is an indictment of Israel for its sins followed by an announcement of God's judgment (for example, 2:6–16). The pattern can be varied with either the indictment or the announcement elaborated and extended. Such oracles are often introduced with the messenger formula "Thus says the LORD." Other patterns of speech found in Amos are exhortations (5:4–6, 14–15, 21–24), hymns (4:13; 5:8–9; 9:5–6), funeral lament (5:1–2), vision accounts (7:1–9; 8:1–3), and promises (9:11–15).

The book of Amos was undoubtedly collected together and edited by followers or admirers of Amos some time after he preached. The materials are not organized in the order he preached them. Some patterns of organization can be seen (e.g., chapters 3—5 all begin with "Hear this word

... "), but for the most part no one has successfully uncovered some grand scheme of organization.

Many have argued that not all of the book of Amos is from the eighth-century prophet himself. They suggest the book is the result of a more complex process of editing in which later generations have added their comments and additions to the original words of Amos. Such proposals have achieved no broad-based consensus for discerning the "original Amos." These attempts seem to us more knowledgeable about what a prophet of the eighth century in Israel could or would have said than we can reasonably claim. Our focus will be more on the book of Amos as it comes to us than on recovering some more authentic Amos hidden within these texts.

THE MESSAGE OF AMOS

The message of Amos is best discussed in the commentary sections as we reflect on the oracles themselves, but it may be useful to identify at least briefly six of the main themes we will encounter.

The End of Israel

Although Israel is God's elect people (2:10; 3:1–2) this election implies moral responsibility and a life lived in accord with God's will. Israel has failed to live such a life and instead lives a life characterized by sin (2:6–16). Therefore, God's judgment has declared an end to Israel (8:2; 9:1). Even God's people are not exempt from God's opposition to sin.

The Sovereignty of God

For Amos, God was supremely sovereign over history and nature. God's sovereignty had, of course, appeared as a theme earlier in Israel, but it might well be said that Amos radicalized this claim to its fullest implications. In particular, Amos made clear that God's sovereignty extended to the nations, and God would hold the nations to moral accountability as well as Israel or Judah (1:1–2:3). God's word of judgment addressed to the nations becomes a common theme in the prophets after Amos until the exile.

Even more surprising was Amos's claim that Israel had no exclusive claim to God's grace. As sovereign over all history, God was active in life-giving events in other nations as well as Israel. In 9:7, Amos dares to equate Israel's deliverance from Egypt with the migrations of Philistines and Aramaeans as God's work even among Israel's traditional enemies. The reign of God is not limited to history for Amos. God is also creator, and all of nature is at God's command. This is clear in hymnic passages in praise of God as creator (4:13; 5:8–9; 9:5–6) and in passages where nature becomes the instrument of God's admonitions and judgments (4:6–12; 7:1–6). The God of Amos is not a warm and friendly God but a roaring lion who strikes fear in the hearts of those who hear (1:2). God's gracious acts are referred to only in the past (2:10–11). Because of Israel's sin, the God of their future is judge, warrior, and destroyer.

The Appeal for Justice

Israel's sin is not announced by Amos arbitrarily and in the abstract. His message concretely documents the ways in which Israel's sin has broken covenant. Amos understood covenant as a relationship established between God and Israel that carried mutual obligations on both parties. Although Amos does not himself speak of the details, Israelite tradition understood this partnership to have been initiated by God on Mount Sinai and mediated by Moses. The obligations could be spelled out by specific laws, such as the Ten Commandments, or ancient law codes, such as found in the book of Exodus, but these obligations also are expressed in terms of commitment to particular principles associated with the covenant. For Amos, the two most central principles were justice and righteousness. We will discuss these principles in greater detail in our comment below (compare esp. comment on 5:21–24).

Amos's most frequent charge against Israel for breaking covenant is that the wealthy and powerful have exploited the poor and weak (2:6–8; 4:1–3), denied them access to the courts and bribed judges so that the complaints of the oppressed cannot be brought (5:10–13), and engaged in false and deceitful business practices (8:4–6). These practices evidence a disregard and a perversion of justice and righteousness. Justice and righteousness are what God demands of God's people (5:7, 15, 24; 6:12). Nothing less will do.

The Hypocrisy of Worship

Prophets before Amos (Elijah) and after (Hosea) singled out purity of worship and the apostasy of idolatry as special concerns. Amos shows almost no attention to the dangers of idolatry, but he has a complaint against

Israel's worship life nonetheless. He charges that Israel loves the sanctuaries and their rituals more than the God they are intended to honor (3:13–15; 4:4–5; 5:4–5). Amos sees in Israel's worship life a piety that has become an end in itself, ritual that has become self-justifying. It is the hypocrisy of ritual piety alongside a lack of justice and righteousness that Amos singles out, and he announces that God hates such worship and will not accept it (5:21–24). Although later prophets do evidence concern for idolatry, many carry on Amos's concern for hypocritical, self-serving worship (for example, Isa. 1:11–17).

The Inevitability of Judgment

Although Amos interceded (7:1–6), he was compelled to understand and announce that God's judgment had been made and the consequences were inevitable (7:7–9; 8:1–3) and comprehensive (9:1–3). Although he uses a variety of images and metaphors for divine judgment (locusts, fire, earthquake, famine), by far the most common images for God's judgment in Amos are those of war, conquest, destruction, and exile (for example, 4:1–3; 7:17; 9:4). Amos seems to believe that although various crises have served to remind Israel of God's potential wrath, the people have not turned back to God (4:6–12) and the most likely form of Israel's fate in judgment will be that of a conquering enemy. Since this is in fact the fate that overtakes Israel a few years later (721 B.C.), it is little wonder that Amos's words were remembered, reflected upon, preserved, and handed on to future generations.

The Promise of Blessing

With almost no prior hint of divine mercy or grace, the book of Amos ends with promises of future restoration and blessing (9:11–15). The hope is held out for a new beginning and a restoration of people and land in the fullness of God's blessing. Because of the reference to the fallen "booth of David," many believe this promise is a later Judean addition reflecting the hope for a return from exile and a rebuilding of Jerusalem (see discussion of 9:11–12). In any case, the promise as it now stands does not change Amos's message. If restored blessing in relation to God is to come, it is after and beyond a judgment that was not stayed. Israel as a nation did perish never to return. But as the book of Amos now stands, it makes plain that this word of death is not God's final word. A further word of life is spoken.

THE INFLUENCE OF AMOS

It is clear from our previous discussion that Amos had a profound effect on the prophets that came after him until the time of the Babylonian exile. Little reference, however, is made to the Amos tradition in the biblical literature that comes after exile. Amos is quoted once in the Apocrypha (Tobit 2:6 quotes Amos 8:10) and twice in the New Testament (Acts 7:42–43 quotes Amos 5:25–27, and Acts 15:16–17 quotes Amos 9:11–12). Amos is not well represented in references from the early church, the Middle Ages, or the Reformation. The church from New Testament times onward was more likely to draw on the prophets for images of hope and promise, and as we have seen, Amos has little of promise to offer.

In the late nineteenth and through the twentieth century the church has been rediscovering Amos and the prophetic message of God's judgment that he represents. The growth of church commitment to moral issues in society around the turn of the century, the rise of the social gospel movement in the early twentieth century, the liberal Protestant interest in economic and social reform prior to World War II, the church involvement in civil rights struggles through the 1960s, and the development of liberation theologies in recent decades have all given a prominent place to Amos and the prophetic concern for social justice as a divine mandate to people of faith. Amos is frequently cited as biblical warrant for understanding faithfulness in social as well as individual terms. He provides firm support for those who would remind us that the faithfulness God demands may best be measured in our regard for and advocacy of the weak and powerless. Some boldly suggest that unless we heed the message of Amos and those who take up his themes, we, too, are subject to God's judgment. Our further assessment of the appropriateness of these appeals to Amos and his message is perhaps now best left to our further reflection on the text of the book that bears his name.

Commentary

THE LORD ROARS FROM ZION
Amos 1:1–2

1:1 **The words of Amos, who was among the shepherds of Tekoa, which he saw concerning Israel in the days of King Uzziah of Judah and in the days of King Jeroboam son of Joash of Israel, two years before the earthquake.**

2 **And he said:**
The LORD roars from Zion,
and utters his voice from Jerusalem;
the pastures of the shepherds wither,
and the top of Carmel dries up.

The book of Amos begins with a superscription (1:1), an opening verse that sets the words of this prophet into a time and place, and a prologue (1:2) that signals the theological mood of those words.

The Superscription (1:1)

Many prophetic books begin with a superscription to give the reader some basic information about the prophet and his setting (Isa. 1:1; Hos. 1:1; Mic. 1:1; Zeph. 1:1). This verse is most closely paralleled in form by Jeremiah 1:1–3, beginning with "The words of Amos" and continuing to give information on hometown, background, and date for the prophet. Some scholars believe that the information about the king of Judah was added at a later time. Since the Northern Kingdom of Israel is destroyed a few years after Amos's preaching, it would stand to reason that his words were preserved and probably edited by Judean admirers who patriotically listed their king first even though Amos preached entirely in the Northern Kingdom.

Verse 1 directs our expectations to the "words of Amos." "Words" here means something like "sayings" and refers to the oracles collected in this book. An oracle is a single unit of prophetic speech, sometimes as brief as a single verse, but at other times a longer, more complex speech (for example, 1:3–2:16). As we will see throughout this book, the words Amos proclaims are considered by him to be the word of God he feels commissioned to bring. Notice that, even though the superscription will give us a bit of information about Amos the man, the emphasis is to be on the message of Amos and not the person of Amos.

The name *Amos* is from a root that means "to carry, bear, or protect." Its form is probably passive, "one who is carried (by God?)," but some think it can also be read as active, "one who carries or bears (God's word?)."

Two phrases give us brief personal information about the prophet. We are told first that he is "among the shepherds of Tekoa." It may be misleading to translate the word for Amos's occupation as "shepherd." Amos does not seem to have been a simple, peasant herdsman, although earlier commentaries and studies on Amos presented him as such and romantically stressed his poor and humble origins. We now know that the Hebrew term suggests a manager or breeder of flocks and herds. But if Amos is not a poor herdsman, neither is he a member of the wealthy elite. His occupation implies responsibility and economic well-being but need not imply wealth and political influence. Amos is a man of ordinary occupation summoned to speak God's word, which means that any of us might similarly be called (compare also 7:14).

If this first phrase tells us of the occupation of Amos, we might say that the second tells us of the vocation of Amos, "which he saw concerning Israel." It may seem odd to think of Amos's "words" as something "he saw." But this is not the ordinary verb "to see." The verb here is from a root that means "to have a vision." The noun derived from this root is "a seer." We are told here that Amos's words have been revealed to him. Indeed, as we will see, visions play an important role in shaping Amos's message (7:1–9; 8:1–3), as they do in many other prophets (Isaiah 6; Ezekiel 1). Thus, Amos has a revealed word to bring, and it is directed to Israel, the Northern Kingdom with its capital in Samaria and its royal sanctuaries in Bethel and Dan.

This prophetic vocation to the Northern Kingdom is somewhat surprising when we learn that Amos's hometown was Tekoa, a Judean town located five miles south of Bethlehem on the edge of the Judean wilderness. Amos was a Judean called to take God's word to the Northern Kingdom of Israel. God's prophetic word is no respecter of our political boundaries. Some may see Amos as an outside agitator (for example, Amaziah in Amos 7:10–13), but God's word is not a parochial, neighborhood matter. The prophetic task sends us to speak God's truth wherever it needs to be heard. We can imagine, and Amos will discover, that this is not always the most popular thing to do.

Finally, the superscription gives us two references intended to place Amos in time and history. His preaching is located during the reigns of Uzziah in Judah (783–742 B.C.) and Jeroboam the son of Joash (thus, Jeroboam II, 786–746 B.C.). Traditionally these kings have been associated with periods of peace, prosperity, and well-being in the two Israelite kingdoms. Jeroboam II is said to have expanded the borders of the kingdom and led it to new levels of influence and wealth (2 Kings 14:23–29). Assyria, Egypt, and Syria were all in periods of weakness or inclined not to interfere in Israelite affairs. This period of outward peace and prosperity has been used frequently as the ironic context for Amos's message that all is not well within the kingdom.

The final note in this verse tells us that Amos preached "two years before the earthquake." This earthquake, which must have been of significant proportions, is mentioned in Zechariah 14:5 and may help with the dating of the book of Amos (see discussion in the Introduction). The reference tells us that Amos's preaching was of relatively short duration, since it must have concluded before the earthquake actually occurred, thus perhaps within a year or less. Some have even argued that Amos preached all the book's material on a single occasion. Since Amos mentions earthquakes as a manifestation of God's judgment several times in the book (3:14–15; 6:11; 9:1, 9), we might suppose that the occurrence of the earthquake was seen as a vindication of his preaching and led to the mention of the earthquake in the superscription.

A Prologue (1:2)

Verse 2 serves as a prologue to the message of Amos, announcing the word of Yahweh in metaphors of roaring lion and sounding thunder that withers and devastates the land. This verse could be an introduction to the oracles against the nations in 1:3–2:16, but there Yahweh speaks in the first person. Further, verse 2 mentions only Israel and not the nations. It is probably best to think of this verse as a prologue to the entire book, appropriately identifying its main theme as God's imminent judgment against Israel.

Are these words from Amos himself? Since the verse mentions Zion and Jerusalem this verse could be placed as an introduction by a later Judean editor. This is possible, but we should remember that Amos was a Judean sent to preach in the Northern Kingdom of Israel. The effects of God's word from Jerusalem felt in the northern area of Carmel fits with the south to north pattern of Amos's brief ministry, and the images of God's coming judgment fit well with the overall theme of the book.

We cannot determine with certainty which passages in the book of Amos are from the mouth of the historical Amos and which are not. Later hands have clearly shaped and edited Amos's preaching (as well as other prophets) for the purpose of preserving and passing his message on to subsequent generations. In general, we will regard the text in its present form as the Amos text we are intended to encounter and interpret. We may observe evidences of editorial work from time to time, but our task will still focus on the full form of the Amos tradition as we now have it in the book of Amos.

The first word presented to us as spoken by Amos is the name of God, Yahweh (NRSV, "the LORD"). This is appropriate because Amos has much to say about who the Lord is and what the Lord is doing or about to do.

We meet the Lord who "roars from Zion." The image is of a lion who roars to strike terror in the heart of its prey. It is an image to which Amos returns in 3:4, 8 and is also used of God by the prophet Hosea (5:14; 11:10–11; 13:7–8). We are properly alerted that in Amos we do not encounter a warm, comfortable God, but a dangerous and fearsome God who demands accountability. It is God, the lion.

In poetic parallel, the next line says that "[The Lord] gives voice from Jerusalem" (NRSV, "utters his voice"). The phrases "give voice" and "voice of the Lord" in Hebrew usually refer to thunder (for example, 1 Sam. 7:10; Job 37:2, 4, 5; Psalm 18:14; 46:7; 68:34). Alongside the image of God's word as roaring lion is laid the image of God's word as thunder from the heavens.

The Lord's thunder does not bring rain. Here the roaring and thundering utterance of the Lord brings withering drought (compare Jer. 12:4; 23:10 where the same verbs are used for the drought on the land). The appearance of God wreaks havoc with the land (compare Nah. 1:3–5). This motif is associated with God's judgment. In fact, variants of this very verse appear in Joel 3:16 and Jeremiah 25:30–38 in connection with God's appearance to judge the nations. Amos gives this a different and chilling twist. Among the nations God appears to judge is Israel itself, God's own people. No one is given privileged immunity from God's judgment—not Israel, not the church—if its sin makes judgment necessary.

The image of God whose appearance (or theophany) has catastrophic effects on nature itself is associated with the image of God as warrior. The divine warrior, an image known in biblical and ancient Near Eastern texts, is associated with divine judgment of enemies. As we shall see in Amos's message, war and its devastation are frequent images of God's judgment against Israel whose disobedient conduct has made them numbered among the enemies of God.

The Lord's word issues forth in frightening form, and it is from Jerusalem and its sacred Mount Zion that it issues. This would be in keeping with Amos's Judean background. Zion in Jerusalem was God's holy habitation (compare Ps. 50:2).

But the effects of the Lord's utterance are devastation in the north. Carmel is the northern range of mountains and accompanying valleys in Israel. It is an area known for its rich and fertile pasture land. The phrase "shepherd's pastures" may not indicate a specific geographic area, but draws generally on Amos's pastoral background to speak of fertile areas devastated by God's utterance.

What are we to make of such a beginning to the preaching of Amos? This is no voice of comfort and caring, no "still, small voice." If this prologue is our introduction to Amos's message, then we are to hear God's word through Amos as an angry roaring and thundering with terrible consequences. What could warrant such divine anger? In our tendency to prefer domesticated and comfortable gods and religion, perhaps we will do well to listen carefully to Amos's indictment of Israel to see how closely we fit the profile of those who kindle God's anger. Divine judgment is not a comfortable theme, but if we truly believe that God opposes evil in the world, we might seek the help of an Amos to see if the roaring and thundering of God is echoing in our own ears.

I WILL NOT REVOKE
THE PUNISHMENT
Amos 1:3–2:16

The roaring of the Lord now becomes a sharply focused word of the Lord through the preaching of Amos. This section is one of the longest and most dramatic oracles in all prophetic literature. Although the setting is not explicitly mentioned, it is easy to imagine that these words were preached at the northern royal sanctuary in Bethel, for this is the place Amaziah, the priest, later tells Amos to leave and cease his preaching

(7:10–12). Bethel was one of two sanctuaries in the Northern Kingdom built and supported by the kings for official religious festivals, sacrifices, and observances. At any time it was likely to be a busy place, and we can imagine Amos taking his position in some public location where he was sure to draw a crowd.

This, in itself, may not have been an unusual occurrence. Many with messages for which they desired attention may have sought an audience here. One cannot help but think of modern places like the famous Speaker's Corner in London's Hyde Park, where on any given afternoon numerous speakers can be found attempting to gain the attention of a crowd through the force of their oratory and the attraction of their cause. The success of these speakers and their causes can be gauged by the size of the audience they attract. It may have been little different in the Bethel of Amos's time, and we can easily imagine that Amos might successfully have gathered quite a crowd about him. His subject at first was the vile and atrocious behavior of Israel's neighboring nations, which Amos denounced with powerful and stinging words.

The Transgressions of the Nations (1:3–2:5)

1:3 Thus says the LORD:
   For three transgressions of Damascus,
      and for four, I will not revoke the punishment;
   because they have threshed Gilead
      with threshing sledges of iron.
   ⁴So I will send a fire on the house of Hazael,
      and it shall devour the strongholds of Ben-hadad.
   ⁵I will break the gate bars of Damascus,
      and cut off the inhabitants from the Valley of Aven,
   and the one who holds the scepter from Beth-eden;
      and the people of Aram shall go into exile to Kir,
                         says the LORD.

   ⁶Thus says the LORD:
   For three transgressions of Gaza,
      and for four, I will not revoke the punishment;
   because they carried into exile entire communities,
      to hand them over to Edom.
   ⁷So I will send a fire on the wall of Gaza,
      fire that shall devour its strongholds.

⁸I will cut off the inhabitants from Ashdod,
>   and the one who holds the scepter from Ashkelon;
> I will turn my hand against Ekron,
>   and the remnant of the Philistines shall perish,
>   says the LORD God.

⁹Thus says the LORD:
> For three transgressions of Tyre,
>   and for four, I will not revoke the punishment;
> because they delivered entire communities over to Edom,
>   and did not remember the covenant of kinship.
¹⁰So I will send a fire on the wall of Tyre,
>   fire that shall devour its strongholds.

¹¹Thus says the LORD:
> For three transgressions of Edom,
>   and for four, I will not revoke the punishment;
> because he pursued his brother with the sword
>   and cast off all pity;
> he maintained his anger perpetually,
>   and kept his wrath forever.
¹²So I will send a fire on Teman
>   and it shall devour the strongholds of Bozrah.

¹³Thus says the LORD:
> For three transgressions of the Ammonites,
>   and for four, I will not revoke the punishment;
> because they have ripped open pregnant women in Gilead
>   in order to enlarge their territory.
¹⁴So I will kindle a fire against the wall of Rabbah,
>   fire that shall devour its strongholds,
> with shouting on the day of battle,
>   with a storm on the day of the whirlwind;
¹⁵then their king shall go into exile,
>   he and his officials together,
>   says the LORD.

2:1 Thus says the LORD:
> For three transgressions of Moab,
>   and for four, I will not revoke the punishment;
> because he burned to lime
>   the bones of the king of Edom.
²So I will send a fire on Moab,
>   and it shall devour the strongholds of Kerioth,

and Moab shall die amid uproar,
   amid shouting and the sound of the trumpet;
³I will cut off the ruler from its midst,
   and will kill all its officials with him,
                  says the LORD.

⁴Thus says the LORD;
For three transgressions of Judah,
   and for four, I will not revoke the punishment;
because they have rejected the law of the LORD,
   and have not kept his statutes,
but they have been led astray by the same lies
   after which their ancestors walked.
⁵So I will send a fire on Judah,
   and it shall devour the strongholds of Jerusalem.

In Israel before the exile, prophets usually spoke in patterned styles of speech that gave their message added drama and impact. This opening speech by Amos is an excellent example. In seven speeches modeled on the same pattern, Amos pronounces judgment on the small nations that were Israel's immediate neighbors. Although there are slight variations in the pattern, the basic effect is an almost hypnotic repetition of phrases and rhythms that draws the reader into the power of Amos's preaching much as his ancient listeners in Bethel must have been held spellbound. One is reminded of the powerful repeated cadences and phrases of Martin Luther King, Jr. or Jesse Jackson in our time.

"Thus says the LORD," begins each of the seven indictments. This phrase, known as the messenger formula, is a constant reminder to the listeners that Amos speaks not for himself but for the God who sent him as messenger to the people. His authority is not his own but his words are to be measured for their faithfulness to what is known of God's will, God's justice, God's righteousness. The first person pronoun, "I," in these speeches is not the "I" of the speaker Amos, but the "I" of the God who sent Amos.

There follows a formula indictment in which each nation is named ("For three transgressions of Damascus, and for four . . . ") and a very specific accusation against each. These are concrete and presumably refer to events known among Amos's listeners. Each speech then announces judgment on the nation named and accused. Four of the speeches end with a brief messenger formula again.

The pattern and the repetition clearly create a building effect and command the attention of listener or reader. It is worth noting the careful crafting of style and form that gives the prophet's message much of its power. Modern preachers and teachers would do well to attend not only to the content of Amos's message but to the care with which he formulates it. Many an important proclamation of God's word falls ineffectually on unlistening ears because the proclaimer spends little time or care on the crafting of a language and form that would make God's word effective.

Indictments against Israel's Neighbors

Seven nations are singled out for indictment. Their order seems to be an intentional pattern. Amos begins with Damascus in the northeast and then moves to Gaza in the southwest. These are home to two of Israel's most persistent historic enemies, the Aramaeans and the Philistines. Moving to Tyre, in the northwest, and Edom, in the southeast, Amos has circumscribed Israel, indicting neighboring nations in four geographical corners. Indictments follow for Ammon and Moab, the two remaining neighbors to the east. Only the sea lies directly to the west. These four—Tyre, Edom, Ammon and Moab—all have kinship or alliance ties with Israel, although relationships were not always cordial. Tyre, the great Phoenician city, was particularly allied with Israel during the time of David and Solomon. King Ahab of the Northern Kingdom later married a Phoenician princess, Jezebel (1 Kings 16:31). Edom was descended from Jacob's brother, Esau (Gen. 36:1). Ammon and Moab were the sons of Lot, Abraham's nephew (Gen. 19:36–38), and gave birth to the nations of their names.

Finally, and perhaps surprisingly since Amos himself was a Judean, comes an indictment against Judah, Israel's closest kin among the nations. Once they had been one nation under Saul, David, and Solomon. They shared the same God and many religious traditions originating in deliverance from bondage in Egypt and covenant making at Sinai. With the oracle against Judah, lying directly to the south, Amos has now geographically encircled Israel with indicted nations. He has also progressed through judgments against enemies, allies, kinsmen, and sibling. All are subject to God's judgment: "For three transgressions . . . and for four. . . ." The formula suggests that the numbering of their transgressions could go on in endless progression. And for none of these will God "revoke the punishment."

Before we even speak of the specific indictments and judgments pronounced on each of these nations we can observe an enormously important presumption behind Amos's preaching. The Lord (Yahweh), the God of Israel, is a universal God who holds all nations accountable for their actions. The God for whom Amos speaks knows and cares about the moral conduct of all peoples, even Israel's enemies. This God is not limited in sphere to Israel alone but is the God of all history.

In our time, many persons show little regard for the problems and crises of nations dissimilar to our own, particularly other nations they think of as different from themselves. Many express moral outrage over the caning of a single American citizen in Singapore while the massacre of hundreds of thousands takes place in Rwanda and receives scant attention from the general public. In a public discussion on violence in Bosnia, a man commented that he saw no reason to risk American lives for Muslims. We have failed to hear the message of Amos that God's justice observes no national or ethnic boundaries. The divine regard for those who might be victimized or oppressed is not limited to those who know and call on the divine name in the manner of our religious practice.

The Crimes and Punishments

Amos does not stop with general accusations. He names the crimes and announces the punishments. Many of the crimes detail the atrocities of war. Terrible deeds have been committed by these nations in pursuit of their self-serving interests, such as enlarging their territorial borders (1:13). Some of this violence has been directed against Israelite territories (for example, Gilead in Amos 1:3, 13) and some against each other (1:9, 11; 2:1). The first six nations named by Amos are all accused of acts of gross inhumanity. Even in the context of war these deeds cross the boundaries of morality. Damascus is charged with torture and cruelty to its victims (1:3); Gaza with dislocation and deportation of entire populations (1:6, one cannot fail to think of ethnic cleansing in our time); Tyre with the disregard for and violation of treaties (1:9); Edom with unwillingness to bring hostilities to an end and unnecessary prolongation of conflict with a brother nation (1:11); Ammon with atrocities committed against noncombatants, in this case pregnant women, in order to expand their territory (1:13); Moab with failure to respect even the dead, by violating the bones of a vanquished enemy king (2:1). It is unfortunate that we still live in a world where examples of similar atrocity and violence are not difficult to come by. Amos's catalog of widespread disregard for human welfare and basic morality in the conduct of nations still seems distressingly pertinent.

One of the judgment speeches is rather different in its specifics. Judah is not accused of wartime violence but is charged with rejecting the law of the Lord and failure to keep God's statutes (2:4). The violation of Judah is one of breached religious commitment and not of violent conduct in international affairs. The crime charged against Judah seems more mildly stated, and, as we shall see, the judgment on Judah is also less detailed. Perhaps this reflects the fact that Amos is himself from Judah. Nevertheless, we should remember that "the law of the Lord" includes extensive concern for a wide range of moral conduct. Judah is thus held accountable to the specific standards of moral behavior that are part of their commitment in covenant with the Lord.

The punishments Amos announces as God's judgment on the nations also follow a pattern. The imagery seems to be drawn from the violence of warfare that figured so prominently in the crimes for which the nations are accused. "I will send a fire," Amos announces for the Lord. To the image of God as roaring lion is added the image of God as consuming flame. Fire will consume the capital or the chief stronghold of each offending nation, including Jerusalem in Judah (a bold declaration later to become reality at the time of Babylonian exile). Many of the judgments go on to announce the doom of the ruler (Damascus, Gaza, Ammon, Moab) and in some the fate of inhabitants (Damascus, Gaza) or officials (Ammon, Moab). The most detailed and thoroughgoing judgment seems to be reserved for Israel's historic enemies, the Aramaeans and the Philistines (Damascus, Gaza).

In these oracles against the nations, God's judgment does not appear to take some supernatural form invading the realm of the historical process. The images are largely of violence ultimately overtaking the violators. There is no timetable, simply a steady assurance that God is also at work in the history of the nations and will not allow their injustices to go unchallenged. In modern times there have been systems of violence that seemed beyond the reach of ordinary historical processes—the recent totalitarian regimes of the Soviet Union and Eastern Europe, the crushing system of apartheid in South Africa, and, earlier in the century, the seemingly irresistible spread of domination by Nazi Germany and imperial Japan. There were many who despaired that anything less than a supernatural intervention could bring liberation. And yet all those violent systems have fallen, some of them meeting their own violent ends. Amos tells us in his oracle against the nations that God's justice is at work in such historic processes. In God's time, violence and oppression will not go forever unchallenged.

At this point, Amos's ancient listeners and we as modern readers of his message might be tempted to self-righteousness. No doubt those gathered in Bethel cheered and urged Amos on in his indictment of moral excesses among the nations. There is something perversely satisfying in pointing our fingers at others. No doubt in our own time it is easier to chronicle the failure and excesses of other groups and nations than our own. The number seven was often considered a number of completion in ancient times. After seven judgments against neighboring nations, the crowd gathered to hear Amos might have thought he was finished. They were content to bask in the self-righteous satisfaction of enjoying this chronicle of their neighbors' sins. But Amos was not through preaching.

The Transgressions of Israel
(2:6–16)

2:6 Thus says the LORD:
  For three transgressions of Israel,
    and for four, I will not revoke the punishment;
  because they sell the righteous for silver,
    and the needy for a pair of sandals—
  7 they who trample the head of the poor into the dust of the earth,
    and push the afflicted out of the way;
  father and son go in to the same girl,
    so that my holy name is profaned;
  8 they lay themselves down beside every altar
    on garments taken in pledge;
  and in the house of their God they drink
    wine bought with fines they imposed.

  9 Yet I destroyed the Amorite before them,
    whose height was like the height of cedars,
    and who was as strong as oaks;
  I destroyed his fruit above,
    and his roots beneath.
  10 Also I brought you up out of the land of Egypt,
    and led you forty years in the wilderness,
    to possess the land of the Amorite.
  11 And I raised up some of your children to be prophets
    and some of your youths to be nazirites.
    Is it not indeed so, O people of Israel?
                              says the LORD.

^{12} But you made the nazirites drink wine,
   and commanded the prophets,
   saying, "You shall not prophesy."
^{13} So, I will press you down in your place,
   just as a cart presses down when it is full of sheaves.
^{14} Flight shall perish from the swift,
   and the strong shall not retain their strength,
   nor shall the mighty save their lives;
^{15} those who handle the bow shall not stand,
   and those who are swift of foot shall not save themselves,
   nor shall those who ride horses save their lives;
^{16} and those who are stout of heart among the mighty
   shall flee away naked in that day,
                              says the LORD.

Amos continues with the same opening formula he had used of the other nations, but this time he names Israel. What a shock this must have been. Amos numbers Israel among the nations just condemned for violent and oppressive behavior. And the opening word of the Lord to Israel is just as unrelenting, "I will not revoke the punishment." This is a surprising turn of events similar to Nathan's confrontation of David. When David unwittingly condemns the man who has unlawfully taken his neighbor's possession the prophet declares, "You are the man!" Here Amos declares to an unsuspecting crowd of listeners, "You, Israel, are the nation!"

How easy it is to take delight in the judgment of others. We can be horrified at reports of violence elsewhere in the world but reluctant to admit anything is wrong in a society with more shootings and violent crimes per capita than any other nation in the world. We demand that courts and governments get tough on crime, especially in the inner city, but we often refuse to support taxes or laws that enable us to address the causes of crime. We will accept almost any responsibility for violence assigned to "them" but resist the notion that any responsibility lies with "us." No doubt Amos would shock us too by suggesting that we can find ourselves judged along with others who have opposed God's will for justice and righteousness.

Domestic Immorality

The crimes for which Israel is judged seem to be domestic rather than international. They speak less of atrocities committed between nations than of the immoral and unjust quality of Israel's life as a community.

Amos accuses Israel first of profiteering on the needs of the poor, apparently selling the poor and needy into debt-slavery for even trivial amounts, "a pair of sandals" (2:6b).

Amos then charges that economic exploitation of the poor is coupled with their abuse and denial of dignity (v. 7a). They "trample the head of the poor into the dust."

Most scholars believe that Amos's next charge, "push[ing] the afflicted out of the way," refers to denial of access to court processes or fair treatment within the courts where those exploited might seek justice.

In verse 7b Amos refers to practices of sexual immorality in which father and son sexually use the same young girl. Although the abuse is clear, the circumstances are less so. This could refer to sexual exploitation of young women hired as household help. Or this could refer to prostitution, and the reference to the profaning of God's name may indicate this is connected with non-Israelite religious practices. This is uncertain, but in any case, Amos clearly indicates God's displeasure with any such sexual exploitation of women and the degrading behavior of the men involved.

Yet another charge against Israel is that garments taken from the poor in pledge for a debt (compare Exod. 22:25–27) or wine taken as fines imposed on the poor (debt, interest) are then piously used for reclining and drinking in the religious places of worship (v. 8). To exploitation is added hypocrisy.

Of course the exact character of the society reflected here for Israel is very different from our own, but the categories of sin and exploitation are not particularly different. We will see those with wealth and power willing to perpetuate their economic advantage at the expense of those with few economic resources. As these lines are written, the newspapers this week have carried articles on long-term care insurance and nursing-home frauds perpetrated on the elderly and on exploitation of Spanish-speaking laborers who are unknowingly manipulated into signing contracts that waive their rights to basic work-related benefits. Access to the legal system is always easier for those who have wealth. Sexuality is used in our society as a marketing commodity, and young teenagers become cynically experienced in sexual practices. Major religious figures in our time have been indicted and imprisoned for the misappropriation of funds and trust bestowed on them by pious common folk. It does not seem that Amos would have too much trouble seeing the Israel of his day in some unjust and immoral practices still present in our time.

It is clear in the speech of judgment to Israel that Amos's God is God not only of all history but also of the weak, the poor, and the powerless.

God's judgment is exercised in behalf of those most vulnerable, most likely to be exploited and manipulated. This is not the God of the powerful and important people of the land. This is the God found among "the least of these" as Jesus later reminded the disciples (Matt. 25:31–46).

Israel's Memory Loss

There is a special section in the oracle of judgment against Israel that was not present in those against the nations. In verses 9–11 God speaks to Israel through Amos of the special relationship that has been established with Israel. God recalls the exodus deliverance out of slavery in Egypt and the leading of Israel through the wilderness to the land they now inhabit (v. 10). God reminds Israel of the divine power that protected them against the hostility of the Amorites as they were establishing themselves in the land (v. 9). God recounts the raising up of committed witnesses to God's grace and care in the form of prophets and Nazirites (v. 11). Nazirites were a group who consecrated themselves to God by a disciplined way of life that among other things involved abstinence from alcoholic drink.

The universal God of the oracles against the nations is now revealed also to be the particular God of Israel's faith story. It was on the basis of Israel's experience of God's grace in this story of liberation and continuing care that they become God's covenant people. Now God's covenant people have become as reprehensible to God as those nations guilty of war crimes.

This section recalling Israel's history of God's salvation implies that Israel has forgotten what God has done. They suffer from a loss of memory. Their own faith story is either unknown or disregarded. Almost as if trying to jar reaction out of a people grown forgetful and apathetic, God demands a response at the end of verse 11: "Is it not indeed so, O people of Israel?"

To the earlier catalog of Israel's sins God now adds a new one (v. 12). The people have corrupted and silenced the very witnesses whose task was to keep memory alive in Israel. They have forced the Nazirites to break their vows and commanded the prophets not to speak. Remembering the covenant and the gift of deliverance from God is also to remember what this covenant demands and to be forced into painful awareness of how far Israel has fallen from those covenant responsibilities. How much easier to silence or co-opt the witnesses.

When memory becomes dim, when we know little of the stories that tell us who God is and what relationship to God requires, then it becomes easy to let our religious practices serve to support the way of life we have chosen rather than call us to God's way of new life. We then want pastors and teachers in the service of a domesticated God who in turn serves our way of life. If an Amos dared to confront us with our sinful patterns of life or dared to call us to remember the history with God that demands of us special responsibility in covenant obedience, then we too might say "You shall not prophesy." But when memory is kept alive in our midst, when we know the story of God's grace and deliverance, we will honor the witnesses to that story and we will see more clearly what relationship to the God of that story requires of us. Morality and justice are not abstract requirements laid on us; they flow naturally from the love and grace of God we have already known.

Israel's Fate

God's judgment on Israel is harsh (2:13–16). Even God's special people fall under divine judgment if they number themselves among those who oppose God's justice. The images are all drawn from the experience of conquest and exile. Israel does not deserve to survive if its behavior is marked by immorality and injustice. Its fate will be to perish. Only a few years after Amos preached, the Northern Kingdom was conquered by Assyria and perished forever. Perhaps this is one of the reasons Amos's words made such an impression that they were preserved and passed on to future generations. Amos thus stands as a reminder to us that relationship to God does not give us special exemption from accountability in that relationship.

HEAR THIS WORD
Amos 3:1–5:27

The next three chapters of the book of Amos (3—5) are collections of oracles introduced by the phrase "Hear this word." It is almost as if the dramatic format of the oracles against the nations in chapters 1—2 with the surprise concluding oracle against Israel was intended to grab our attention, and now Amos has a few matters he wants to address as the proclaimer of God's word. As a child, I had a neighbor who always demanded our attention by exclaiming, "Listen up now!" The prophet is using a similar exclamation that insists we give attention: "Hear this word. . . . "

The oracles in this section were not spoken at the same time or in this order by Amos. They seem to be grouped by subject matter and to presuppose that the reader has first read Amos's oracles against the nations and Israel in chapters 1—2.

You Only Have I Known (3:1–2)

3:1 **Hear this word that the LORD has spoken against you, O people of Israel, against the whole family that I brought up out of the land of Egypt:**
² **You only have I known**
  of all the families of the earth;
 therefore I will punish you
  for all your iniquities.

Those who heard Amos's speeches against the nations with the surprise judgment on Israel itself must have been shocked. One of their reactions was probably to say, "These things can't happen to us. We're God's special chosen people." They thought their special relationship to God gave them a privileged position, certainly some sort of immunity from God's wrath. In fact, this has been a common attitude among religious folk through the ages, including our time. We think God's judgment is for "them" but not directed at "us."

In these two short but very important verses, Amos addresses the issues of identity (Who is Israel?) and responsibility (What is required of Israel?). In these questions, addressed by Amos to ancient Israel and passed on to us as scripture, the church is forced to confront similar questions about its understanding of identity and responsibility in relationship to God.

Identity

No doubt many Israelites shouted at Amos, "Don't you know who we are?" Amos's response in these verses seems to be "Yes, I do, but have you forgotten what that really means?" His reminder is blunt and compact but remarkably broad. The prophet uses language that draws on three different themes to remind Israel of its identity. These themes can help us reflect on the identity of the church as God's people.

The first is the image of family. Out of all the families of the earth (v. 2) Israel is a family in special relationship to God. Amos is not thinking of blood kinship here, but of the kinship that comes from mutual relationship to one another in covenant with God. The image of family suggests

that the relationship to God and to others in community must be understood as personal and intimate. In family relationships, the members are
mutually attached and responsible in caring for one another. Such family
caring comes from within and is not limited by external requirements
alone. The wholeness of each family member is bound to the well-being
of the whole family. In family we simply care for one another as whole
persons in every aspect of life and without end. When we understand
covenant relationship as family, then we cannot fulfill our obligation to
God and others by simply attending religious services, paying our financial
pledge, and not actively breaking the law. Amos is calling Israel and us to
a deeper standard of mutual caring and responsibility by using the image
of family for covenant relationship to God and to one another.

A second theme appears when Amos refers to Israel as the family "that
I brought up out of the land of Egypt" (v. 1a). The relationship between
God and Israel was initiated by God's deliverance. Israel became a family
in their common experience of God's gift of grace in the exodus from
Egypt. This is the language of faith story. To be God's special people is
to share and cherish this story—to remember that once they were slaves
but the Lord God brought them out. In the speech against Israel, God in-
vokes this memory (2:10) of God's grace to Israel when they were oppressed and needy to contrast with Israel's present behavior in afflicting
the weak and vulnerable among them. The covenant law codes make clear
that remembrance of deliverance from Egypt is to provide a motivation
for compassion and care for others who are dispossessed, afflicted, or in
need (for example, Exod. 23:9; Deut. 10:18–19). The words of Amos are
a reminder that neither Israel nor the community of faith in any generation could exist by their efforts alone. We are a community established by
the graciousness of God, and our lives are therefore to be marked by cor-
responding graciousness lived out in the world. In American culture, the
romantic attraction to the myth of the "self-made man" and the elevation
of the individual to central importance tends to value self-fulfillment and
self-indulgence. This makes it important for the church to remember the
story of our deliverance and be reminded that we are a community who
owes its life to God's grace, and therefore, we are bound in care and compassion to one another.

A third theme is suggested in God's statement through Amos that "you
only have I known of all the families of the earth" (v. 2). The language of
God's "knowledge" of Israel (or of the church) in this context is covenant
language. God not only delivered Israel but entered into mutual relationship with them in covenant. Israel is God's covenant people.

What does it mean when Amos says, "you *only* have I known"? Does it mean God does not care for other nations and is not active in their histories? Does it mean Israel has some sort of exclusive claim on God's grace? No, for Amos was clear in chapters 1—2 that God is the God of all history and is concerned for the behavior of the nations and not just Israel. Further, at a later point (9:7), Amos clearly argues that God's grace is present in the life of the nations and not just in Israel. Even the Philistines and the Aramaeans have experienced moments of grace similar to Israel's exodus event (compare discussion of Amos 9:7–10).

The key to understanding this verse is in the verb "to know." In Hebrew this verb is not limited in meaning to cognitive knowing, the activity of the mind. "To know" in Hebrew often means "to experience or interact with someone or something mutually." What distinguishes Israel from the nations is the establishment of covenant relationship that allows for mutual knowing and being known. God is active in the life of all nations and all creation, but only in Israel has mutual knowing been established. God in covenant has revealed (become known) the divine power that lies behind the experiences of life and wholeness in the world. A later prophet during the Babylonian exile spoke of Cyrus, the king of Persia, as an instrument of God's grace and said "I [God] arm you, though you do not know me" (Isa. 45:5). To be known by God is to be in mutual, acknowledged relationship to God.

Such covenantal knowing implies responsibility. Israel is indeed chosen, but not for privilege. God's covenant people are chosen for responsibility in the world. Chosenness is not for the sake of exclusive benefits but for the sake of God's mission to restore wholeness to a broken world. The obligation of covenant knowing is made clear in Genesis 18:19.

> No, for I have chosen [Hebrew, "known"] him, that he may charge his children and his household after him to keep the way of the LORD by doing righteousness and justice; so that the LORD may bring about for Abraham what he has promised him.

For God to know Abraham and his seed after him (Israel, the church) is connected here with the obligation of righteousness and justice. These two words will loom large in the message of Amos as part of his understanding of covenant obligation also (see especially the discussion of Amos 5:21–27). To be God's covenant people is not a matter of exclusive privilege but of obligation to responsible mission. For those in the modern church who think the church exists for the sake of their personal needs alone, Amos's word here is a harsh one. Such narrow and self-centered understanding of special relationship to God leads not to fulfillment and well-being but to judgment.

Responsibility

The special relationship to God implied by the language of family, deliverance, and covenant knowing does not, for Amos, lead to God's indulgence of our sin. It leads instead to special accountability. God cannot look the other way because God has especially revealed to Israel what is required of them, as family, as delivered people, and as covenant community. God is much like the familiar image of the parent who hears a child argue of a misdeed, "Everyone does it." The parental response is "Yes, but *you* should have known better." In Amos's preaching, all the nations are judged and held accountable for their moral violations, but Israel especially should have known better. They had the covenant tradition to guide them and a faith story through which to keep their distinctive calling in view. Their special relationship to God grants no immunity. God will oppose and judge oppression and iniquity even when it is found in Israel or the church.

Surely it is evident that this portion of Amos's message has a special pertinence to the church in the American setting. From colonial days to the present, there have been many who described our nation as "God's New Israel" and saw in the successes of the nation and its way of life the deserved blessings of a people whose virtue had given them privileged relationship to God. On the occasion of the American Bicentennial, President Gerald Ford said, "Our greatness is because of our goodness. Should we cease to be good we will soon cease to be great." Amos's word to Israel in 3:1–2 should stand as a warning against the self-deception that tempts us in such attitudes. Nations, denominations, or congregations can all begin to think of themselves as having claim on God for the special blessings of privilege.

When that happens, we run the risk of ignoring our own "iniquities," the places where we have opposed the righteousness and justice of God. We lose the power of self-examination in the blind faith that as God's people we can do no wrong.

When that happens, we regard those with fewer material blessings and more broken lives as less good or less deserving when they are the very "least of these" that Jesus and the prophets call us to give special care.

When that happens, we tend to substitute fulfillment and happiness for mission. We do not want to be reminded of those left out of the American dream. We do not want to be reminded of those left outside our congregational walls. We do not want a faith that offers both comfort and accountability.

Amos forces us to understand our identity as God's chosen people in a disturbing and challenging way.

Who Can but Prophesy (3:3–8)

3:3 **Do two walk together**
    unless they have made an appointment?
  4 **Does a lion roar in the forest,**
    when it has no prey?
Does a young lion cry out from its den,
    if it has caught nothing?
  5 **Does a bird fall into a snare on the earth,**
    when there is no trap for it?
Does a snare spring up from the ground,
    when it has taken nothing?
  6 **Is a trumpet blown in a city,**
    and the people are not afraid?
Does disaster befall a city,
    unless the LORD has done it?
  7 **Surely the Lord GOD does nothing,**
    without revealing his secret
    to his servants the prophets.
  8 **The lion has roared;**
    who will not fear?
The Lord GOD has spoken;
    who can but prophesy?

Those who heard Amos preach in Bethel not only would have taken offense at what he said but also surely would have challenged his right to speak at all. "Who are you to say these things?" In this oracle, Amos justifies his speaking by saying he is responding to the urgency of the divine call to prophesy.

This passage is an excellent example of the skill of Amos as a speaker and his ability to draw on a wide range of materials to serve his purposes. He draws his listeners in by a series of obvious and insignificant rhetorical questions. The listener is forced to make an obvious response to each question. Each question names an effect and asks if its cause is not apparent.

Would two people take a walk if they had not agreed to do so? Of course not! Would the lion in the forest or the young lion in the den roar if it had caught no prey to roar about? Of course not! Seven questions drawn from situations in nature or human affairs (vv. 3–6) force the listener or reader to conclude that the effect naturally and necessarily follows from the cause. Question six does reverse the order and name the cause first, followed by the effect: If a trumpet is blown (presumably a warning) will the people be without fear? Of course not! Still, the building effect is the growing conviction that some things are inevitable. In question seven (v. 6b) Amos begins to suggest that his rhetorical questions are leading somewhere. For the effect of disaster befalling a city Amos cites as obvious cause that the Lord has done it. Cities and their rise or fall are within the sovereignty of God over history. For Amos, as the oracles against the nations in chapters 1—2 make clear, the fall of cities has something to do with God's judgment and the moral failings of such cities.

In verses 7–8 Amos comes to the point of his sequence of questions. Each verse makes a climactic point that Amos wants to emphasize, verse 7 as a statement and verse 8 as a final pair of pointed cause-and-effect questions.

Those Who Dare to Speak for God

Verse 7 is a statement that interrupts the flow of questions that Amos asks. It is like a parenthetical statement, and perhaps Amos considered it the necessary preface to his final questions. It does reveal crucial understandings for Amos of the relationship between God and the prophets.

At first reading the statement is problematic. It says God does nothing without revealing it to "his servants the prophets." Surely this cannot be true. The activity of God encompasses all times and places. No human group, even the prophets, could know all that God does. Certainly prophetic pronouncements on the activity of God cover only a small portion of what we know and can imagine God is constantly doing in creation and history.

Part of the problem here lies in the ambiguities of language. The Hebrew term here can mean "thing" or "word." Thus, the phrase could be read "does not a thing" or "makes/establishes not a word." The phrase could indicate that God's word is always made known through the prophets. There are, of course, many things God is doing about which no human can fully know, but those events of divine activity that God desires be understood and made meaningful are established through God's word revealed to the prophets. James Ward says helpfully of this verse, "Not every act of God requires a prophet. But if an historical event is to be a *meaningful* act of God, it must be interpreted in the light of the prophetic faith" (Ward, *Thus Says the Lord*, 17).

God is constantly at work in human history whether we know or acknowledge this divine activity. If we are to recognize and understand what God is doing, there must be those who are open to the revealing of God's word and are then proclaiming it. Such prophets are as needed in our time as in that of Amos. This verse states the conviction that God will reveal the word to such prophets. It remains for the church to raise up those who will be open to the receiving of that word, who will dare to interpret the course of human events in light of that word, and who will challenge the church to respond to the address of that word. There must be those who dare to speak for God and take on the role of prophet.

Speaking for God Is a Scary, Fearful Thing

How are such prophetic speakers for God to be found? Verse 8 speaks to Amos's conviction that they are summoned by God—compelled to speak God's word, to prophesy. To the list of cause-and-effect questions Amos adds two final ones. When the lion roars, can we escape fear? Of course not! When the Lord speaks, can we do anything but prophesy? Of course not!

Amos uses the lion image first, and although he used lions as observations from nature earlier in this passage (v. 4), here he seems to use the lion as a metaphor for God. The book of Amos opened with the image of God as a roaring lion (see the discussion on 1:2). Coming between the statement of verse 7 and the question of verse 8b there can be little doubt that Amos gives us God as roaring lion again in verse 8a. God's speaking is a roaring and it strikes fear in the heart as surely as if we encountered a roaring lion in the wild. The word God reveals to the prophets is not without risk. To feel compelled to proclaim the roaring word of God is a fearful thing.

This is a difficult word for the church to hear. So many want God's word reduced to the safe and the comfortable. So many who would exercise leadership do not want to undertake the risky, fearful venture of prophetic speaking that Amos suggests here. We want a safe God. C. S. Lewis in *The Chronicles of Narnia* addressed this issue by making Aslan, the lion, his God/Christ character in the story. When Lucy is told of Aslan, she timidly asks:

"Is—is he a man?"

"Aslan a man!" said Mr. Beaver sternly. "Certainly not. I tell you he is the King of the wood and the son of the great Emperor-Beyond-the-Sea. Don't you know who is the King of Beasts? Aslan is a lion—*the* Lion, the great Lion."

"Ooh!" said Susan, "I'd thought he was a man. Is he—quite safe? I shall feel rather nervous about meeting a lion."

"That you will, dearie, and no mistake," said Mrs. Beaver, "if there's any-one who can appear before Aslan without their knees knocking, they're either braver than most or else just silly."

"Then he isn't safe?" said Lucy.

"Safe?" said Mr. Beaver. . . . "Who said anything about safe? 'Course he isn't safe. But he's good. He's the King, I tell you."

Amos's God is not safe and comfortable, but to hear God's speaking truly is to feel the urgent compulsion to prophesy—to proclaim God's roaring word (v. 8b). Amos says that God's speaking and the prophet's proclaiming are as obvious and inevitable in cause and effect as all the other examples he used in verses 3–6. If God speaks, then the prophet must prophesy.

Amos clearly numbers himself among those who must respond to God's speaking and who are compelled to prophesy. He sees his speaking as prophetic in character even though he later dissociates himself from the formal role or office of prophet (see discussion below on 7:14). He did not choose to be a prophet, but God's word chose him and he prophesied.

God's word is always urgent and compelling. But there is much in the life of the church that lacks any sense of urgency or any genuine conviction that our preaching and teaching make a crucial difference. One suspects that God's word is just as compelling today, but we do not always choose to hear it. It is easier to shut out and ignore what God is saying to us because if we allow ourselves to hear it we will be compelled by it. As the apostle Paul writes, " . . . an obligation is laid on me, and woe to me if I do not proclaim the gospel" (1 Cor. 9:16b). What might God be speaking to us about that we would rather not hear? What fears of risk are causing us to limit God's activity only to the safe and the comfortable? Does our speaking for God carry any urgency?

They Do Not Know How to Do Right (3:9–4:3)

3:9 **Proclaim to the strongholds in Ashdod,**
and to the strongholds in the land of Egypt,

and say, "Assemble yourselves on Mount Samaria,
    and see what great tumults are within it,
    and what oppressions are in its midst."
[10] They do not know how to do right, says the LORD,
    those who store up violence and robbery in their strongholds.
[11] Therefore thus says the Lord GOD:
An adversary shall surround the land,
    and strip you of your defense;
    and your strongholds shall be plundered.

[12] Thus says the LORD: As the shepherd rescues from the mouth of the lion
two legs, or a piece of an ear, so shall the people of Israel who live in Samaria
be rescued, with the corner of a couch and part of a bed.

[13] Hear, and testify against the house of Jacob,
    says the Lord GOD, the God of hosts:
[14] On the day I punish Israel for its transgressions,
    I will punish the altars of Bethel,
and the horns of the altar shall be cut off
    and fall to the ground.
[15] I will tear down the winter house as well as the summer house;
    and the houses of ivory shall perish,
    and the great houses shall come to an end,
                                        says the LORD.
4:1 Hear this word, you cows of Bashan
    who are on Mount Samaria,
who oppress the poor, who crush the needy,
    who say to their husbands, "Bring something to drink!"
[2] The Lord GOD has sworn by his holiness:
    the time is surely coming upon you,
when they shall take you away with hooks,
    even the last of you with fishhooks.
[3] Through breaches in the wall you shall leave,
    each one straight ahead;
    and you shall be flung out into Harmon,
                                        says the LORD.

This section of the book of Amos consists of four separate pieces that
in some way denounce the degenerate and immoral lifestyle of the
wealthy and privileged people of Samaria. They all suggest a contrast between that lifestyle and the moral demands that have been violated to
maintain a privileged way of life. They all describe God's coming judgment for violation of covenant. The form of this judgment is described

as defeat by a foreign power and the violence associated with such conquest. Despite these common themes, the four pieces are not connected in any organized literary fashion. It may be that the editors who collected Amos's words grouped these separate, unconnected pieces here because they have some common themes. It seems best to discuss each of the four pieces briefly and then to reflect on their word to Amos's time and to our own.

Violence and Robbery

In 3:9–11 Amos uses mockery and sarcasm to make a case for judgment against Samaria, the capital of the Northern Kingdom of Israel and the location of its greatest palaces and royal fortresses. He begins with a mocking invitation to each great empire before whom most of the ancient world trembled—Assyria (Ashdod) and Egypt (v. 9a). They are invited to come from their fortresses, presumably with their armies, and to assemble at the mountain on which Samaria stands. There they are to observe the "great tumults" and the "oppressions" that mark the life of this capital city. The phrase "great tumults" translates a term associated with the terrors of war when panic and confusion reign (for example, Deut. 7:23; 1 Sam. 5:9). It suggests a situation in which no one is secure, safe, or at peace. Oppression grips the city, presumably in the form of the vulnerable exploited by the powerful in the many ways described elsewhere by Amos (compare 2:6–8; 8:4–6). Both Assyria and Egypt are known for their harsh treatment of enemies, but the implication is that even they will be shocked by what they find in Samaria.

Verse 10 combines moral pronouncement with sarcasm to telling effect. Amos announces a verdict on what has gone wrong. The people of Samaria have lost their sense of moral direction. "They do not know how to do right" (v. 10a). What a shocking indictment. They have strayed so far from God's covenant norms that the knowledge of right itself has been lost. The result is summed up in Amos's sarcastic pronouncement that the strongholds (fortress/storehouses) of Samaria are filled not with treasures and supplies but with violence and robbery. Violence implies crimes against persons and robbery implies crimes against property. The implication may be that the wealth of Samaria is at the cost of such exploitation of persons and economic goods. Clearly Amos sees such exploitation as the natural outcome of the previously mentioned moral confusion.

Judgment

Verse 11 begins with a traditional formula for announcing God's judgment, "Therefore thus says the Lord GOD." The form judgment takes in this pronouncement is conquest by an enemy, presumably either Assyria or Egypt who have been invited to come to Samaria (v. 9). The three phrases of this verse make a comprehensive description of the fate that awaits conquered peoples. Their land will be occupied; their cities and fortresses will be destroyed; they will be plundered of their wealth. Land, cities, and possessions will be lost. Such a violent end seems to match the abuse and violence of Samaria's life.

Verse 12 is a brief word picture that furthers the description of Samaria's violent end. It seems to be only a fragment of a speech and is surely placed here because of the description in verse 11 of judgment on Samaria by conquest. Amos first describes the bleak picture of a shepherd trying to rescue a sheep of the flock from a ravaging lion and succeeding only in the saving of torn body parts. It is surely not insignificant that Amos chooses the metaphor of the ravaging lion since he has twice before described God as a roaring lion (1:2; 3:8). The prophet then says straightforwardly that this is what will happen with the inhabitants of Samaria. All that will be left of their former wealth and possessions will be broken fragments—the corner of a couch, a part of a bed. Whereas the common population sat and slept on mats, the wealthy could afford opulent furnishings. But the day of judgment will bring a bleak picture with the rescue of torn remnants representing no hope of rescue at all.

Transgressions

Courtroom language opens the oracle in 3:13–15: "Hear, and testify against. . . . " In verses 14–15 the prophet then speaks directly for God using the first person, "On the day I punish Israel for its transgressions. . . . " It is God's own testimony in a covenant lawsuit. In this passage it seems more the rendering of God's verdict on Israel than the citing of evidence against it.

Amos uses two significant titles in the opening of this brief speech, one for Israel and one for God. Israel is cited as the "house of Jacob." Jacob was the ancestor identified particularly with the Northern Kingdom. He was the first to bear the name Israel and is one of the ancestors to whom God's promise is given before Israel ever became a people (see especially

Gen. 28:10–22; 32:22–32). To use this title is to focus on Israel as community in relation to God, not on Israel as political kingdom. It is to remind Israel of identity based in faith story, not identity formed by wealth and power. In ominous contrast God is identified as "the Lord GOD, the God of hosts" (or "the Lord, Yahweh, the God of armies"). This is God, the warrior—the God whose heavenly armies will vanquish those who oppose God's righteousness and justice. In this oracle it becomes clear that this God will bring judgment even on "the house of Jacob" if Israel's transgressions place it among those who oppose God's purposes.

The verdict of judgment itself is pronounced directly in the voice of God against Israel's cult (its institutions and practices of worship, v. 14) and against Israel's wealth (v. 15). The transgressions of Israel are left unspecified here, although they are amply identified elsewhere in Amos.

God's punishment for these transgressions is directed first at the "altars of Bethel." Bethel is the site of one of the Northern Kingdom's two royal sanctuaries, and these were presumably dedicated to the worship of Israel's covenant God, Yahweh. Amos later has a confrontation with Amaziah, the priest at Bethel, who ordered him to cease prophesying there (7:10–17). Some think the use of the plural "altars" indicates the practice of idolatry and the worship of multiple deities at Bethel. This is not certain. Amos says little about idolatry, but more often he charges the cult with hypocrisy and with indifference to the lack of justice and righteousness in the land (see comment on 5:21–24). In any case, Bethel clearly is not the center of covenant faithfulness that it should be. The horns of the altar are protrusions at the corners of the altar that serve two significant purposes. When an accused person grasps the horns of the altar, he can be granted asylum and mercy (Exod. 21:13–14; 1 Kings 1:50; 2:28). It was also where the blood of sacrifice was spilled to bring expiation of sin (Lev. 4:7; 16:18). For the horns of the altar to be cut off means that Israel can no longer obtain mercy or expiation. The religious life of Israel is under irrevocable judgment.

God's judgment will also be felt in the destruction of Israel's economic wealth. The great houses, the palaces and homes of the powerful and the influential, will be destroyed. "Winter house," "summer house," "houses of ivory," and "great houses"—all these testify to the ostentatious wealth that stood in stark contrast to the needs of the poor and the afflicted that Amos champions elsewhere (see 4:1 immediately following this passage). In the face of unmet human need, the palatial homes of the rich are only a sign of Israel's corruption and forgetting of covenant. The material possessions in which Israel took such pride will also perish in God's judgment.

Luxurious and Decadent Lifestyles

The theme of ostentatious and corrupt lifestyles continues in 4:1–3, but this time addressed to a particular group—the wealthy women of Samaria. With biting sarcasm, Amos addresses them as "cows of Bashan." Bashan is a region in Transjordan known for its fat, well-fed cattle. While it is true that ancient terms of flattery sometimes seem strange in our ears (many mention the endearments of the Song of Songs in connection with this passage), it is evident that Amos's purpose here is not flattery but sarcastic indictment. Amos intends to be rude. The high-born, well-bred women of Samaria with their luxurious and decadent lifestyles are addressed as fattened and pampered beasts.

Amos is not simply concerned with appearances, nor with the contrast of these rich women with the condition of the poor. Amos charges that their lifestyle has been purchased at the cost of direct oppression and exploitation of the poor and needy (v. 1). Their excesses have denied the possibility of enough for others. They may not do this directly since the last portion of verse 1 suggests that they goad their husbands into the indulgence of their every desire. But for Amos the effect is the same. Their luxuries have involved them and their husbands in unacceptable abuse of others.

The announcement of judgment in verses 2–3 begins with unusual solemnity. The Lord God swears an oath based on God's own holiness that the time of their judgment will come. The images for this judgment are those of captivity and exile. This completes the picture of conquest begun in verse 11. Land, cities, possessions, and now inhabitants are forfeit. The rich women of Samaria are led captive through the breaches in the walls, goaded ahead with hooks like the cows Amos likened them to.

It is not easy to hear harsh words such as these that Amos used to address the wealthy and the powerful of Samaria. We live in a prosperous nation by the world's standards, and the churches in which we worship are equally prosperous. The majority of citizens and members are comfortable in that prosperity and get most uncomfortable when national or denominational budget crises threaten to erode that comfortable lifestyle. We do not want to hear the words of Amos, and yet we are the very people he most urgently addresses.

Amos reminds us in these passages that there is a connection between moral behavior and historical well-being. As people of faith, we do not believe that history is simply the product of impersonal, secular forces. Our faith assumes with Amos that God is both sovereign and active in history.

God is pursuing the divine purposes of righteousness, justice, and peace, and to oppose these is to oppose God. Thus, there is no immunity, no privileged position apart from accountability to God.

The tendency, especially in the American cultural setting, is to believe that we make our own destiny, and we even romanticize the ruthless, powerful figures that seem to do so. We even like to think of our nation in a similar mold. We believe we have earned our wealth and the right to enjoy it. Of course, God's judgment does not operate in some simple retributive fashion. There is no immediate moral report card that triggers immediate rewards or punishments. Even Amos speaks in phrases that trust in God's ultimate timing, "the day will come . . ." or "on that day. . . ." But the message of Amos to us is that God will not let evil and iniquity go unchallenged. In God's own time, even those nations that seem most secure in their power will be held to account. In recent years, oppressive regimes that seemed impregnable and enduring in their power have fallen or been removed, for example, the apartheid system of South Africa, or the communist rulers of the Soviet Union and Eastern Europe. When nations act as if "they do not know how to do right," then the seeds of God's judgment are already sown. The question for us is whether we will be numbered among those who suffer such moral amnesia.

The measure of our moral life as a people, according to Amos, can be seen in the welfare of the poor and the needy, those who for any reason are vulnerable and easily abused or exploited. We tend to celebrate our successes and give them moral valuations. But what of those who are somehow left out of the American dream? The words of Amos sound ominous in our ears when we consider some realities of our life. The number of families below the poverty line and the number of homeless persons on the street are growing not shrinking. These poor in our midst are disproportionately African American and Hispanic, women and children. Violence grips our cities and has invaded the countryside. Gun-related deaths are at an all-time high. Public schools are installing metal detectors. The extensive savings and loan frauds have been called the most widespread instance of public robbery in the nation's history. Many will not recover their funds. Political campaigns are waged on the comparative indictment records of officials in rival parties. Have we become "those who stored up violence and robbery in their strongholds" (3:10), or those "who oppress the poor, who crush the needy" (4:16)?

Amos also makes clear that God's judgment is not only for those who actively exploit the weak and the powerless but also for those whose luxurious and self-centered lifestyle is without regard for the contrast between their well-being and the suffering of the dispossessed. We live in a culture dominated by the promotion of conspicuous consumption of goods. We are a consumer society that holds up wealth and luxury as an appropriate life goal. Amos tells us that in the face of poverty and injustice such an unexamined lifestyle is itself an affront to God. Those who would be the covenant people must be among the first to see the connections between lifestyles of excess for some and denial of basic needs to others. The disparities are great in our society and they grow greater when viewed in global perspective. Amos will not allow us to use our economic well-being to insulate ourselves from responsibility.

Come to Bethel—and Transgress (4:4–5)

4:4 **Come to Bethel—and transgress;**
> **to Gilgal—and multiply transgression;**
bring your sacrifices every morning,
> **your tithes every three days;**
⁵bring a thank-offering of leavened bread,
> **and proclaim freewill offerings, publish them;**
for so you love to do, O people of Israel!
> > **says the Lord GOD.**

Amos turns his focus on Israel's religious life and does so in his usual attention-getting way. His speech is a parody of an invitation to worship. It is probably modeled on liturgical patterns known to his listeners, much like the call to worship that begins the service in so many of our churches. One can imagine Amos dramatically positioning himself near the entrance to one of the important sanctuaries of Israel and piously calling out to the approaching worshipers and others passing by, "Come to Bethel . . . ," "Come to Gilgal . . ." (4:4). Bethel was one of the two royal sanctuaries established for the Northern Kingdom by Jeroboam I (1 Kings 12:28–32). It was a shrine with a long history as a holy place associated with their ancestor Jacob (Gen. 28:10–22). The name Bethel itself means "house of God." Gilgal is also a holy place with a long tradition. It was associated with Israel's entry into the land (Joshua 4—5) and the first king, Saul, was anointed there (1 Sam. 11:14–15). The summons to worship at these holy places would have been welcomed.

Then comes the shock. Amos calls them to Bethel and Gilgal not for worship but for transgression. Can you imagine the shock of someone who approached you to say, "I'd like to invite you to our church for some sin!" We might be appalled but they would have our attention. Amos suggests that what passes for pious religious activity at these holy places only amounts to transgression. The word translated here as transgression is used elsewhere in connection with the most blatant forms of rebellion against God. Those who have come bringing sacrifices to seek peace and communion with God are told that their worship accomplishes the opposite. It has become an obscenity before God. Their worship actually increases their alienation from God ("multiply transgression").

Why is this so? What does Amos mean? The prophet continues his mocking invitation with a listing of the sacrifices and offerings normally brought to the sanctuaries. He mentions "sacrifices." The term here refers to any offering for which an animal is slaughtered. The most common sacrifice would be one in which the animal is killed and part of the offering is eaten in a meal of communion with God. On a pilgrimage to one of the shrines it would be customary to offer this on the first day. On the third day the worshiper would present the tithe, the offering of a tenth of the produce of the land to be brought to the sanctuary regularly. Bethel had an ancient connection with this practice through the ancestor Jacob (Gen. 28:22). These two are prescribed offerings required periodically for all Israelites, but even here Amos's words are a mocking parody. He invites his listeners to bring sacrifices *every* day, and their tithes *every* three days as if they were on constant religious pilgrimage to the holy places. Imagine the equivalent in our terms. To us an irreverent Amos might say, "Why don't you pious folk go to church and pay your pledge *every* day?"

Amos continues by naming the thank offering of leavened bread and freewill offerings. These are voluntary rather than prescribed offerings, the gifts above and beyond the necessary. And finally, in verse 5b, we begin to understand the objection Amos has to these religious acts of worship and devotion. They are not objectionable in themselves. They are objectionable because their purpose is the elevation of the worshiper not the honoring of God. "Punish them!" Amos cries, "For so you love to do!" Amos charges that Israel is not engaged in true worship because its purpose is only to enhance the people's reputation for piety. They do it for recognition and self-importance. The sacrifices and offerings have become ends in themselves rather than serving to glorify God. Ritual has become empty and hollow.

To engage in religious acts when the inward motivation is only self-promotion and public reputation for piety is to engage in rebellion. For such transgressions God's judgment is also directed against Israel's religious institutions, such as we have seen already in 3:14: "On the day I punish Israel for its transgressions, I will punish the altars of Bethel. . . . "

Hollow religious practice is not a temptation limited to Amos's day. It is routine for public officials to lace their speeches with pious rhetoric and appear publicly at churches and cathedrals for special occasions, and yet many have no discernible ongoing relationship with the church or its commitments. A noted pastor of a large church in a major city recently revealed that he copyrights his Sunday liturgies because people use these materials without giving proper recognition to his labors in writing them. Denominations exhibit more concern over membership statistics than evidence of faithfulness in mission and service. Many individuals seem to believe that church attendance and pledging financial resources are sufficient as the extent of the religious life. Obligation is often felt more to the congregation or denomination as institutions than to the praise and honor of God.

Amos has indicted both the religious practices and the moral behavior of Israel. He will soon tell us that these are connected (see especially 5:21–24). Ritual piety undertaken only for self-righteousness will inevitably contribute to the deadened morality of people whose practices of manipulation and exploitation suggest that they no longer "know how to do right" (3:10). Amos will have more to say to us about this connection.

You Did Not Return to Me (4:6–13)

4:6 I gave you cleanness of teeth in all your cities,
     and lack of bread in all your places,
   yet you did not return to me,

                              says the LORD.

   7 And I also withheld the rain from you
        when there were still three months to the harvest;
   I would send rain on one city,
        and send no rain on another city;
   one field would be rained upon,
        and the field on which it did not rain withered;
   8 so two or three towns wandered to one town
        to drink water, and were not satisfied;
   yet you did not return to me,

                              says the LORD.

   9 I struck you with blight and mildew;
        I laid waste your gardens and your vineyards;
        the locust devoured your fig trees and your olive trees;
   yet you did not return to me,

                              says the LORD.

[10] I sent among you a pestilence after the manner of Egypt;
    I killed your young men with the sword;
I carried away your horses;
    and I made the stench of your camp go up into your nostrils;
yet you did not return to me,
                           says the LORD.

[11] I overthrew some of you as when God overthrew Sodom and Gomorrah,
    and you were like a brand snatched from the fire;
yet you did not return to me,
                           says the LORD.

[12] Therefore this I will do to you, O Israel;
    because I will do this to you,
    prepare to meet your God, O Israel!

[13] For lo, the one who forms the mountains, creates the wind,
    reveals his thoughts to mortals,
makes the morning darkness,
    and treads on the heights of the earth—
    the LORD, the God of hosts, is his name!

This final portion of chapter 4 seems liturgical in character and consists of three parts: a litany with a recurring refrain (vv. 6–11), a declaration (v. 12), and a doxology (v. 13). Perhaps the sarcastic call to worship in verses 4–5 also goes with this section. At least the two pieces seem complementary in the present arrangement.

The litany of verses 6–11 is a list of failed warnings that have come to Israel from the Lord in the form of catastrophes. All represent common fears in the ancient world, but in each instance Amos claims that God has been active in these disastrous events to provide an opportunity for Israel's return to covenant obedience. The list of crises includes: famine (v. 6), drought (vv. 7–8), crop failure through disease or insects (v. 9), disease or pestilence followed by the devastation of war (v. 10), and finally an undefined but devastating calamity such as that which destroyed Sodom and Gomorrah (v. 11).

All these disasters are portrayed as hostile acts of the Lord. This is consistent with the covenant tradition on which Amos seems to draw. The solemn concluding of a covenant relationship between God and Israel entailed moral and religious obligations. When those obligations were carried out, blessing would ensue, but if the obligations are broken and ignored, then curses for the breach of covenant are invoked. Leviticus 26 and Deuteronomy 28 contain long lists of such curses for the breaking of covenant, and the list in Amos's litany is consistent with these catalogs of covenant curses. The covenant cannot be breached without consequences.

Amos earlier had made use of a recital of God's saving events (2:9–11; compare also 3:1) as a reminder of God's grace toward Israel. Now alongside that salvation recital Amos lays a kind of warning recital as a reminder that God the deliverer is also God the judge. Those who might have thought God was primarily to be found in the sanctuary in the context of religious ritual (see 4:4–5; 5:21–24) are reminded that God is Lord of all creation. The conclusion of this section with a doxology of praise to God as Creator serves to underline this. The earlier oracle against the nations (chaps. 1—2) reminded the hearers of Amos that their God was also the Lord of history. This litany in 4:6–11 serves to emphasize the understanding that Israel encounters God in the world as well as the sanctuary.

"Yet you did not return to me, says the LORD" (4:6b). With this refrain after the recitation of every disaster, Amos announces the people's failure to see crisis as an occasion for renewal of relationship to God. The covenant curses already have been actualized, but total disaster has not yet overtaken Israel. Yet the people continue unchanged in their ways. Relationship to the Lord is broken, but Israel has not taken the opportunities afforded for restoring that relationship. "To return" to the Lord would be to resume relationship with God as covenant partner. "To return" to the Lord would be to recognize the obligation to honor God by justice and righteousness in all life and not simply by sacrifice in the sanctuary (see 5:21–24).

In verse 12, the word "therefore" announces God's judgment, but it is not very specific in its declaration. "Thus I will do . . . , I will do this. . . ." Perhaps "thus" and "this" refer to further catastrophic events similar to those cataloged in the litany. Perhaps we are left to supply images of God's catastrophic judgment from other texts where Amos spoke of this in greater detail (for example, 2:13–16; 3:11, 14–15). One thing is made clear, however. A central element in Israel's coming judgment will be the Lord's direct appearance. It will be a theophany (a direct manifestation of God's presence). "Prepare to meet your God, O Israel" (12b). It is as if God is saying, "You would not return to me, so I will come to you." And God's coming will be in judgment.

Verse 13 is a brief doxology, a hymn in praise of the Lord. The God Israel will meet is the Creator. The verbs of this brief verse of praise are direct and powerful. God forms, creates, reveals, makes, and treads. All things are from this Creator God and answer to this divine reality. Who is this Creator God? "The LORD [Yahweh], the God of hosts [armies], is his name." The God of Israel whom they have rejected is Creator and commander of the heavenly armies whereby judgment against enemies may be executed. With Israel we should tremble at the prospect of meeting this God.

This passage in Amos raises an important and difficult question for us as modern persons of faith. Does God directly cause natural disasters to discipline or warn us? The outcry of protest a few years ago when a well-known televangelist claimed that the spread of the AIDS virus was a direct moral judgment of God on certain lifestyles shows that many Christians cannot hold the view that diseases, earthquakes, floods, and other natural disasters are direct punishments by God. Many Christians believe that such catastrophes claim many innocent victims. There are, of course, consequences to foolish and irresponsible acts such as exposing oneself to a disease or refusing to evacuate a dangerous location in the face of a hurricane or flood. But most Christians do not believe that disease, drought, war, tornado, or other natural disasters are themselves the intentional creation of God for our discipline.

In the ancient world, including Israel, all events were directly attributed to divine hands. It was a prescientific world with little concept of the laws of physics or the world of the microbe. Most Christians still believe that God as Creator and Sustainer is ultimately responsible for all things, but most no longer believe that God is intentionally creating each event. God is the ultimate cause of all things, but there are secondary causes as well. These secondary causes may or may not have to do with our moral behavior. The slipping of great cleavages in the earth's crust that caused the Los Angeles earthquake of 1993 was not a comment on the morality of Los Angeles. But the rise of crime and violence in our cities does have something to do with the lack of moral resolve to address effectively the causes of such violence.

But we do not need to share the conviction of Amos that natural disasters are direct divine interventions in order to take seriously his conviction that crises should be occasions of self-examination and renewal. We do have a choice about how we respond to the crises through which we experience brokenness. There are many whose experience of pain or loss spurs them to renewed commitment in relationship to God and altered priorities that flow from that renewal. Whole nations and peoples have been brought together in renewed moral commitment through national tragedies. The rapid passage of important civil rights legislation in the wake of the assassination of John F. Kennedy might be an example. If we have a different understanding of the complex causes for crisis events, we still share Amos's conviction that God is in the midst of these and cares about our response to them. On recent television coverage of the fiftieth anniversary of the invasion of Normandy in 1944 an interviewer asked a survivor of the costly landing if it had affected his life. The response was quick: "Anyone who lives through that experience and fails to reexamine his life is a fool!" Amos was no fool, but he thought many in Israel had been, and there are consequences then and now for such foolishness.

Special Note:
Doxology in Amos 4:13; 5:8–9; 9:5–6

Almost all scholars are agreed that the brief hymnlike texts in praise of God as Creator that are found in Amos 4:13; 5:8–9; and 9:5–6 are portions of a common hymn of praise (doxology). Whether they are the complete hymn or how the pieces originally fit together is impossible to determine, but the similarities are too great to deny some relationship. Each develops a strong theological statement affirming God as Creator of all things; each has a similar poetic structure; each concludes with the affirmation "The LORD [Yahweh] is his name."

Many scholars have argued that these hymn fragments interrupt the flow of the text where they presently stand and must be the editorial insertion of later hands. These scholars believe the creation theology reflected in the doxologies arose at a later time than that of Amos. The opinion on this matter has shifted somewhat in recent scholarly work on Amos. Some now argue that the creation theology reflected here need not be considered a later development and have defended the notion that these doxologies have been used here by Amos himself although he may have been using a well-known hymn for this purpose.

It seems best to consider these doxology texts as an important part of Amos's message. Nothing in their form or content argues definitively to the contrary. If these hymn texts are used by Amos himself, it would seem to serve as emphasis to texts where Amos is announcing a theophany (divine appearance) of judgment against Israel. The one who will appear to judge Israel is none other than the Creator of all things. Further, the context for this judgment, reinforced by testimony to God's power as Creator, is in all three instances related to criticism of the great sanctuaries and the hypocritical worship that takes place there (4:4–5; 5:5; 9:1). Amos seems to be suggesting that God is not limited to the sanctuary and therefore cannot be controlled by the sacrificial system practiced there. God is at work in all creation. It is this universal God who is the true focus of worship and not the religious rituals themselves (see 4:4–5 and 5:21–24). This makes the use of the doxology passages consistent with the larger effort of Amos constantly to refocus Israel's loyalty to God and relationship to God as covenant partner. In a modern climate in which institutional church program efforts are so elaborate and extensive, it may be well for us to listen carefully to Amos's use of these hymns to God the Creator. We, too, may often lose sight of God as the only true object of our worship. We, also, may have shifted loyalty to our programs and away from our God at the cost of focused covenant partnership in God's work of justice and righteousness in the world. We would do well to heed Amos's call to pause in our religious "business as usual" for the simple praise of God.

Seek the Lord and Live (5:1–17)

5:1 **Hear this word that I take up over you in lamentation, O house of Israel:**
     [2] **Fallen, no more to rise,**
        is maiden Israel;
     forsaken on her land,
        with no one to raise her up.
     [3] **For thus says the Lord GOD:**
     The city that marched out a thousand
        shall have a hundred left,
     and that which marched out a hundred
        shall have ten left.

     [4] **For thus says the LORD to the house of Israel:**
     Seek me and live;
     [5]   **but do not seek Bethel,**
     and do not enter into Gilgal
        or cross over to Beer-sheba;
     for Gilgal shall surely go into exile,
        and Bethel shall come to nothing.

     [6] **Seek the LORD and live,**
        or he will break out against the house of Joseph like fire,
        and it will devour Bethel, with no one to quench it.
     [7] **Ah, you that turn justice to wormwood,**
        and bring righteousness to the ground!

     [8] **The one who made the Pleiades and Orion,**
        and turns deep darkness into the morning,

and darkens the day into night,
who calls for the waters of the sea,
    and pours them out on the surface of the earth,
the LORD is his name,
9who makes destruction flash out against the strong,
    so that destruction comes upon the fortress.

10 They hate the one who reproves in the gate,
    and they abhor the one who speaks the truth.
11 Therefore because you trample on the poor
    and take from them levies of grain,
you have built houses of hewn stone,
    but you shall not live in them;
you have planted pleasant vineyards,
    but you shall not drink their wine.
12 For I know how many are your transgressions,
    and how great are your sins—
you who afflict the righteous, who take a bribe,
    and push aside the needy in the gate.
13 Therefore the prudent will keep silent in such a time;
    for it is an evil time.

14 Seek good and not evil,
    that you may live;
and so the LORD, the God of hosts, will be with you,
    just as you have said.
15 Hate evil and love good,
    and establish justice in the gate;
it may be that the LORD, the God of hosts,
    will be gracious to the remnant of Joseph.

16 Therefore thus says the LORD, the God of hosts, the Lord:
In all the squares there shall be wailing;
    and in all the streets they shall say, "Alas! alas!"
They shall call the farmers to mourning,
    and those skilled in lamentation, to wailing;
17 in all the vineyards there shall be wailing,
    for I will pass through the midst of you,
                     says the LORD.

This long section is made up of several speeches of Amos. They do not seem to be parts of one longer speech because they do not flow smoothly from one to another. They do seem arranged in an intentional pattern that gives impact to the message of this chapter. The arrangement is symmetrical and can be visualized as follows:

A. Lament over maiden Israel, verses 1–3
   B. Seek God and live, verses 4–6
      C. Announcement of sins, verse 7
         D. Doxology to God the Creator, verse 8a
            E. The LORD is his name, verse 8b
         D'. Doxology to God the destroyer, verse 9
      C. Announcement of sins, verses 10–13
   B'. Seek good and live, verses 14–15
A'. General lamentation over Israel, verses 16–17

This arrangement may be the work of those who collected and edited Amos's preaching, but it certainly reflects his concern to call Israel back to a central focus on God and away from practices that break covenant and sanctuaries that have become self-serving. The Lord stands at the center of this chapter and Amos's message. We must look more closely at several elements of this important section.

Amos's Lament over Israel

Imagine yourself sitting comfortably in your church pew on a Sunday morning as the preacher rises to begin the sermon. However, instead of giving a sermon, the preacher begins the keening wail of a funeral dirge. This is what Amos does here. Verses 2–3 are in the style and traditional poetic meter of a lament for the dead, the moaning chant of the mourners. Amos announces his lament over Israel as if Israel had already died, and he begins the dirge as if he is already present at the mourning ceremonies. He seems to say in this way that Israel's end is certain.

Israel is pictured by Amos as a young woman, collapsed and desolated on her own land with no help in sight (v. 2). Since his images of judgment and the ultimate fate of Israel have to do with military conquest, the image of a maiden is surely intended to convey powerlessness and vulnerability in the face of an enemy army. In his lament, Israel has already fallen. In verse 3 Amos also describes Israel's conscript army as already decimated. Only a tenth of those men who went out to meet the threat straggle back as survivors. Of fallen Israel, Amos makes a point of saying that there is "no one to raise her up" (v. 2b). It is the Lord who raises up those in trouble (1 Sam. 2:6–8; Hos. 6:2; Amos 9:11). Israel has turned from the

Lord, and this lament makes clear that the consequence is death. This sets up the prophet's poignant plea for the Lord in verse 4 (also v. 6), "Seek me and live."

There is an important shift of mood in this moving lament that would be easy to miss yet seems especially important to those who would speak a prophetic word in and to the modern church. We have seen Amos address those who have abused and exploited others, those who have manipulated religion for their own benefit, and he has often done so in harsh and sarcastic tones. But that is not the mood here. The traditional poetic form of the mourning song is an expression of genuine grief. Amos takes no delight in the death of Israel that he must announce. He cries out in grief and surely wishes it could be otherwise. One cannot help remembering the moving lament of Jesus near the time of his own passion, "Jerusalem, Jerusalem, the city that kills the prophets and stones those who are sent to it! How often have I desired to gather your children together as a hen gathers her brood under her wings, and you were not willing! See, your house is left to you, desolate" (Matt. 23:37–38). Too many of those who seek to speak prophetically in the life of our churches and our nation fall into the trap of self-righteousness. They become the "us" condemning the "them." The message frequently comes out glib and distant from those they address. Prophets like Amos, Jeremiah, and Jesus grieved over the words of judgment they pronounced because they were part of the communities they addressed and shared their brokenness. They spoke to that brokenness out of their own broken hearts. Amos's lament over fallen Israel is a cry of grief-stricken pain that does not compromise his confrontation with the sin and evil of his time. There is a lesson here for those who would address the sin and evil of our time.

Seek God and Live

In contrast to the portrait of Israel's death in verses 1–3, Amos announces a life-giving summons from the Lord (v. 4b): "Seek me and live," which is repeated in the third person in verse 6a, "Seek the Lord and live." In God is life rather than death. For the first time, Amos suggests that Israel has an alternative. This may not mean for him that judgment can be averted. He often announces God's judgment as certain in light of Israel's sin and recalcitrance. This exhortation may, however, hold out hope for life through and beyond judgment for those who seek the Lord.

What does it mean to "seek the Lord"? How do we do this? For Israelites this usually meant going to a sanctuary. The verb "seek" is often associated with going to the sanctuary, particularly in time of trouble or need, as a way of turning to the Lord (see Psalm 24:6; 27:8). The sanctuary was thought of as the place of access to God's presence. There the blessing of life that comes from God would be pronounced by the priest. (See Deuteronomy 30 for the association of life and blessing.) We are not so different in the modern church. It is often the case that families somewhat sporadic in their church attendance become suddenly regular in church attendance during times of trouble, illness, or loss. We also tend to associate the seeking of God with going to church.

But this is not what Amos has in mind. In his customarily abrupt way, he tells the people not to go to Bethel, or Gilgal, or Beersheba. Simply going to these holy places is not to "seek the Lord." We spoke of the long history of Bethel and Gilgal as holy places in our discussion of Amos 4:4–5. Beersheba is in the very southern portion of Judah, the Southern Kingdom, yet Amos suggests that pilgrims from Israel still go there, no doubt because Beersheba was associated with all three of the ancestors of the promise, Abraham, Isaac, and Jacob (Gen. 21:31–34; 26:23–33; 46:1–7). The context of this chapter suggests that Amos believes the sanctuaries have become ends in themselves, offering life in the name of the Lord that has little to do with the life demanded beyond the sanctuary for those who seek the Lord. Liturgies in the Psalms, such as Psalm 15 or 24, make clear that those who seek the Lord at the sanctuaries are called to a demanding life of covenant obedience beyond the sanctuary. Because the sanctuaries have become self-serving, Amos announces that they will perish: Gilgal to exile and Bethel to nothingness, devoured by fire (vv. 5b, 6b). The whole "house of Joseph" (Israel) is liable to a similar fate unless they seek the Lord and the true source of life rather than the sanctuary (v. 6a). This is a sobering thought for those in the modern church who associate life (success) with membership and church attendance figures rather than with faithfulness to God's call in the world.

If not by going to the sanctuary, how do we seek the Lord? In a related and parallel passage later in this chapter Amos tell us, "Seek good and not evil, that you may live" (v. 14a). To seek the Lord is to seek good and not evil. In fact, it is to "hate evil and love good" (v. 15a). Further, for Amos, to seek and love good is involved with justice: "establish justice in the gate" (v. 15a). We will speak further of justice and its connection with righteousness in the discussion of 5:7 and 5:24 below. Here, Amos echoes a theme taken up in a similar fashion by his slightly later contemporary, Isaiah: "Cease to do evil, learn to do good; seek justice, rescue the oppressed, defend the orphan, plead for the widow" (Isa. 1:17). It is the moral quality of Israel's life and not participation in sanctuary rituals that evidences the finding of the Lord and the gift of life that comes from the Lord (see further my discussion of 5:21–24).

Amos has been called the Bible's most thoroughgoing prophet of judgment, and it is true that he seldom speaks of hope. Yet, in these verses that call on Israel to seek the Lord and to seek good there is the promise of life (vv. 4, 6, 14). Even in the face of God's judgment, God continues to offer life to those who will claim it. Perhaps to some this seems a grim hope, for verse 15b suggests that it may be only a "remnant" who will claim the life the Lord offers. Perhaps only a few will survive the consequences that Israel's sin brings on the nation. Yet, even this suggests that God does not give up on the covenant people. Beyond God's judgment, God's power for life is still available. As we shall see, the note of hope is where the book of Amos ends (9:11–15).

Good Defined as Justice and Righteousness

This arrangement of short speeches by Amos also includes some more specific help in identifying the good we must love and the evil we must hate. The good is defined as justice and righteousness (5:7, 15; see also later 5:24; 6:12). The evil is identified through Amos's condemnation of numerous practices that break covenant and exploit the neighbor (5:10–13).

We have already discussed Amos's positive admonition to establish justice in the gate as a way of hating evil and loving good (v. 15a). In verse 7 he laments those who have turned justice into wormwood and cast righteousness to the ground. Wormwood is a plant known for its bitterness and it is often used as an image for the bitterness of trouble. Amos returns to a similar image in 6:12: "But you have turned justice into poison and the fruit of righteousness into wormwood."

The linked concepts of justice and righteousness are centrally important in the message of Amos (in addition to 5:7 and 6:12, Amos links the two in 5:24). Both terms are related to the covenant responsibilities that Israel has failed to observe, and each of the three texts in which Amos refers to this pair of concepts is in the context of condemning hypocritical worship that substitutes piety for the exercise of justice and righteousness.

The Hebrew word for *justice* refers to the claim of all persons to full and equitable participation in the structures and dealings of the community, and especially to equity in the legal system. It is by appeal to the principle of justice that one person can be judged to have wronged another, and it was often in the judicial process that this was determined and restitution or penalty was set. In Israelite towns, these judicial proceedings were often conducted in the gate, an entrance structure to a fortified town with rooms or recesses where public gatherings could be held. Here the men of the town gathered to hear cases where wrong was claimed. The system depends not on professional officers (judges or lawyers) but on the integrity of the citizens (perhaps like the notion of being tried before peers in our legal system). When Amos calls for Israel to "establish justice in the gate" (v. 15a), he is asking for an honest and equitable court system where those who are exploited and wronged can seek help. By the same token, his condemnation is harsh for those who "hate the one who reproves in the gate, and they abhor the one who speaks the truth" (v. 10). This speaks of those who seek to avoid and circumvent the jurisdiction of the courts, who resist truthful witness and fair adjudication of cases. Those who "trample on the poor and take from them levies of grain" (v. 11) exploit the poor and do not wish to be held accountable for their actions. Those "who afflict the righteous, who take a bribe, and push aside the needy in the gate" (v. 12b) are those who, as citizen-judges, are swayed in their opinions by bribes or as influential citizens seek to deny access to the judicial process. When the judicial process itself is corrupt, Amos suggests that prudent citizens simply keep quiet. They lose hope of justice. Such a time is indeed "an evil time" (v. 13).

It is out of righteousness that justice flows. Amos later says that justice is the "fruit of righteousness" (6:12). Righteousness is not the fulfillment of some list of rules or adherence to a set of standards. Righteousness is a relational term. It refers to the expectation in relationships that persons will, in their intentions and actions, seek the wholeness of the partner in that relationship. Thus, righteousness can refer to a relationship to God or any of the many human relationships that make up our lives. Doing justice is one of the ways in which we might seek to fulfill our obligation to righteousness in the relationships of neighbor, community, and nation.

Amos pairs these two concepts because they are closely interrelated as part of covenant faithfulness, and he pairs them in his context to confront Israel with denying justice and corrupting righteousness. Instead of covenant obedience, Israel has multiplied sin and transgression (v. 12a), but in God's judgment they will not enjoy the fruits of ill-gotten material gain (v. 11). In the end of this arrangement of short speeches, Amos again takes up the theme of lament for Israel (vv. 16–17). Now, however, we understand better the distortions in Israel's life that have brought it to this lamentable state.

To read this section of Amos's message (vv. 1–17) today forces us to apply the measures of justice and righteousness to our institutions, communities, and relationships. Do we operate with the concerns embodied in these concepts as central principles and commitments? Do we examine the extent to which our material comfort has been purchased at the expense of equitable distribution of economic resources? Are we concerned that study after study shows the judicial system of our land to be more accessible and more hospitable to the wealthy than to the poor? What would doing justice look like in our churches and communities? Who are being denied full participation and recognition? Who are being taken advantage of or manipulated for others' gain? How are we seeking wholeness in all our relationships to take seriously the call to righteousness? Are we willing to put the welfare of the other in relationship alongside or even above our own self-interest? Would this make a difference in parenting, marriages, friendships, electoral office, church boards and committees, international policies? Or does our idea of relationship to God simply entail going to church? Amos will return to these themes later in this chapter (vv. 21–24).

Is Not the Day of the Lord Darkness? (5:18–20)

5:18 **Alas for you who desire the day of the LORD!**
     Why do you want the day of the LORD?
   It is darkness, not light;
 ¹⁹   **as if someone fled from a lion, and was met by a bear;**
   or went into the house and rested a hand against the wall,
     and was bitten by a snake.
²⁰ **Is not the day of the LORD darkness, not light,**
     and gloom with no brightness in it?

Once again Amos reverses a popular idea in Israel and forces his listeners to think of that idea in a new way. The concept here is the day of the Lord (Yahweh). This is the earliest reference to the day of the Lord, but many later prophets refer to the concept (for example, Isa. 2:12; Jer. 46:10; Joel 1:15). Although its origins are unclear, the day of the Lord is a time expected in Israel's history when God will vanquish those who oppose the divine will in the world. It is an expected day of battle in which the natural assumption of most Israelites is that those to be defeated are their national enemies. This expectation was probably celebrated on particular feast days at the important cultic centers, such as Bethel. It seems likely that this oracle would have been preached by Amos to the gathering crowds on such an occasion, probably at Bethel. Amos turns the people's expectation completely upside-down. It would be much like standing at the annual July 4th celebration to catalog the ways in which the nation deserves condemnation rather than praise.

Amos opens with a series of questions. Why are you people looking forward to the day of the Lord? Then he makes a shocking statement. The day of the Lord is darkness, not light (v. 18). Light is associated in prophetic imagery with God's victory and the forces of divine power. Darkness is associated with the enemies God will vanquish. Amos says that Israel's experience will be on the darkness side of this cosmic conflict! They will be numbered among God's enemies! It is they whom God will arise to oppose! What a shock!

To underline this reversal that Amos announces, the prophet uses a striking sequence of images. The prophet pictures a man who escapes great dangers only to find himself fatally attacked after he thought he had reached safety (v. 19). He runs from a lion—only to meet a bear. He escapes the bear and relaxes in the safety of his own house—only to be bitten by a snake. The first encounters were dangerous. The last is fatal. Israel is like this man. They think they are safe. They think as God's people that they have been delivered, but they are in danger of God's own judgment. The danger comes in the very house where they complacently thought they were safe. Can it be that we too as readers of Amos are not as safely protected in relationship to God as we think we are? Have we made ourselves the enemies of what God is at work doing in the world? Amos ends with a question just as he began. Isn't the day of the Lord really darkness and gloom rather than light and brightness?

Why is this so? What has caused this reversal? We must look for explanation to verses 21–27. Scholars are divided on whether verses 18–20 go with verses 21–27 as a single piece, but in the present arrangement they are complementary in any case. Verses 21–27 make clear why Israel finds itself among the enemies of God.

Let Justice Roll Down (5:21–27)

5:21 **I hate, I despise your festivals,**
       and I take no delight in your solemn assemblies.
    ²² **Even though you offer me your burnt offerings and grain offerings,**
       I will not accept them;

and the offerings of well-being of your fatted animals
    I will not look upon.
²³ Take away from me the noise of your songs;
    I will not listen to the melody of your harps.
²⁴ But let justice roll down like waters,
    and righteousness like an everflowing stream.

²⁵ Did you bring to me sacrifices and offerings the forty years in the wilderness, O house of Israel? ²⁶ You shall take up Sakkuth your king, and Kaiwan your star-god, your images, which you made for yourselves; ²⁷therefore I will take you into exile beyond Damascus, says the LORD, whose name is the God of hosts.

Amos 5:21–24 is probably the best-known passage in the book of Amos and is thought by many to summarize the central core of Amos's message. Its theme of Israel's futile and unacceptable worship, contrasted with what God truly desires of Israel, is not new at this point in the book of Amos (see 4:4–5; 5:4–7), but this is the most comprehensive and striking statement of that theme. Verses 25–27 were probably a separate saying of Amos but have been placed here by the editor because it builds on the theme of 21–24.

God Despises Israel's Worship

God is the speaker in verses 21–24, and the harshness of the language used to describe the divine reaction to Israel's worship is stunning. "I hate, I despise . . . ," God begins. Stronger words could not be found. "Hate" implies total rejection and opposition; "despise" includes revulsion and disgust. The four verbs that follow in describing God's reaction are all negations of the usual verbs that describe God's positive response to Israel's sacrifices and praise: "I take no delight in . . ." (literally in Hebrew, "I do not like the smell of . . ."); "I will not accept . . . "; "I will not look . . . "; "I will not listen. . . ." Taken collectively, they represent the closing of a divine sense (smell, touch, sight, hearing) to Israel's religious practices. God has become numbed to Israel's efforts to draw God's regard toward them.

What are the objects of these harsh divine responses? It is the entire range of Israel's liturgical and devotional practice that draws such displeasure. Israel's worship and piety fell into three primary categories and all three are represented here. First, there were the festival observances (festivals, solemn assemblies, v. 21). These are associated with the pilgrimage feasts of Unleavened Bread, Weeks, and Booths (or Tabernacles). These feasts were held annually and required pilgrimage to the great worship centers such as Bethel. Second, there were the regular sacrifices and offerings in the rituals presided over by the priests at local shrines as well as at the great sanctuaries. These are represented in the catalog of God's rejection by burnt offerings, grain offerings, and offerings of well-being (peace offerings, v. 22). Finally there was the offering of praise in music, which could be part of sanctuary ritual but was not limited to formal gatherings at holy places (v. 23). Here the songs are described as "noise," and God refuses to listen to them. A very similar passage on the same theme in Isaiah includes God's rejection of personal prayer: "When you stretch out your hands, I will hide my eyes from you; even though you make many prayers, I will not listen" (Isa. 1:15). The final impression of the passage in Amos is that God has rejected the whole range of worship practices common in Israel. Traditional expressions of religious life in festival, sacrifice, offering, and praise do not impress God. In fact, God refuses them and is repulsed by them. The question left for Amos's hearers, and for us, is perhaps best expressed by the prophet Micah. He addresses this same theme and pictures Israel asking in exasperation, "With what shall I come before the LORD . . . ? Shall I come before him with burnt offerings, with calves a year old? Will the LORD be pleased with thousands of rams, with ten thousand rivers of oil? Shall I give my firstborn for my transgression . . . ?" (Mic. 6:6–7). Micah has an answer. "He has told you, O mortal, what is good; and what does the LORD require of you but to do justice, and to love kindness, and to walk humbly with your God?" (Mic. 6:8). In similar fashion, Amos, too, suggests that what God truly desires of Israel lies in the realm of morality rather than ritual.

What God Desires

Verse 24 is the climax of this passage and one of the best-known lines in all prophetic literature. Its images are powerful, but there have been two different ways of understanding these images. Some have argued that these are images of God's judgment. It is God's justice and righteousness that will overtake Israel like an overwhelming flood, ending the hypocrisy of Israel's worship. This does not seem convincing. Every other reference to justice and righteousness in Amos (5:7, 15; 6:12) has to do with what is expected of Israel in covenant relationship with God. It is far more likely that verse 24 represents God's alternative to the self-serving worship condemned in verses 21–23.

What God truly desires is justice and righteousness. The verse is a dramatic divine call to moral commitment rather than pious ritual. We have discussed justice and righteousness earlier in connection with 5:7 and 15. Amos is especially concerned with justice as the integrity of the judicial process in the gates, the guarantee of access to a forum where wrongs can be confronted and put right. He is concerned with righteousness as the regard due to God and neighbor in relationship, the concern for the welfare of the other. It is fulfillment of the moral demands of the covenant and not the ritual obligations that please God. This same contrast is a theme common to all the eighth-century prophets (Isa. 1:10–17; Hos. 6:6; Mic. 6:1–8). With them, Amos calls for attention to the quality of Israel's life and not the quantity of its sacrifices or praise.

Not only is Israel's life to be marked by justice and righteousness but justice and righteousness should also flow forth like the powerful torrents that sweep through following the rains. Yet, they should not fail as these floods quickly do but persist as an enduring stream. The images are of power and persistence. Justice and righteousness require no less than both these qualities. "Let justice roll down like waters, and righteousness like an everflowing stream" (v. 24).

Verses 25–27 are almost anticlimactic following the forceful poetry of verses 21–24. Verse 25 suggests that sacrifices and offerings were not necessary in the wilderness. No doubt there was some worship life even then, but perhaps Amos is thinking that in this early period of Israel's life there were no fixed sanctuaries with their control of ritual observance and their tendency to draw loyalty to themselves rather than God. In verse 26 there is a clear reference to idolatry although the exact details are obscure because the verse is difficult to translate. In general, Amos does not mention idolatry much. His problems with Israel's worship life have more to do with its separation from lives lived in obedience to covenant moral demands. His slightly later contemporary Hosea places a far greater emphasis on idolatry as a problem in Israel. Finally, verse 27 concludes with the threat of judgment in the form of exile, a theme we have seen previously in Amos (for example, 4:2–3).

What Makes Worship Authentic

Does this text mean that God finds all forms of worship inherently objectionable? Does God reject ritual piety in general? It must be admitted that Amos is quite sweeping in his indictment of Israel's worship, but in every instance it is coupled with Israel's failure to live as covenant obedient people. There is no critique of festival, sacrifice, or praise as such. It is the notion of these rituals as sufficient in and of themselves in order to establish relationship to God that is objectionable. It is also the notion of the sanctuaries as holy places in the center of Israel's religious life rather than God as the holy one in the center. The question for Amos is what makes worship authentic. If Israel's life were characterized by justice and righteousness, then the offerings and praises of Israel would be representative of whole lives offered to God. But without the context of a righteous and just life, Israel's worship becomes hollow, meaningless, and offensive to God. Amos would seem to stand in a tradition evidenced in the liturgical materials of the Psalms that tied authentic worship to the moral qualifications of the worshiper.

> O LORD, who may abide in your tent?
>   Who may dwell on your holy hill?
> Those who walk blamelessly, and do what is right,
>   and speak the truth from their heart;
> who do not slander with their tongue,
>   and do no evil to their friends,
>   nor take up a reproach against their neighbors;
> in whose eyes the wicked are despised,
>   but who honor those who fear the LORD;
> who stand by their oath even to their hurt;
> who do not lend money at interest,
>   and do not take a bribe against the innocent.
> Those who do these things shall never be moved.
>   (Psalm 15:1–5; see also Psalm 24:3–6)

The Relationship between Worship and Ethics

The question of authentic worship and its relationship to the moral life of the faith community that occupies Amos in this passage has been an issue of perennial concern in the history of the Christian church beginning with the ministry of Jesus himself. This was one of the central points of focus in his conflict with the Pharisees and others in authority.

"Not everyone who says to me, 'Lord, Lord,' will enter the kingdom of heaven, but only the one who does the will of my Father in heaven." (Matt. 7:21)

"Woe to you, scribes and Pharisees, hypocrites! For you tithe mint, dill, and cummin, and have neglected the weightier matters of the law: justice and mercy and faith. It is these you ought to have practiced without neglecting the others." (Matt. 23:23)

Throughout the centuries of church history, the relationship between the gathered institutional life of the church (especially its worship) and the ethical life of the church lived out in the world has been a matter of concern. One of the issues that led Martin Luther to break with the church in Rome was the degree to which the institutions of the church had become self-serving. The emphasis was on the church as a dispenser of salvation rather than on the church as a proclaimer of God's salvation already accomplished and available. The results were lives lived for the church rather than lives lived for God in the world. Centuries later, his namesake Martin Luther King, Jr. stirred the conscience of churches across the nation with his challenge to come out of comfortable pews where people sang of God's justice and to join in the effort to make justice a reality for all races in the fabric of the nation.

To read Amos 5:21–24 today is to be faced with this perennial issue in our own time. It challenges us as it has generations in the church before us. The challenge is to examine the integrity of our worship and the seriousness of our commitment to justice and righteousness as God's covenant people by the following:

1. *Reexamining Our Focus.* Too many congregations are too concerned with success as measured by church attendance and program participation. Too seldom is it asked how the church and its programs serve the saving and healing work God is doing in our broken world. Amos challenges us to move beyond the self-serving tendencies of our holy places.

2. *Promoting Integrity in Worship.* Is our worship truly focused on God? At the present time there is considerable discussion on the need to provide dynamic and creative worship experiences in order to reach new generations of potential believers. The danger is that the experience of worship can become an end in itself. We can end up attracting audiences and performers rather than believers and disciples. Amos challenges us to keep God at the center of our worship life so that our creativity in liturgy and music is directed to praise and not entertainment.

3. *Committing Ourselves to Justice and Righteousness.* The most dynamic worship experience imaginable becomes hollow and unacceptable to God if persons are not sent from the sanctuary empowered to live as God's covenant people in the world. Taught the meaning of commitment to justice and righteousness, church people are then challenged to embody it in their lives.

4. Serving All Believers. The life of the scattered church is to be honored and supported as fully as we do the life of the gathered church. So also the church is to act in ways that serve those in need rather than recruiting those who can serve the church's needs, making clear that the doing of justice and the living of righteousness mean serving the whole family of God's creation and not just fellow believers. Amos challenges us to "let justice roll down. . . . "

5. Decompartmentalizing. The compartmentalization of worship and ethics constantly reappears all too often in various guises: prayer versus social action; spirituality versus liberation; worship versus mission; identity versus involvement. These are all false dichotomies. Worship is only authentic if it is rooted in lives lived out of covenant partnership in God's enterprise in the world. Our efforts to seek justice and live out righteousness cannot be undertaken as individual ego trips cut off from sustenance and accountability in the community of God's people. The church is not a cafeteria line where some may legitimately select worship and others select social action. The inner and outer lives of the church must interrelate and nourish each other. Amos challenges us to hold praise and justice together in the constant partnership that gives each integrity before God. Praise without justice is hollow; justice without praise is rootless.

ALAS, FOR THOSE AT EASE IN ZION
Amos 6:1–14

6:1 **Alas for those who are at ease in Zion,**
 and for those who feel secure on Mount Samaria,
 the notables of the first of the nations,
  to whom the house of Israel resorts!
 ²**Cross over to Calneh, and see;**
  from there go to Hamath the great;
  then go down to Gath of the Philistines.
 Are you better than these kingdoms?
  Or is your territory greater than their territory,
 ³**O you that put far away the evil day,**
  and bring near a reign of violence?

 ⁴**Alas for those who lie on beds of ivory,**
  and lounge on their couches,

and eat lambs from the flock,
   and calves from the stall;
⁵who sing idle songs to the sound of the harp,
   and like David improvise on instruments of music;
⁶who drink wine from bowls,
   and anoint themselves with the finest oils,
   but are not grieved over the ruin of Joseph!
⁷Therefore they shall now be the first to go into exile,
   and the revelry of the loungers shall pass away.

⁸The Lord GOD has sworn by himself
   (says the LORD, the God of hosts):
I abhor the pride of Jacob
   and hate his strongholds;
   and I will deliver up the city and all that is in it.

⁹If ten people remain in one house, they shall die. ¹⁰And if a relative, one who burns the dead, shall take up the body to bring it out of the house, and shall say to someone in the innermost parts of the house, "Is anyone else with you?" the answer will come, "No." Then the relative shall say, "Hush! We must not mention the name of the LORD."
¹¹See, the LORD commands,
   and the great house shall be shattered to bits,
   and the little house to pieces.
¹²Do horses run on rocks?
   Does one plow the sea with oxen?
But you have turned justice into poison
   and the fruit of righteousness into wormwood—
¹³you who rejoice in Lo-debar,
   who say, "Have we not by our own strength
   taken Karnaim for ourselves?"
¹⁴Indeed, I am raising up against you a nation,
   O house of Israel, says the LORD, the God of hosts,
and they shall oppress you from Lebo-hamath
   to the Wadi Arabah.

This chapter consists of a very pointed oracle of indictment by Amos of those who enjoy the comforts of wealth while exhibiting arrogant indifference to the demands of justice and righteousness (vv. 1–7), followed by a miscellaneous collection of short sayings or fragments that in general elaborate God's judgment on these same arrogant upper classes (vv. 8–14). We will treat the opening major piece more fully and look only briefly at the several small pieces in the second half of the chapter.

A Lament for the Wealthy and Powerful (6:1–7)

In the time of Amos, the wealthy, ruling class probably felt as though they had never had it so good. The great powers in Egypt and Assyria were not very strong or assertive for the moment. Trade and commerce were thriving. Politically and economically, the rulers and the wealthy, upper class of Israel surely felt comfortable and in control of their destiny. Amos does not see this picture through the same eyes. In verses 1–7 he denounces their attitudes and lifestyle, first for pride and arrogance (vv. 1–3) and then for self-indulgence and indifference (vv. 4–6). He then announces God's judgment on these comfortable wealthy (v. 7).

Each part of this indictment is introduced by the lamenting cry "Alas!" (other translations have traditionally rendered this exclamation as "Woe!"). We saw Amos use this cry once before in 5:18, and it is probably associated with mourning for those named. Amos is crying in lament for the wealthy and powerful much as he sang a funeral dirge for Israel in 5:1–3. This must have been a surprise to the upper classes who surely thought they were more likely to be envied than lamented.

Israel and Judah Deluded by Pride and Arrogance

In verses 1–3 Amos pictures the ruling class of both Israel and Judah as arrogant, boastful, and supremely self-confident. Although somewhat unusual, Amos includes the privileged classes of both capitals, Jerusalem and Samaria, in his damaging picture. Amos speaks of those "who are at ease in Zion," and those "who feel secure on Mount Samaria" (v. 1a). These "notables" (v. 1b) can't imagine that they have anything to worry about. In fact, they think of themselves as the "first of the nations" (v. 1b). Verse 2 is their boastful claim to prominence. Calneh and Hamath are important city-states and trading centers to the north of Israel in northern Syria. Gath is one of the important Philistine cities. The boast here is that these prominent cities are no greater than Israel or Judah. (The reading of verse 2b suggested in the NRSV footnotes is the better reading here and is consistent with the Hebrew text for this verse: "Or is their territory greater than your territory?") These tiny kingdoms actually imagine that they are first in importance among the nations. With such a perspective it is no wonder they think the day of reckoning announced by Amos is "far away" (v. 3a), but Amos suggests that in such an attitude they are actually bringing the "reign of violence" near (v. 3b).

There is an absurdity to what Amos is describing here. In a recent World Cup soccer tournament hosted by the United States, the underdog team from a small country won a first-round game that was their nation's first victory ever in World Cup competition. Several players and then numerous fans in the stands took up the chant familiar at many sports contests, "We're number one! We're number one!" It was an absurdity when many more powerful teams were left in the competition and only one victory had been won, but it was an enthusiasm of the moment. Amos is dealing with the same kind of absurdity, but transferred to the deadlier realm of national illusions. It was an arrogant delusion to think that tiny Israel and Judah were the "first of the nations." Since only a few years later mighty Assyria would destroy Israel, it is clear how dangerous such a delusion can be. But history has shown the power of the temptation for nations in times of prosperity and well-being to imagine that they are number one, that they are first in all the things that matter. Amos's portrait of the "notables" stands as a reminder of the dangers of national pride, the desire to be first, to win, at all costs. In a documentary on the Vietnam War, an army colonel is asked whether he ever questioned the policies he was implementing. His chilling response was, "In war it is more important to win than to be right." Patriotism and national pride are not qualities to be rejected, but Amos suggests that they cannot be purchased at any cost. The desire to be "first of the nations" cannot be allowed to fuel an arrogant and blind self-confidence that renders us incapable as a nation of engaging in self-assessment, self-criticism, and genuine renewal. We cannot be blinded to the ways in which we might in our pride and arrogance "bring near a reign of violence."

Israel and Judah Consumed with Apathy and Indifference

Verses 4–7 have the same wealthy classes of the kingdom in view but the focus has shifted to their luxurious and excessive lifestyle and the indifference to social conditions that seems to accompany such self-indulgence. They are at leisure amid opulent furnishings (v. 4a), and eat meat regularly, which only the wealthy could afford (v. 4b). They amuse themselves with musical entertainment (v. 5), drink wine from bowls rather than drinking cups (v. 6a), and anoint themselves with costly oils or perfumes (v. 6a). The picture is one of conspicuous consumption for its day. It is a lifestyle of material well-being not available to all. It is a lifestyle of privilege and self-indulgence.

Is Amos condemning wealth and material well-being? Perhaps the description itself is pejorative in its portrayal of excess. But the real indictment here is that these privileged folk are so busy feeding their aesthetic and bodily desires that they "are not grieved over the ruin of Joseph!" (v. 6b). They do not care what is happening in Israel (Joseph). Elsewhere Amos has described social conditions in which the poor and weak are exploited, the law courts are corrupted, illegal business practices abound, worship has grown hypocritical, and justice is not honored. But these privileged folk have been insulated from these realities by their capacity to buy material well-being. It is their apathy and indifference that draws Amos's indictment. They simply don't care.

The judgment of God announced by Amos in verse 7 refers back to both the arrogance of verses 1–3 and the materialistic indifference of verses 4–6. Those who wanted to be first will get their wish. They will be the first to go into exile (v. 7a). Those who thought life could be an endless enjoyment will find that "the revelry of the loungers" cannot endure (v. 7b).

The important lesson Amos teaches in this passage is that indifference to injustice is as sinful in the eyes of God as active exploitation. The apathy of those who do not care allows the flourishing of evil and immorality. The materialistic lifestyle of the privileged creates the illusion that they are not affected by the brokenness of community. This is the same theme Jesus takes up in his teachings. In Matthew 25:31–46 he condemns those who stood idly by and did not feed the hungry, clothe the naked, visit the prisoner; who did not care for the "least of these." In Luke 16:19–31, Jesus tells the parable of a rich man who feasted every day and paid no heed to the poor beggar, Lazarus, who lay in need at his doorstep each day. The poor man is taken up into paradise and the rich man is condemned to Hades. The issue in each of these is not active exploitation but indifference to injustice and human need.

It is of particular importance that we hear Amos's message on this matter because we live in a nation and worship in churches that are among the most privileged in all human history. The cultural context of our lives is one of emphasis on material well-being. Material comfort is the most common measure of success in our society, and degree of success is usually measured by the extent of material resources we have beyond the meeting of basic human needs. It is easy in such a context to lose sight of priorities urged on us as God's covenant people. The requirement to love God and neighbor constantly urges us beyond the temptation to settle for self-fulfillment or self-indulgence. As God's people, we must "grieve over the ruin" of any whose lives are broken by injustice, exploitation, oppression, poverty, and need. We cannot afford to be "at ease in Washington" or any of our other towns or cities, bragging about our national accomplishments while ignoring areas of social brokenness. Amos's word is uncompromising. God's judgment will be as surely directed to those who stood by and did nothing as to those who actively perpetrated evil. God's wrath will be directed equally at churches who sought only the comfort of their own sanctuaries and the resourcing of their own programs without regard to the brokenness of the world to which they were sent.

God's Judgment on the
Upper Classes (6:8–14)

The last half of this chapter consists of short speeches, perhaps fragments in some cases, that in general serve to reinforce the imagery of judgment announced against the privileged classes in verses 1–7.

Verse 8 speaks of the pride of the Northern Kingdom and suggests that strongholds and cities will not provide security against God's wrath.

Verses 9–10 are difficult to understand fully. The images seem to be of a city sacked and destroyed with few survivors, and those that do survive fearful of mentioning the name of the Lord lest further judgment come upon them.

Verse 11 tells us that in the day of God's wrath great houses as well as small shall be destroyed.

Verse 12 uses rhetorical questions to make a point. The questions juxtapose absurd things. Of course horses do not run on rocks. Of course oxen do not plow the sea. This dramatically prepares the listener for the equal absurdity of Amos's next statement: Justice has been turned to poison and the fruit of righteousness (also a reference back to justice) into wormwood. Justice and righteousness, which should have been a source of hope for those in need, have now become deadly and bitter. That this should happen is as unthinkable as imagining that elephants can fly. We discussed the meaning of justice and righteousness in some detail in connection with Amos 5:7, 15, and 24. The text of 5:7 is a particularly close parallel to this verse.

The final verses of this chapter (13–14) again mock those in Israel who think by their own strength they can gain security. "Lo-debar" and "Karnaim" are towns in the trans-Jordan where Israel may have been successful in victories over the Aramaeans, a traditional enemy. Amos pictures Israel as boastful of these successes and sarcastically twists their boast. He mispronounces "Lo-debar" as "Lo-dabar," which means "no-thing." They boast over nothing! "Karnaim" means "horns" in Hebrew and is a common image for strength. Israel's boast is that by their own strength they have gained strength. But Amos's rejoinder to this boasting ("We are the masters of our fate") is that it is not so. Because they have corrupted justice and righteousness and made them into absurd things (v. 12) they are not at all secure—in spite of their strength. God is raising up a nation against them (v. 14a), and this nation will oppress Israel from one end of its territory to the other (Lebo-hamath to Arabah). Only a few years after Amos's preaching, the Assyrians destroyed and ended the Northern Kingdom of Israel. This no doubt convinced those who remembered and preserved Amos's words that it was Assyria Amos had in mind as the instrument of God's judgment in sayings such as this one.

THIS IS WHAT
THE LORD SHOWED ME
Amos 7:1–9; 8:1–3

7:1 This is what the Lord GOD showed me: he was forming locusts at the time the latter growth began to sprout (it was the latter growth after the king's mowings).
2 When they had finished eating the grass of the land, I said,
"O Lord GOD, forgive, I beg you!
How can Jacob stand?
He is so small!"
3 The LORD relented concerning this;
"It shall not be," said the LORD.

4 This is what the Lord GOD showed me: the Lord GOD was calling for a shower of fire, and it devoured the great deep and was eating up the land.
5 Then I said,
"O Lord GOD, cease, I beg you!
How can Jacob stand?
He is so small!"
6 The LORD relented concerning this;
"This also shall not be," said the Lord GOD.

7 This is what he showed me: the Lord was standing beside a wall built with a plumb line, with a plumb line in his hand. 8 And the LORD said to me, "Amos, what do you see?" And I said, "A plumb line." Then the Lord said,

"See, I am setting a plumb line
    in the midst of my people Israel;
    I will never again pass them by;
⁹ the high places of Isaac shall be made desolate,
    and the sanctuaries of Israel shall be laid waste,
    and I will rise against the house of Jeroboam with the sword."

8:1 This is what the Lord GOD showed me—a basket of summer fruit. ²He said, "Amos, what do you see?" And I said, "A basket of summer fruit." Then the LORD said to me,

"The end has come upon my people Israel;
    I will never again pass them by.
³ The songs of the temple shall become wailings in that day,"
                                    says the Lord GOD;
    "the dead bodies shall be many, cast out in every place. Be silent!"

Many prophets are associated with visions (for example, Isaiah 6; Ezekiel 1—2). They are not only speakers of God's word but also seers of God's vision, and these often dramatically shape the prophet's message. In his famous confrontation with Amos, Amaziah, the priest of Bethel, calls him a "seer" (7:12). It may be on the basis of the four visions reported in this passage (7:1–9; 8:1–3 and a fifth vision in 9:1–4 of a different type that we will discuss separately) that Amos was given this title. The visions certainly explain why Amos's message took some of its characteristic emphases and may represent Amos's own account of the beginnings of his ministry. Amos understood his role to grow out of an experience of direct revelation in which God's intention to judge Israel became unmistakable.

These visions are not, however, a peek into the private diary of Amos. The prophet may have experienced them privately, but he is now using them publicly as part of his proclamation. He recounts his visions as a way of claiming authority from God. He speaks not his word but God's. In fact, given the final outcome of the visions—the pronouncement of Israel's doom—Amos may have been eager to say that this outcome was not what he wished. In fact, he tried to intercede for Israel, but the final word is God's. We know that the account of the visions was part of the public ministry of Amos because the announcement of judgment against the house of Jeroboam attached to the third vision provokes an encounter with Amaziah the priest of Bethel. Because this confrontation is a direct response to Amos in 7:9, the narrative about this event is inserted between the third and fourth visions (7:10–17). We will discuss this narrative in the next section.

Amos Recounts Two Visions of Events (7:1–6)

Each vision opens by saying, "This is what the Lord GOD showed me. . . ." The language is of seeing, not of hearing the word of God. The first two visions are events that Amos is shown. In the first, a swarm of locusts devours the grass of the land (7:1–2). In the second, a great fire consumes the land (7:4), and even the great deep (the watery chaos out of which creation was begun, Gen. 1:2). Both of these events were catastrophic events that were feared by all ancient peoples and could wreak unprecedented devastation on whole populations. The locusts are swarms of insects more like our grasshoppers, that occasionally formed into gigantic clouds of insects that ate everything in their path. Nothing was left of vegetation on the land and it could even be dangerous to human life. Locusts are used elsewhere in the Bible as an image of God's wrath (Exod. 10:12–15; Joel 1; Amos 4:9). Uncontrolled fire, as in the second vision, could sweep unchecked across the landscape, particularly during the dry season, leaving nothing in its wake. We are reminded of the fire used as image of God's judgment in the oracles against the nations (Amos 1—2).

When Amos sees these visions of locusts and fire, he does not have to ask for interpretation. He immediately understands these events as images of judgment against Israel, events signaling Israel's destruction. His response is to intercede. Amos quickly moves to appeal to God's mercy and compassion. "O Lord GOD, forgive . . ." he implores after the locusts; "O Lord GOD, cease . . ." he pleads after the fire. The basis of his appeal is the weakness and insignificance of Israel: "How can Jacob stand? He is so small!" (7:2, 5). What an ironic statement this is in light of the pompous bragging that just preceded in 6:1–2 and 13. Amos sees correctly that in the larger scheme of things Israel is not great and important. He appeals to God's concern for the weak and the powerless, and says that Israel is really, for all its pomposity, only a small, weak nation. Amos here takes on the role of mediator. Whereas we often think of prophets speaking for God to the people, we are reminded here that prophets also speak for the people to God. Much like Moses in the wilderness, Amos finds that God has allowed him a vision of the true situation. Israel is in danger. He alone can attempt to stand in the breach and attempt to avert disaster.

Perhaps surprisingly, God does respond in mercy. Amos is successful as a mediator. One voice raised in appeal has been heard. God relents; the meaning here is "to change one's mind." Twice Amos intercedes, and twice God says the destruction shall not be (7:3, 6).

Do such visions of catastrophe still have meaning for us? We do not live in fear of locusts and fire in the same way as did ancient peoples. But we can still identify with images of catastrophe as judgment. Nevil Shute's novel *On the Beach* struck a responsive chord with millions of readers at the height of the cold war. It was a tale of nuclear apocalypse told from the perspective of temporary survivors in Australia waiting helplessly while clouds of radioactive particles left from a nuclear war gradually covered the earth. The image was one of judgment on the unthinking policies that could risk such a fate, and the story cried out for intercession in behalf of a humanity rendered pitifully small and helpless by the course of events. More recent scenarios of ecological disaster carry the same sense of potential catastrophe as judgment, and those who paint such scenarios are often attempting intercession, not with God, but with those who make policies that run dangerous risks. We may not see God as directly causing natural disasters in judgment of our covenant failures, but we still find meaning in thinking of God as one who holds us accountable for our failures to do justice and righteousness. God's judgment may still be seen and understood in the harmful and even disastrous consequences that come from self-indulgent and self-centered national life.

Amos's first two visions also tell us something important about the prophetic role. It is common to think of prophetic witness in the church in terms of confrontation and judgment only. In our popular conceptions, the prophet speaks against the sin of the people. Amos is reminding us that prophets also speak for the people. They are advocates and mediators for the people's needs before God. And equally important, the divine role is not fixed. God's compassion can be stirred by our prayers and appeals in behalf of human need. God is truly responsive; relationship is genuine and two way. Amos's visions tell us that even in the face of circumstances that call for judgment, God's predilection is to mercy and grace. God's wrath is a last resort not God's desired response. For those concerned with the issues of justice and righteousness in the human community, which are also so important to Amos, there is an important witness here. Our efforts to confront injustice must not be separated from our prayers for God's mercy in spite of injustice. Social action and prayer can and must go together because what we can do is then coupled with our appeal to what God's grace can do. My grandmother had a needlepoint sampler in her hallway that said "Prayer Changes Things." Amos suggests that one thing it might change is God's mind as God responds in compassion to our appeals.

Amos Recounts Two Visions
of Objects (7:7–9; 8:1–3)

The third and fourth visions are of a different type. In each vision Amos is shown an object rather than an event, and the object is associated with a key word for understanding the meaning of the vision. This type of vision is often difficult to understand in English translation because the meaning depends on words that have similar sounds in Hebrew—the key is a play on words.

In the third vision, Amos sees God standing by a wall holding a plumb line. Amos is asked what he sees and he responds, "A plumb line" (vv. 7–8a). Then the Lord must interpret to Amos the meaning of what he sees. This is not as obvious to him as in the first two visions. Verses 8b–9 are a short oracle based on the image of the vision. In recounting his vision Amos is also obviously proclaiming this oracle from the Lord to a wider public.

A plumb line is a cord with a weight (often lead) on one end. It enables the measurer to see if a wall is vertically true. Gravity will make the cord perpendicular to the ground, and when one end of the cord is held at the top of the wall, a clear visual judgment on the wall can be made. If the wall is not straight, the cord will hang out from the wall rather than along its side. The word used in this text is really the word for the lead weight on the end of the cord. Amos sees what he is intended to see, but he makes no other response than to name the object. Its meaning is not clear.

The Lord then says, "I am setting a plumb line in the midst of my people Israel . . ." (v. 8b). Israel is to be measured. When God says, "I will never again pass them by . . ." it is clear that Israel has not measured up. The time for relenting from judgment has passed. The phrase "my people," which God uses here for the first time in Amos, is a covenant phrase and suggests that covenant is the standard set in the midst of Israel by which this measurement has been made. Israel does not stand true by this measure. God's judgment becomes explicit in verse 9: The high places and the sanctuaries are to be destroyed, and the dynasty of Jeroboam II is to be ended. The religious and the political institutions of Israel are to bear the weight of God's wrath. The images of this judgment (made desolate, laid waste, with the sword) suggest judgment in the form of a conquering enemy. This is, of course, how the Northern Kingdom is ended at the hands of Assyria a few years later. Amos speaks no further. He does not intercede. God has held judgment back before, but no longer. In the face of the finality of God's pronounced judgment Amos is silent.

God's compassion and mercy are not without bounds, and without ultimate accountability covenant would have no meaning. Dietrich Bonhoeffer spoke of such nondemanding grace as "cheap grace." But covenant does ask much of those who would be God's people. God may in mercy give many opportunities for faithfulness, but ultimately we, like Israel, will be measured.

The plumb line is one of the best-known images from the prophet Amos. He is often depicted by artists carrying a plumb line, and the effect of this image has always been to imagine how we might measure up. Have we, like Israel, bent far from the path that God or even we ourselves intended? When and how do we experience our measuring moments?

One interesting thing about walls and plumb lines is that until the line is held up the eye cannot always tell the true character of the wall. In the school where I teach, a decision was made to add an elevator as part of renovations being done. An elevator shaft was constructed alongside the building. Bricklayers carefully laid each row of brick, but when it was finished, the elevator car could not be installed. The entire shaft was out of plumb. The measurements were carefully made from a beginning point that was not level. It looked straight but had to be demolished and rebuilt. This is part of the symbolism of Amos's vision as well. People, whether ancient Israel or ourselves, can easily fool ourselves and others into thinking things are all right. We look past or refuse to see the things that are out of line, not right. We extol the virtues and accomplishments of our families, communities, and nation, but we often think it disloyal to engage in critical examination of our problems and failures. It often takes a courageous, even discordant voice, to tell us things are not just as we hope or wish or delude ourselves in thinking they are. For Israel it was an Amos, wanting to intercede, but finally having to pronounce God's hard word of judgment. For us it might be a courageous preacher, or teacher, or politician, or citizen, but someone always has to tell us the truth eventually. Do we measure up to the standard or will we just pretend we do? We might remember the lesson of the well-known fable *The Emperor's New Clothes*. In the name of fashion and going along with the crowd, everyone, including the emperor, pretended that everything was all right and the emperor was wearing a fabulous set of new clothes, until a child cried, "He is wearing no clothes at all!" The truth had been told and could no longer be avoided.

When Amos told the truth and suggested that one consequence would be the fall of the royal dynasty, he was reported to the king, Jeroboam II, and confronted by Amaziah, the priest at Bethel. The account of this event is placed at this point in the book of Amos (7:10–17) interrupting the flow

of the four visions. We will look ahead to the fourth vision in 8:1–3 and
return to discuss the encounter with Amaziah in the next section.

In a fashion similar to the third vision, God shows Amos an object—a
basket of summer fruit—and asks Amos what he sees. Again Amos responds only by naming the object. The Lord speaks, again pronouncing a
divine word of judgment based on the image of the summer fruit. Amos
makes no attempt at intercession. The finality of God's judgment is clear,
and the time for God's mercy has passed.

The meaning attached to the image of a basket of summer fruit may operate at several levels. It may be intended to represent the offerings of first
fruits brought to the sanctuary at Bethel in thanksgiving for past gifts of
God and in the hope of blessing for future prosperity. But this image of
hope is turned on its head when God's pronouncement in verse 2b relates
the Hebrew word for summer fruit (*qayits*) to the similar appearing and
sounding Hebrew word for end (*qets*). "The *end* has come upon my people Israel." The play on words makes the summer fruit a visual reminder
of the coming destruction of Israel as God's judgment. The singing in the
temples will become the wails of lament; death will replace hope, and in
the end there will be only silence (v. 3). Perhaps the summer fruit is an apt
image for this coming end in another way. The fruit of the late summer is
attractive and delicious, but it does not last long. It spoils quickly, and fruit
that looks beautiful in the basket one day can be rotting the next. Perhaps
the image of Amos's vision suggests that Israel may think all is well, but
the nation is suffering moral decay within. The end is closer at hand than
appearances might suggest.

As with the third vision, we are reminded again that God's compassion
is not unlimited. Disregard for the covenant demands of justice and righteousness will not go forever ignored or without consequence. The image
of the summer fruit might be a particularly apt one for the church in our
American setting. The tendency to optimism and positive thinking that is
so strong in our culture affects both church and nation. We tend to extol
our virtues and successes while paying too little heed to signs of injustice
and failure of righteousness in our midst—those things that might suggest
all is not well and attention must be paid. Why is violence so prevalent in
our society, extending now in new and deadly ways even to children in our
schools? Why is the population of homeless people on the streets of our
cities growing rather than shrinking? Why have there been renewed and
seemingly more extensive outbursts of racial tensions and intolerance?
Why do important studies of our national life such as *Habits of the Heart*
suggest that the balance of individual and communitarian interests so im-

portant to our cultural experience is being thrown out of balance by the erosion of community commitments? Amos's shift in these four visions from intercession to acceptance of judgment suggests that there comes a time when excuses and mitigating circumstances are not enough, and we must face the tough questions that suggest all is not well. Such a message is one of difficulty and disruption. It will often be seen as negative thinking and doom-saying. But Amos's visions suggest that if we wait too long to examine the difficult and disruptive questions that focus on the problems of our church and societal life, we run the risk of being too late.

I AM NO PROPHET
Amos 7:10–17

7:10 Then Amaziah, the priest of Bethel, sent to King Jeroboam of Israel, saying, "Amos has conspired against you in the very center of the house of Israel; the land is not able to bear all his words. 11 For thus Amos has said,

'Jeroboam shall die by the sword,
    and Israel must go into exile
    away from his land.'"

12 And Amaziah said to Amos, "O seer, go, flee away to the land of Judah, earn your bread there, and prophesy there; 13 but never again prophesy at Bethel, for it is the king's sanctuary, and it is a temple of the kingdom."

14 Then Amos answered Amaziah, "I am no prophet, nor a prophet's son; but I am a herdsman, and a dresser of sycamore trees, 15 and the LORD took me from following the flock, and the LORD said to me, 'Go, prophesy to my people Israel.'

16 "Now therefore hear the word of the LORD.

You say, 'Do not prophesy against Israel,
    and do not preach against the house of Isaac.'

17 Therefore thus says the LORD:

'Your wife shall become a prostitute in the city,
    and your sons and your daughters shall fall by the sword,
    and your land shall be parceled out by line;
you yourself shall die in an unclean land,
    and Israel shall surely go into exile away from its land.'"

This passage is unique in the book of Amos. It is the only piece of narrative storytelling about the prophet Amos. Everything else in the book is the collected message of Amos. This passage is the account of a dramatic confrontation between Amos and the priest of Bethel, Amaziah. The drama of this encounter surely explains why the event was remembered and included in the collection of Amos's words.

This narrative falls into three distinct parts: Amaziah's charge against Amos, made to Jeroboam, the king (vv. 10–11); Amaziah's command to Amos (vv. 12–13); Amos's response to Amaziah (vv. 14–17). All of this took place at Bethel, which was one of the royal sanctuaries in Israel, the place where the king worshiped and particular national religious observances were held. It may be that Amos chose one of these festival occasions at Bethel for his preaching. From Amaziah's point of view, his preaching there is particularly unwelcome.

This episode has been of particular interest in the life of the church. It gives one of the clearest statements of a prophet's call from God to the vocation of prophetic ministry, and this statement is occasioned by a dramatic example of the threat prophetic preaching poses to established religious and political institutions. Both of these issues are worthy of ongoing reflection in the life of the church.

Amaziah Addresses Amos (7:10–13)

Although he is described only as "the priest of Bethel" it seems clear that Amaziah is the priest in charge of the shrine at Bethel. He has the king's ear, and clearly sees it as part of his duties to look out for the king's interests. After all, Bethel is "the king's sanctuary, and . . . a temple of the kingdom" (v. 13) as Amaziah reminds Amos in his rebuke to him. Amaziah serves as priest in Bethel at the pleasure of the king. National interest and religious interest are wedded in Israel.

In keeping with this close convergence of interests, Amaziah reports to Jeroboam, the king of Israel, that Amos is preaching treason and sedition against the king. "Amos has conspired against you . . . the land is not able to bear all his words" (v. 10). He then quotes a segment of Amos's preaching in which Jeroboam is condemned to die by the sword and Israel is to be taken into exile. This statement from Amos is very similar to the oracle of judgment attached to the vision of the plumb line in 7:9, which is why the editors have placed this story of confrontation with Amaziah in this place in the book. But Amaziah has either missed or intentionally distorted an important element of Amos's preaching. He reports to Jeroboam that these utterances come as the personal conspiracy and the personal utterances of Amos ("Amos has conspired . . . his words"). But Amos announced the fate of Jeroboam and Israel as God's judgment, not his own. Amaziah is either unable or unwilling to recognize the authority of God's word in the words of Amos. Perhaps he knows all too well what the granting of such authority to Amos's preaching might mean. In the Northern Kingdom of Israel, prophets have often announced the judgment and overthrow of kings. The words of prophets have often heralded rebellion and conflict leading to the end of kingships and dynasties (for example, 1 Kings 11:29–40; 19:15–18; 2 Kings 8:7–15; 9:1–13). When Amaziah reports, with some exasperation, that the "land is not able to bear all his words," he is not lamenting the loquaciousness of Amos. He is fearing that such words can indeed affect the political course of events in the land. The political and religious stability of the land is disturbed by such harsh and judgmental words. Therefore, they are judged treasonous, and Amos is held personally responsible no matter that he claims to speak God's word.

After reporting to Jeroboam, Amaziah turns to Amos and, in effect, tells him to go home! "Go back to Judah where you came from," he says. Many have felt that Amaziah treats Amos with some deference considering that he had just reported him to the king for treason. This may indicate the respect given to the role of prophet in ancient Israel even when tension and conflict arose. Amaziah may be reluctant to be too harsh with one who speaks in the name of God even if he felt his words to be seditious. He begins with some reticence by addressing Amos as "seer" (v. 12), a term used as an interchangeable alternative to the term "prophet" in ancient Israel. Many prophets were "seers" of visions as well as proclaimers of God's word, and the use of this title indicates a measure of respect. In urging Amos to go back to Judah to earn his keep, Amaziah certainly was trying to rid Bethel of a problem, but he may also be intending to warn Amos that he has been reported and it is dangerous to stay in Bethel. Although he reported what he considered treasonous words to Jeroboam, Amaziah does not confront Amos at all with objections to the content of his preaching. He just wants the problem of Amos's preaching removed from Bethel because Bethel is a royal shrine. His concern seems to be more with propriety than with truth.

Before even considering Amos's reply, we can reflect on the way in which this text reminds us of the ease with which religious institutions seek peace and harmony at the expense of truth. This may be particularly the case when the church has become the beneficiary of political and cultural privilege. It is not of small consequence that the framers of the American constitution and its Bill of Rights sought to prevent the establishment of any religion or its institutions. They knew that privileged position leads to intolerance of divergent views and willingness to compromise truth for the sake of maintaining that privileged status. Although the legal separation of church and state remains in place, there are many informal ways in which religious perspectives have become captive to particular political and cultural views. At the present time, some segments of the religious right refer to those with liberal political views as "pagan liberalism" suggesting that religious faithfulness requires a particular political allegiance.

When religious institutions like the church become privileged by those in political power, as in the time of Amaziah and Amos, the danger of being co-opted becomes great. It is hard to speak the truth to power when enjoying the privileges of power. Only a small segment of the church in Nazi Germany (the Confessing Church) avoided the temptation to remain silent to the abuses of the Third Reich while enjoying its privileges. When Martin Luther King, Jr. and other courageous leaders of the civil rights movement in the American South spoke the truth about racism, it was at the expense of their own security and disturbed the external peace and harmony of southern and later northern communities. Like Amos, civil rights leaders and workers were called outside agitators and told to go home. Like Amaziah, many churches and church leaders suggested that the peace and harmony of the status quo was more important than truth and justice. But in Amos's time and our own, the prophetic truth is that peace purchased at the price of injustice is no true peace. The violence beneath the surface of such a false peace will eventually exact judgment against co-opted political and religious institutions alike. That judgment is the judgment of God, and it is this divine judgment with which Amos must confront Amaziah.

Amos Responds to Amaziah
(7:14–17)

It may seem odd at first that Amos does not respond directly to Amaziah's order to leave town. Instead, he tells of his call to proclaim God's word. But Amos has clearly seen the issue in a way Amaziah has not. Amaziah is worried over what to do with Amos, but Amos sees that the deeper issue is what to do with the God whose word Amos speaks. To silence God's prophet is to silence God. Thus, the issue is not the place of Amos's speaking (Bethel or Judah?) but the authority by which Amos speaks. To address that deeper issue, Amos briefly tells the story of his call.

His opening response to Amaziah is one of the best-known and most enigmatic statements in prophetic literature. "I am no prophet, nor a prophet's son" (v. 14). What does Amos mean by this? He seems to refer to his activity as "prophesying" (3:8; 7:15). What is he if not a prophet? The clue to Amos's meaning probably lies in understanding the phrase "sons of the prophets." This was a phrase used to describe guilds of professional prophets such as those associated with Elijah and Elisha (1 Kings 20:35; 2 Kings 2:3–8; 4:1, 38). Members of such guilds seem to have functioned as prophets in a professional sense as an ongoing role, perhaps from early in their adult lives, and as members of a professional guild of prophets. It at least seems clear that Amos is dissociating himself from these professional groups of prophets.

In fact, he goes on to say that he was engaged in quite ordinary vocations from which God called him. He was a herdsman and a dresser of sycamore trees, but the Lord took him from the flock (v. 15). The word "herdsman" in Hebrew suggests cattle and the word "flock" suggests sheep (as does the reference in 1:1). In any case, Amos was involved in the management of livestock, probably not as a simple shepherd but as a manager or overseer of flocks. The tree translated as "sycamore" here is really a member of the mulberry family and to be a "dresser" of such trees probably involved some sort of husbandry, puncturing or pinching the fruit to enable it to develop more fully and sweetly. Both indicate an ordinary agrarian life, but Amos says God called him from this life and commanded him, "Go, prophesy to my people Israel." Here Amos obviously sees his activity as prophecy following God's command.

The phrase "I am no prophet" in verse 14 has no verb at all in Hebrew (literally "no-prophet-I"). The translator must supply the verb as understood from the context. Thus, the footnote in the NRSV translation suggests that this phrase could be rendered "I *was* no prophet, nor a prophet's son." This use of the past tense makes sense in light of verse 15. Amos is not refusing the designation of prophecy for his message. He is simply saying that he speaks not because he was already engaged in a professional prophetic role, but because God called him to that vocation from his previous occupation. He may be intentionally contrasting himself to Amaziah. His authority comes not by virtue of holding an institutional role or office, but directly from the command of God.

The implications of this passage have been perennially important in the life of the church. As an institution, the church has understandably sought to exercise appropriate judgment on the qualities and qualifications for leadership in the life of the church, particularly those who seek ordination as clergy. This witness by Amos is a constant, humbling reminder that calling and vocation are ultimately from God and not simply through our programs of candidacy and qualification. John Wesley faced harsh criticism for his decision to send lay preachers and superintendents of their work to the American colonies. He responded to his critics by saying,

"The preaching of God's word where it is clearly needed cannot wait on the councils of the Church of England." Clericalism has been a constant temptation and danger in the history of the church, and still manifests itself in patronizing attitudes toward the laity and the predominance of institutional rather than vocational concerns in the ordination process of many church bodies. Amos's testimony to his call reminds us that all persons are potential instruments of God's work in the world, and the call to participate in that work can and does come in unexpected times and circumstances. This is actually a very prominent biblical theme. The stories of Moses, Gideon, Saul, Isaiah, Jeremiah, Ezekiel, Jesus' disciples, and Paul testify to God's willingness to work through persons who might in others' eyes have been considered unlikely or unqualified.

Unfortunately for Amaziah, Amos had more to say. After reasserting the divine authority by which he spoke, Amos then pronounces a judgment on Amaziah for his attempt to silence God's prophet. The accusation against Amaziah in verse 16 is reminiscent of the charge against Israel in 2:11–12 that God had raised up prophets but the people had commanded them not to prophesy. Accusation is followed in verse 17 by judgment, and it is very harsh. Amaziah's wife shall become a prostitute, his children killed, his land taken, and he will himself be taken into exile. This should not be taken simply as Amos's personal vendetta against Amaziah. These harsh circumstances are consistent with the picture of judgment by foreign conquest so commonly evoked by Amos as the form of God's judgment on Israel. If such were to happen, Amaziah, as a high religious official, would be among the first to suffer this harsh fate. In effect, Amaziah has placed himself among the judged by his attempt to deny and silence God's prophetic warning through Amos. Amos makes clear the consequences. If we are horrified at the harshness of Amaziah's fate, is it enough to make us reluctant to silence the discordant voices that are sometimes raised to disrupt the concord of our churches? Is it enough to make us listen long enough to decide whether we too tend to purchase peace and harmony at the expense of truth?

YOU THAT TRAMPLE ON THE NEEDY
Amos 8:4–14

8:4 **Hear this, you that trample on the needy,**
and bring to ruin the poor of the land,
⁵**saying, "When will the new moon be over**

so that we may sell grain;
and the sabbath,
    so that we may offer wheat for sale?
We will make the ephah small and the shekel great,
    and practice deceit with false balances,
6buying the poor for silver
    and the needy for a pair of sandals,
    and selling the sweepings of the wheat."

7The LORD has sworn by the pride of Jacob:
Surely I will never forget any of their deeds.
8Shall not the land tremble on this account,
    and everyone mourn who lives in it,
and all of it rise like the Nile,
    and be tossed about and sink again, like the Nile of Egypt?

9On that day, says the Lord GOD,
    I will make the sun go down at noon,
    and darken the earth in broad daylight.
10 I will turn your feasts into mourning,
    and all your songs into lamentation;
I will bring sackcloth on all loins,
    and baldness on every head;
I will make it like the mourning for an only son,
    and the end of it like a bitter day.

11 The time is surely coming, says the Lord GOD,
    when I will send a famine on the land;
not a famine of bread, or a thirst for water,
    but of hearing the words of the LORD.
12 They shall wander from sea to sea,
    and from north to east;
they shall run to and fro, seeking the word of the LORD,
    but they shall not find it.

13 In that day the beautiful young women and the young men
    shall faint from thirst.
14 Those who swear by Ashimah of Samaria,
    and say, "As your god lives, O Dan,"
and, "As the way of Beer-sheba lives"—
    they shall fall, and never rise again.

In the first speech directed to Israel in the book of Amos, the prophet singles out exploitation of the poor as central among the reasons for God's judgment on Israel (2:6–7). He returned to that theme in 4:1–3, and now he takes it up again in this passage near the end of the book of Amos (8:4–6). In this indictment Amos adds new specificity to his charges. The business community is as corrupt as the courts (5:10–15). Amos follows the naming of these abuses with a long, multifaceted description of the consequences that God will exact of Israel in judgment (8:7–14).

Israel's Exploitation of the Poor

Amos focuses his charges in this passage (vv. 4–6) on the business community in the urban, trading centers of the Northern Kingdom of Israel. His perspective on these businessmen is not that of a neutral observer. His opening summons to listen ("Hear this . . .") already makes a moral judgment on those he addresses (". . . you that trample on the needy, and bring to ruin the poor of the land, . . ." v. 4). Exploitation of the "needy," the "poor," and the "afflicted" was already a major concern of Amos's preaching in 2:6–7 (also the "poor" and the "needy" in 4:1).

Behind the charges Amos levels in this passage lies a fundamental economic shift in Israel's life. The growing commercial life of the kingdom with its aggressive business practices has driven many Israelites off the land that was their family inheritance. An elite class of wealthy landowners and merchants arises while a growing number of Israelites are forced to sell their labor and buy basic goods from the commercial interests of the cities. Many of these Israelites live on the edge of poverty and need. They are the "poor of the land" (v. 4). Amos charges that the needs of these poor in Israel have been exploited ruthlessly and dishonestly. In fact, his choice of words may suggest that the wealthy are aiming to exterminate this lower economic class because the phrase "bring to ruin" means literally "to do away with."

Amos follows his general indictment in verse 4 with precise statements of oppressive attitudes and practices in Israel's business life (vv. 5–6). His first two charges deal with greed covered thinly with religious hypocrisy (v. 5a). These merchants scrupulously observe the sabbath and the new moon (the first day of the new cycle of the moon each month was also a religious day of rest; see Ezek. 46:1). No doubt they are prominent in religious observance, but beneath this religiosity they chafe at giving up a day of profits. They can hardly wait to resume their buying and selling.

Furthermore, their pious activities seem to have little effect on the moral quality of their business practices. They are the very people whose sacrifices and praise are unacceptable to God because they do nothing to embody justice and righteousness (5:21–24). Quite the opposite! The measure of volume (ephah) by which grain and other commodities is sold is made small, while the weight (shekel) for payment is made heavy, and the balance scales for weighing other goods are rigged (v. 5b). These practices are in outright defiance of the law requiring honest weights and measures (Deut. 25:13–16; Lev. 19:35–37). Such practices must have been widespread since other prophets of Amos's time also mention these deceitful business dealings (Hos. 12:7; Mic. 6:9–11).

These dishonest merchants then have the audacity to sell into servitude those who fall into the slightest debt (v. 6a). For no more than the worth of a pair of sandals a poor man or woman can lose freedom (see the same charge in v. 2:6b). Finally, these same unscrupulous merchants sweep up the chaff left from the threshing of the grain and sell it for a profit, although it is worth little as food (v. 6b). They may mix this in with good grain to dilute and stretch their goods dishonestly or they may sell it outright to the desperately poor who can afford no better quality food.

Reading about such flagrant abuses in the Israel of Amos can, of course, remind us that the poor are most vulnerable to abuse in our time as well. Misleading bait-and-switch advertising, high-pressure sales tactics, misrepresentation of inferior goods, loans made at exorbitant rates, complex credit schemes for purchase of high-price goods, high prices for doing business in the inner city, redline real estate practices—all these practices and more find a disproportionate majority of their targeted population among our society's poorest families. In addition, public financing practices such as lotteries and sales taxes are largely put in place with the political support of the well-to-do and the influential while the economic burden of these falls most heavily on the lowest levels of income. By contrast white-collar fraud on income tax returns (especially those returns filed by computer) has reached record levels. Such continuing practices truly "bring to ruin the poor of the land."

Behind and beneath the issues of economic exploitation, however, lies an issue fundamental to faith communities in any age—those of Amos's time or our own. It is the issue of correspondence between the practice of religion and the practice of our lives. We have frequently heard the clichés: we should practice what we preach; we should not be Sunday-only Christians. But the clichés arise because this matter lies so close to the heart of the matter in determining the integrity of our faith. It is so easy to substitute attention to the institutions, rituals, observances, and trappings of religion for the necessary living of one's faith through every moment of daily life. The dishonest businessmen of Amos 8:4–6 are probably pious, religiously respectable men. So too, in our time, were most of the men and women implicated in the Watergate scandal, the savings and loan frauds, the Iran-Contra scheme, the Bakker televangelism organization. But apart from headline-grabbing cases, the degree to which ordinary church people compartmentalize their piety away from the practice of their daily lives is a scandal. We live in a society that is at the same time one of the world's most overtly religious nations (measured by church membership and professed belief in God), and one of the most individualistic and materialistic nations in the world. This nation of church members makes best-sellers out of books with titles like *Looking Out for Number One*. Robert Bellah and his team of sociologists did an extensive study of American values (*Habits of the Heart*) in which they concluded that the necessary balance between individual goals or values and communitarian goals or values was going out of balance from the erosion of communitarian interests and commitments. In too many congregations and church judicatories the measure of success is seen in terms of membership, attendance, financial giving to the church, attractive facilities, and internal church program rather than in mission, outreach, justice ministries, or simple personal and social ethics. It remains a fundamental question for every generation: How much does our practice of religion make a difference in the practice of our lives?

The Coming Day of God's Judgment (8:7–14)

By this point in the book of Amos, we are not surprised that the prophet's indictment is followed by a strong statement of the divine judgment that comes as a consequence of continuously broken covenant. Verses 7–14 all deal in some way with the coming day of God's judgment. Many images here have been encountered earlier in Amos's preaching, but there are a few surprising and new images as well.

The statement of God's judgment in this chapter is made particularly strong and direct by the swearing of a divine oath ("The LORD has sworn by the pride of Jacob . . .") and a divine resolve to "never forget any of their deeds" (v. 7). The "pride of Jacob" has been thought by some to be a divine title, since God frequently swears by God's own divine self (4:2; 6:8), or to be a reference to what Israel (Jacob) was ideally intended to be as God's covenant partner.

What follows describes the experience of this coming divine judgment and some elements sound familiar from earlier passages in Amos. The language of mourning is used frequently as in 5:1–3, 16–17. Here Israel's mourning is contrasted to the celebration of festivals and the singing of songs in Israel's worship (v. 10a). Piety will be displaced by lamentation. None will escape mourning (v. 8a), and it will be as bitter as the lament for an only son (v. 10b). The death of an only son means the end of family name and inheritance; this is to be the fate of Israel. At several points coming human tragedy is mirrored in natural upheavals. The land will tremble (v. 8a), and it will rise and fall like the Nile (v. 8b, perhaps an earthquake?). The sun will darken in midday (v. 9, as in an eclipse of the sun?). These verses remind us of the natural tragedy through which God hoped Israel might turn back to God in 4:6–12. Now the moment of turning back seems past. Three times Amos uses phrases that remind us of his earlier words about the coming day of the Lord, which he understands as a day of God's judgment (5:18–20). "On that day . . ." (v. 9a), "The time is surely coming . . ." (v. 11a), and "In that day . . ." (v. 13a) all suggest that Amos continues to think in terms of a coming and inescapable day of reckoning for those who have placed themselves in opposition to God's purposes in the world. All these images are sobering reminders that God's patience with sin is not without limit.

Toward the end of this chapter comes a brief portrait of the coming day of God's judgment that is unique in the book of Amos. In verses 11–12 we are reminded that the consequences of sin are spiritual as well as physical and social. While Amos most often draws on images of national defeat and exile in describing the coming day of judgment, he pictures here a day of spiritual famine. He says that on that day God will send a famine, not of bread, and a thirst, not for water, "but of hearing the words of the LORD." No matter how strenuously they seek the word of the Lord they shall not find it. In Israel's time prophets not only volunteered the word of the Lord in their preaching but might also be entreated by individuals or even the nation through its representatives for the word of the Lord. The prophet then might respond with an oracle that addressed the need brought before God (for example, 2 Sam. 21:1; 1 Kings 22:5). Amos's oracle here is filled with irony. The people of Israel have not thought they needed God's word, perhaps not desired it or sought it. The word of the Lord preached to them by Amos has been rejected. He has been ordered to take his preaching elsewhere (7:12–13). When the day of judgment comes, many will seek the word of the Lord, but it will be too late. It will not be found. Sin leads not only to the experience of broken community but to brokenness of spirit as well. The word of the Lord cannot be simply turned on and off as crises rise and wane. Those who fail to hear God speaking in and through their lives day to day are unlikely to hear or recognize God's word for them in time of crisis. This is the tragedy observed so often by pastors who are suddenly sought out by families in crisis who have not previously taken their faith seriously. Such families often want and hope for spiritual resources suddenly available, when in reality they have spent little or no time building and nurturing such resources. They are likely to conclude that God has no word for them, when the truth is that God's word was available to them much earlier and cannot easily be found in the moment of crisis. For all the harshness of other images in Amos for God's judgment perhaps this is the saddest and most poignant. As a consequence of sin, we are separated from God's word as a source of life in the midst of our lives. We experience famine and thirst for the living bread and water that sustains the spirit.

The final verses of this chapter are difficult and enigmatic. The youth of Israel, its promise for the future, will faint from thirst (v. 13). But verse 14 concludes this chapter by saying that those who swear by the holy places or images of Samaria, Dan, and Beer-sheba shall perish. Is this a reference to idolatry in these places? The NRSV translators suggest that is so, at least for Samaria, by translating the phrase in verse 14a as "Ashimah of Samaria." Other translators render this phrase as the "shame/guilt of Samaria." Amos does not speak much of idolatry. He is more concerned with hypocrisy in worship and the inordinate trust placed in sanctuaries and holy places than with the god to be worshiped there (4:4; 5:4–5). We cannot resolve the technical issues of this verse, but one thing is clear. For Amos, these shrines were not places characterized by the authentic worship of Israel's covenant God. Whether God's true worship had been pushed out by idolatry or by the self-centeredness of the sanctuaries themselves matters little. Where God has been denied or pushed to the side, sinful and abusive practices, as mentioned in the beginning of this section of Amos (vv. 4–6), will thrive, and in the coming day of God's judgment such a community cannot endure.

ARE YOU NOT LIKE
THE ETHIOPIANS?
Amos 9:1–10

> 9:1 I saw the LORD standing beside the altar, and he said:
> Strike the capitals until the thresholds shake,
>   and shatter them on the heads of all the people;
> and those who are left I will kill with the sword;
>   not one of them shall flee away,

not one of them shall escape.

[2]Though they dig into Sheol,
  from there shall my hand take them;
though they climb up to heaven,
  from there I will bring them down.
[3]Though they hide themselves on the top of Carmel,
  from there I will search out and take them;
and though they hide from my sight at the bottom of the sea,
  there I will command the sea-serpent, and it shall bite them.
[4]And though they go into captivity in front of their enemies,
  there I will command the sword, and it shall kill them;
and I will fix my eyes on them
  for harm and not for good.

[5]The Lord, GOD of hosts,
he who touches the earth and it melts,
  and all who live in it mourn,
and all of it rises like the Nile,
  and sinks again, like the Nile of Egypt;
[6]who builds his upper chambers in the heavens,
  and founds his vault upon the earth;
who calls for the waters of the sea,
  and pours them out upon the surface of the earth—
the LORD is his name.

[7]Are you not like the Ethiopians to me,
  O people of Israel? says the LORD.
Did I not bring Israel up from the land of Egypt,
  and the Philistines from Caphtor and the Arameans from Kir?
[8]The eyes of the Lord GOD are upon the sinful kingdom,
  and I will destroy it from the face of the earth
  —except that I will not utterly destroy the house of Jacob,
                                        says the LORD.

[9]For lo, I will command,
  and shake the house of Israel among all the nations
as one shakes with a sieve,
  but no pebble shall fall to the ground.
[10]All the sinners of my people shall die by the sword,
  who say, "Evil shall not overtake or meet us."

The text of 9:1–10 is almost certainly not a single, unified composition. It is composed of at least four separate parts that were probably preached separately by Amos. However, there seems to be a pattern and relationship in their present arrangement by the editors of Amos's oracles. The first section (vv. 1–4) and the last section (verses 8–10; although verse 8 may belong with verse 7 as we will discuss below) make the finality and the completeness of God's judgment on Israel clear. The center of the section focuses on the nature of the God who does this: God is sovereign over both nature (vv. 5–6) and history (v. 7). The outline of the whole, therefore, is as follows:

> 1–4 Vision of God's final judgment on Israel—no escape
> 5–6 Testimony to God's radical sovereignty over nature
> 7 Testimony to God's radical sovereignty over history
> 8–10 Sinful among the nations will be separated and destroyed—even Israel

The time is past for detailing charges of sin against Israel. These texts are renderings of the verdict and are testimony to the divine authority by which judgment is given.

God's Judgment Is Clear
(9:1–4, 8–10)

Amos opens this oracle (vv. 1–4) as if he is reporting a vision, "I *saw* the LORD. . . ." It is not much like the visions recounted earlier by Amos (7:1–9; 8:1–3), however. Almost the entire text of these verses is a first-person address by the Lord, and the content does not seem dependent on any event or image that comes to Amos through the medium of a vision. It could have been reported simply as a "word" from the Lord. Perhaps the only real function of the verb indicating a vision is to allow Amos (and us as readers) an important place to visualize this word of final judgment. Amos saw the Lord "standing beside (or on) the altar." We are not told where this altar is located, although we might surmise it is the altar of the royal sanctuary in Bethel, which is the only place we know for certain that Amos preached. Perhaps it does not matter which altar. It is simply significant that the holy altar in the sanctuary where Israelites would expect to find the help and mercy of God is now the place for God's word of uncompromising judgment. Amos has been harsh in his condemnation of the sanctuaries of Israel as places of hypocrisy in light of Israel's sinful life. He has been clear that piety at the sanctuaries cannot save (4:4–5; 5:4–5, 21–24), and now the sanctuary altar has become the place for God's announcement of Israel's death.

Even after the many expressions of God's judgment on Israel by Amos the harshness of this passage is shocking. It is a divine sentence of death on the nation that will not even allow refugees or survivors. The key lines of this passage appear at the end of verses 1 and 4: "... not one of them shall escape" and "I will fix my eyes on them for harm and not for good." This is a shocking word from God at the altar of the sanctuary. The altar is precisely the place one would seek divine aid for escape and to ask there for God's eyes to fall on one is normally to seek blessing. This word of Amos is clear. In covenant terms the time of blessing is now forfeit to Israel's sin, and God now announces not the covenant blessing but the covenant curses.

The language of verse 1 at first sounds like an earthquake, pulling down pillars and thresholds on the heads of people, but it quickly shifts to the language of conquest and death by the sword, the most common image of judgment in Amos and the eventual fate of the Northern Kingdom. Perhaps even the first half of verse 1 refers to the razing of buildings in conquest.

Those who survive the initial onslaught will be hunted down and killed with the sword—no exceptions (v. 1b). Verses 2–4 then detail in poetic imagery all the places survivors might seek to hide from God's wrath, all to no avail. Sheol, heaven, mountaintop, sea bottom—there is no hiding place. Even captives will not survive their captivity. Israel will perish. This passage is made all the more shocking when we realize that we know another text very much like it. It is Psalm 139 with its testimony to God's constant but sustaining presence: "Where can I go from your spirit? Or where can I flee from your presence? If I ascend to heaven, you are there; if I make my bed in Sheol, you are there . . ." (Ps. 139:7–8). The psalmist celebrates the ability of God's grace to seek him out from birth to old age. How different is the picture in Amos. It is from God's wrath that there is no escape. Undoubtedly Amos is drawing on the same tradition reflected in Psalm 139. Perhaps he also knew that part of the psalm tradition that implores "O that you would kill the wicked, O God. . . . See if there is any wicked way in me . . ."(Ps. 139:19a, 24a). For Amos, Israel is now numbered among the wicked.

We do not like being reminded of God's wrath. It is very uncomfortable to hear God speak in such harsh and unrelenting tones. Must we include these elements in our portrait of God? We must remember that Amos does not suggest that God's wrath and judgment are capricious or unwarranted. Amos's God was disposed to relent (7:3, 6). God's harsh verdict comes only in relation to Amos's detailed accounting of Israel's sinful and cynical breaking of covenant, and after a demonstrated unwillingness to change these patterns. God is opposed to sin and evil in the world, even when it appears in God's people (see further on 9:8). It should be a hopeful thing that this is so. A well-known Nazi holocaust death camp survivor was often asked how he came out of that experience without being consumed by bitterness and hatred. He responded that, of course, there were times when bitterness welled up within him and he felt that he would like to devote his life to seeking out his surviving tormentors and exacting vengeance. But he said what allowed him to escape such bitterness was the knowledge that they could not escape the wrath and judgment of God. God is opposed to evil in the world and that freed him from believing that it was all up to him. We can take comfort from God's declaration, through Amos, that sin cannot hide itself from the opposition of a sovereign God. The sobering question that must accompany this thought is whether we have persistently broken covenant, and like Israel, numbered ourselves among the enemies of God.

God Sovereign over Nature (9:5–6)

In 9:5–6 we find another fragment of a hymn in praise of the Lord that seems related to 4:13 and 5:8–9, perhaps pieces from the same hymn (see our earlier discussion of these doxology passages on pp. 209–210). Each of these brief doxologies uses the refrain, "the LORD (Yahweh) is his name." Like the earlier passages in Amos, this one stresses God's sovereignty over nature. God both creates and controls the power inherent in nature. In 9:5–6 the stress is more on nature as testimony to the power of God than on God's creation of nature. The power of storms, the rise and fall of the Nile River, and the fearful movement of the earth itself (an earthquake?) are all evidences of the sovereign power of the God who is judging Israel. No wonder there is no escape from God's wrath when God is creator and controller of the whole created order of things.

God Sovereign over History (9:7)

The Lord sovereign over nature is also in control of all history. Verse 7 is probably one of the most startling and radical statements of God's reign over all history to be found in the Old Testament. It suggests that for Amos, the Lord is a universal God, and that God does not simply exercise moral judgment over the nations (as in 1:3–2:5), but is active in life-giving ways in the midst of the nations as well. In other words, God's story is larger than Israel's story. God's life-giving grace is not held as an exclusive possession by Israel.

Amos does not affirm this about God in the abstract. He states God's universal sovereignty in history through a set of boldly concrete affirmations about where God has been at work. These affirmations are made through a series of rhetorical questions that can only be answered in the affirmative. "Are you not like the Ethiopians to me, O people of Israel?" is the first of these such questions. The Hebrew text reads Cushites, which some translate as Ethiopians and others as Nubians. We know that Cush was a kingdom south of Egypt and that the people of this land were dark-skinned, but precise identification of the geographic area is difficult. Cush may have included the areas of both Nubia and Ethiopia. It is clear that Cushites were perceived as very different from Hebrews. Moses marries a Cushite woman to whom both Miriam and Aaron object (Num. 12:1). Other references suggest that Cushites were considered somewhat exotic and quite alien to Israel (for example, Jer. 13:23; 38:7). Amos boldly declares that a Cushite and an Israelite are alike in the eyes of God. Election of God's people Israel bestows no special privileged status in the regard of God.

To make this point absolutely clear God declares through Amos that Israel's deliverance from bondage in Egypt and their migration to the promised land is matched by God's work bringing the Philistines from Caphtor (probably Crete) and the Aramaeans from Kir (in Mesopotamia). The exodus experience is not unique. God is at work bringing new possibilities for life even in the histories of Israel's enemies. The Philistines and Aramaeans are traditional enemies of Israel and were named first in the oracles of judgment against the nations (1:3–5, Aram, and 1:6–8, Philistia). This is one of the most radical statements to be found in the Old Testament on the universality of God and of God's sovereignty over all history. God chose Israel not for privileged status but for obedience, responsibility. Israel had a mission as God's covenant people, but they did not gain exclusive access to God's grace as a result. This declaration by Amos suggests that God is constantly active in all human history, actualizing possibilities for life and wholeness. Israel was to honor this God as known through the exodus and Israel's own salvation history, but Israel could not possess this God or take relationship to God for granted.

This remarkable statement in Amos 9:7 is truly an affirmation of divine freedom. The God of Israel and our God will not be possessed or domesticated. The temptation of religious communities and nations, in Israel's time and our own, is to think that our relationship to God gives us some control over God. The temptation is to think that a covenant relationship somehow obligates God and places covenant people in privileged positions with God. But Amos tells us here that God is radically free and is active in the whole of history and not just our own. Israel's kings and people often tried to domesticate God through idolatry or nationalized religion. Amos and other prophetic voices say no! Some Jews of Jesus' time tried to control God through their righteousness and obedience to the law. The teachings of Jesus and Paul say no! Constantine made Christianity the official religion of the empire and countless "Christian nations" declared that God was on their side in one crusade or another. Many prophetic and reforming voices were raised through the history of the church to say no! God will not be possessed or domesticated, and a radically free God will constantly surprise us with unexpected contexts for the grace of God at work. In our own time, concern over civil religion, the appropriation of our faith symbols and God language for the purposes of the national interest, is but a reappearance of the same issue addressed by Amos. God will not be possessed by the American national interest, or any particular party or ideology. God is not "on our side." God is on the side of righteousness and justice, life and wholeness in all nature and history. There are no privileged positions. All are judged by faithfulness to God's purposes or sinful opposition to them.

The Sinful Will Be Separated and Destroyed (9:8)

Verse 8 may belong with 9:7. It states that the eyes of God are on the sinful nation and will destroy it. The implication is that this will be so even if the sinful nation is Israel or any other people who imagine themselves privileged in relationship to God. At least it would seem that verse 8 is placed here because it follows naturally from the declaration of verse 7. The last portion of the verse (8b) is probably to be understood as a later addition by Judean (Southern Kingdom) editors from the time of exile or later. They knew that although Judah had also suffered judgment for its sinful disobedience, a small remnant did return to rebuild Jerusalem and start again. They were not utterly destroyed and added their note to that effect as they passed on the text of Amos.

Verses 9–10 continue the theme of judgment even against God's people Israel by developing a metaphor for the thoroughness of God's sentence against Israel. Along with all the nations, Israel will be shaken in a sieve and no pebble will fall to the ground (v. 9). The image here is taken from agricultural life, as are many images in the book of Amos. Near the end of the process for threshing the grain, the kernels are swept up from the threshing floor and passed through a sieve. The mesh is fine enough to allow the edible kernels of grain to pass through but pebbles and other debris are trapped and discarded. Those who are the sinners in Israel will be trapped and destroyed by the sword as impurities among the nations. This shall be so in spite of the unwillingness of Israel to hear of this possibility. Those who say "Evil shall not overtake or meet us!" (v. 10b) will nevertheless perish. It is a sobering word to remember as we near the end of Amos. Amos is not an easy book to study. Its words are harsh and unwanted. We would rather disregard these possibilities of God's wrath and judgment. "That's not going to happen to us. Preach something positive and uplifting." In this last verse on judgment in the book of Amos, the prophet reminds us that God will judge the sinners in our midst whether we choose to consider it or not.

I WILL RESTORE THE FORTUNES
OF MY PEOPLE ISRAEL
Amos 9:11–15

9:11 On that day I will raise up
    the booth of David that is fallen,
  and repair its breaches,
    and raise up its ruins,
    and rebuild it as in the days of old;
12 in order that they may possess the remnant of Edom
    and all the nations who are called by my name,
    says the LORD who does this.

13 The time is surely coming, says the LORD,
    when the one who plows shall overtake the one who reaps,
    and the treader of grapes the one who sows the seed;
  the mountains shall drip sweet wine,
    and all the hills shall flow with it.
14 I will restore the fortunes of my people Israel,
    and they shall rebuild the ruined cities and inhabit them;
  they shall plant vineyards and drink their wine,
    and they shall make gardens and eat their fruit.
15 I will plant them upon their land,
    and they shall never again be plucked up
    out of the land that I have given them,
                says the LORD your God.

Unexpectedly, the book of Amos concludes with two oracles of promise in 9:11–12 and 9:13–15. They do not seem to be parts of a single piece and do not share any common characteristics except that they both promise restoration from God in a book that has relentlessly announced God's judgment and the end of the nation Israel. Each oracle of promise begins with a phrase associated with the announcement of God's future ("On that day . . ." v. 11, and "The time is surely coming . . ." v. 13), but in every other instance in the book of Amos that coming future is one of judgment and destruction (for example, 2:16; 8:3, 9, 13). These promises at this point are especially surprising in light of the strong message in the earlier verses of chapter 9 that "not one of them shall escape" (v. 1b). Has Amos changed his mind? Are these verses perhaps the addition of a later editor as many have suggested? We will have to raise these questions as we look more closely at each oracle in turn.

Restoration and Hope (9:11–12)

Verses 11–12 speak of restoration and hope. But whose restoration is promised? In verse 11 God says that "I will raise up the booth of David that is fallen. . . ." A booth is a frame structure covered by branches that was used in the observance of the Festival of Booths (or Tabernacles) to remember the booths that afforded shelter during the time Israel was in the wilderness. Booths were also used to shelter troops in the field and watchers over flocks or vineyards. Here "booth of David" is used as a metaphor for the kingdom of David or the city of David's reign, Jerusalem. The language that follows speaks in terms appropriate to the restoration and repair of a conquered and destroyed city. But in this text the city or kingdom is clearly fallen and will be restored in the future. The viewpoint seems to be after the destruction of Jerusalem at the time of the Babylonian exile in 587.

The following verse (12) seems to promise that the restored kingdom of David will extend to its fullest borders at the time of David ("all the nations who are called by my name") for the nations that were part of the Davidic kingdom at its height were all promised to David and his descendants in God's name (2 Samuel 7). Edom is singled out in particular for inclusion in this restored kingdom. This would seem again to fit well with the period of Babylonian exile when Edom had taken advantage of Judah's weakened state to plunder for its own gain. Judean bitterness was great toward Edom during and after the exile (Psalm 137:7; Lam. 4:21–22; Obad. 10–14). Shortly after Jerusalem's fall, Edom also experienced reversals as a nation, which may explain the reference to "the remnant of Edom."

Neither of these verses seems likely to have been a concern for Amos in his preaching to the Northern Kingdom, and neither verse would have made much sense to an eighth-century audience. It seems best to regard them as the addition of a Judean editor during or after the Babylonian exile. This does not, however, make them unimportant as part of our present book of Amos. On the contrary, those who preserved and cherished the words of Amos, handing them on as meaningful to later generations, knew something that Amos's hearers did not yet know for certain. Amos was right! The Northern Kingdom of Israel did perish, and it did not return. If God's people were to have a future, it would be with the restoration of Judah and Jerusalem. Yet, they too had tasted of God's judgment. They knew the sober reality of Amos's warning to those who disregarded God's covenant. This may be a reason they cherished and handed on his words. But if the Northern Kingdom had been totally extinguished, this was not yet true for Judah, and they dared put their own testimony to God's hopeful future alongside Amos's warning of God's judging future. Through other prophetic voices who came after Amos (Hosea, Isaiah, Micah, Jeremiah) they knew a prophetic tradition of promise alongside the prophetic preaching of judgment. It remains (along with vv. 13–15) as a reminder to us that through God's grace death will not have the final word; life has a further word to speak. This is a theme close to the heart of Christian belief.

A brief word should be said about the use of this text in James's speech at the Council of Jerusalem recorded in Acts 15:16–17. This is one of only two references to the book of Amos in the New Testament. (Amos 5:15–27 is cited in Acts 7:42–43.) James is citing this passage as support for approval of Paul's mission to the Gentiles. This use of Amos 9:11–12 is possible only because James (and the writer of Acts) used the Greek version of the text. The Greek translators read the word for Edom as the generic word for humanity ('adam, a very similar word in Hebrew), and read the word for "possess" as the similar Hebrew word for "seek." This allowed the Greek version to translate verse 12 as James cites it, "so that all other peoples may seek the Lord—even all the Gentiles over whom my name has been called."

The New Age (9:13–15)

The book of Amos closes with an eloquent portrait of a hoped-for new age of God's blessing (9:13–15). If God's judgment is inevitable when covenant is broken and sin abounds, it does not necessarily mean that judgment is

God's final word. In the present book of Amos it is not! God's final word is a promise of restored people and land in the midst of God's bountiful blessing. Whereas verses 11–12 focus on restored political kingdom and its capital, the focus here is on people and land in a manner reminiscent of the theme of the "promised land" in the Pentateuch. The coming time will be marked by peace and prosperity. The land will be so fertile that the harvest hardly has time to be completed before another crop has its planting (v. 13a). The fields and hills will yield only abundance (v. 13b). God will restore "my people" and they will rebuild their settlements and enjoy the abundance of the land (v. 14). Indeed, God will "plant" them as a people on the land, one of its bountiful crops, and they will never again be "plucked up" (v. 15). It is a glorious picture, harmonious with the portrait of God earlier in chapter 9 as sovereign over both nature and history. But here nature and history are used by God for blessing not for judgment. It is life and not death that speaks the final word in the book of Amos.

Is this word from Amos himself? Was it preached to eighth-century Israelites in the Northern Kingdom? Many scholars have thought that this oracle of promise was a later Judean addition (like vv. 11–12) sometime after the experience of Babylonian conquest and exile. Certainly it is true that Amos nowhere else speaks in the voice of God's promise. When he speaks of the day to come, it is a day of judgment and death for Israel. The rebuilding of ruined cities in verse 14 sounds as if destruction has already taken place. On the other hand, there is nothing in these verses that is distinctly Judean or limited in reference to exilic times. Verse 14 speaks of God's restoration of Israel, the name of the Northern Kingdom, and not Judah. Although Israel can be a term for all the people of God looking back to times before the division of the kingdoms, Amos does not use the term Israel in this larger sense.

It is, of course, impossible to know whether this final promise is a later addition or not. But Amos does suggest that a remnant of Israel may survive judgment and find God's mercy (5:15). All the other prophets of the eighth century (Hosea, Isaiah, Micah) include strong images of hope and renewal alongside their announcement of God's judgment. It seems best to put the question of authorship aside and ask how this final promise of renewal and blessing affects our reading of the book of Amos. Is this a softening of God's judgment? No, this seems to be a hope for renewal after the judgment Amos announced as inevitable and final. It does not promise a restoration of political kingdom. Israel's end is final as Amos announced it, but God's grace is not exhausted. The promise here is not of renewed kingdom but of renewed covenant between God and the people and land.

The promise grows out of God's faithfulness beyond judgment, not out of God's contradiction of the announced word of judgment. Perhaps it was the presence of a hopeful promise of God's renewed grace here at the end of the book of Amos that attracted the Judean addition of verses 11–12. It was returned exiles who saw in the rebuilding of Jerusalem and Davidic kingdom the hope for the actualizing of this new age of blessing that is promised beyond judgment.

Whatever the history of these texts, it is fitting that the book of Amos ends by reminding us that Amos's announcement of death for God's people in judgment on their sin is not the final word. It is a true word, and even God's people cannot escape the harshness of God's opposition to sin and evil, but it is not the last word. God will judge, but God chooses also to redeem. As Christians, we cannot help pondering a truth visible already here in Amos that God's redemptive journey leads first to a facing of the reality of death before the promise of life can be actualized.

For Further Reading

Hosea

Limburg, James. *Hosea–Micah*. Interpretation. Atlanta: John Knox Press, 1988.

Mays, James Luther. *Hosea: A Commentary*. Old Testament Library. Philadelphia: Westminster Press, 1969.

Staton, Cecil P., ed. *Interpreting Hosea for Teaching and Preaching*. Macon: Smyth & Helwys Publishing, 1993.

Ward, James M. *Thus Says the Lord: The Message of the Prophets*. Nashville: Abingdon Press, 1991.

Yee, Gale A. "Hosea: Commentary and Reflection," *The New Interpreter's Bible*, vol. 7. Nashville: Abingdon Press, 1996.

Joel

Crenshaw, James L. *Joel*. The Anchor Bible. New York: Doubleday, 1995.

Dillard, Raymond. "Joel," *The Minor Prophets: An Exegetical and Expository Commentary*, vol. 1. Grand Rapids: Baker Book House, 1992.

Hiebert, Theodore. "Joel, Book of," *The Anchor Bible Dictionary*, vol. 3. New York: Doubleday, 1992.

Limburg, James. *Hosea–Micah*. Interpretation. Atlanta: John Knox Press, 1988.

Amos

Hasel, Gerhard F. *Understanding the Book of Amos: Basic Issues in Current Interpretations*. Grand Rapids: Baker Book House, 1991.

Limburg, James. *Hosea–Micah*. Interpretation. Atlanta: John Knox Press, 1988.

Mays, James Luther. *Amos: A Commentary.* Old Testament Library. Philadelphia: Westminster Press, 1969.

Paul, Shalom M. *Amos.* Hermeneia. Minneapolis: Fortress Press, 1991.

Ward, James M. *Thus Says the Lord: The Message of the Prophets.* Nashville: Abingdon Press, 1991.

Printed in the United States
29467LVS00007B/167

9 780664 252717

Made in the USA
Middletown, DE
18 February 2015